4/1/87
3-

Ray—

Thanks for the help!

Harry Popple

Information
Technology

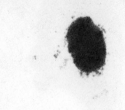

Information Technology

The Trillion-Dollar Opportunity

Harvey L. Poppel

Bernard Goldstein

With foreword by
John Sculley
Chairman, President, and Chief Executive Officer
Apple Computer, Inc.

McGraw-Hill Book Company
New York St. Louis San Francisco Auckland Bogotá
Hamburg Johannesburg London Madrid Mexico
Milan Montreal New Delhi Panama
Paris São Paulo Singapore
Sydney Tokyo Toronto

Library of Congress Cataloging-in-Publication Data

Poppel, Harvey L.
  Information technology.

  Includes index.
  1. Computer industry.   2. Telecommunication equipment
industry.   3. Market surveys.   I. Goldstein, Bernard.
II. Title.
HD9696.C62P623   1987   338.4′7004′0973   86−27782
ISBN 0−07−050511−X

1234567890   DOC/DOC   893210987

ISBN 0-07-050511-X

The editors for this book were William A. Sabin and Nancy Young,
the designer was Naomi Auerbach, and the production
supervisor was Thomas G. Kowalczyk. It was set in Baskerville
by Saybrook Press.

Printed and bound by R. R. Donnelley & Sons Company.

To our wives, Lee and Pat,

and our children—
Marc and Clinton Poppel and
Mark, Bruce, and Nancy Goldstein

Contents

Foreword by John Sculley   xi
Preface   xv
Introduction   xvii

Part 1   Infotrends: Why IT's Happening   1

1. The Five Infotrends: Go for IT   3

Content   3
Interoperability   5
Disintermediation   6
Globalization   7
Convergence   8
Summary   14

2. Content: The Substance of IT   15

Knowledge Work: What's in IT for Me?   15
Home: Can't Get Away from IT All   28

3. Interoperability: Making IT Happen   34

The IT-Integrated Factory   35
Standardizing IT   40
Summary   44

4. Disintermediation: IT Power   46

Connecting to IT   47
Paying for IT Now   56
Summary   62

5. Globalization: Thinking the World of IT   64

North American and Japan: Racing for IT   64
Europe: Lagging IT   71
Summary   76

6. Convergence: Homing in on IT   77

IT Grid   78
Getting IT On   85
Summary   95

Part 2   Clusters: The Winners and Losers of IT   97

7. Communications Services: Going IT Alone   99

Surviving the Aftershocks of Divestiture   99
Five Strategic Challenges   101

8. Information Services: Getting with IT   105

High-Tech IMS Market Evolution   108
IMS Competitive Structure   109
Critical Success Factors   112
Summary   113

9. Entertainment Services: For the Fun of IT   115

Segmenting the Market   116
Video Performance Media   116
Traditional Broadcasting   117
Cable TV   118
Participative Video Media   119
Segmenting in the Changing Video Marketplace   121
Summary   123

10. Consumer Electronics: Home Is Where IT's At   124

Infotainment: Is IT There?   125
Home Computers: Proving IT   126
Playstations: Having Your Cake and Eating IT   128
Transtations   129

11. Office Equipment: IT's Wonderful, IT's Marvelous, But... 131

Lessons Learned   133
Roadblocks   135
What Can Users Do about IT?   136
IT's Urgent   139
What Can IT Suppliers Do?   139

12. Business Operations Equipment: Embedding IT   142

Getting to the Heart of IT   143
Network Telecommunications Suppliers: Getting IT Out There   145
Industry-Specific Marketing Segmentations: Taking IT Apart   147
Summary   150

Part 3   Succeeding at IT   151

13. Measuring IT   153

Shareholder Rewards   153
Stakeholder Perceptions   161
Perceptions versus Performance   165
Success Attributes   166

14. Doing IT Right: The Strategic Management Challenge   168

Managing IT   168
Different Views of IT   171
Summary   174

15. Humanizing IT: The People-Culture Challenge   175

On Top of IT   175
What Is in IT for the Rest of Them?   178

16. What IT's All About: The Product Quality and Technology Challenge   184

Wanting IT   184
Innovating IT   186
Summary   189

17. Working IT In: The Marketing and Sales Challenge   190

Analyzing IT   190
Getting More out of IT   193

Index   199

Foreword

I believe the world is going through a fundamental change. We are migrating from an economy built on the foundations of the petrochemical industrial revolution to a new and different economy in which the building blocks are computers, communications, and the media—what the authors call information technology (IT).

In 1939, the year I was born, a World's Fair was held in New York. Very detailed predictions were documented about the next 50 years. Yet the computer was never mentioned. The microchip was not even hinted at—nor were lasers. Television, already extant in 1939, was viewed as little more than a curiosity.

All this suggests that predicting the future is extremely difficult. Within this context of unpredictable change, new visions of the individual, of education, of the corporation and, indeed, of the entire IT industry are materializing. The new vision of the individual permeates the other three so I will start with and dwell mainly on it.

Some estimate that the world's information is doubling every 3 to 4 years, whether it is in business, education, or the home. If we fail to redefine our concepts, this geometric progression combined with more powerful desktop computing, multivendor choices, and broader networking is going to overwhelm each of us. Conversely, we can unleash the opportunity to manage information in new ways if we redefine individual IT use perhaps analogously to how automobile use evolved.

In its earliest days, the automobile industry depended on the "machine enthusiast"—the kind of person who could tinker with a car and who did not mind cranking it up, shifting all the gears, and turning the steering wheel without power, one who took great pride in a car.

But eventually the industry became accessible to the mass public. To make the transition, more than the automobile had to be changed.

The technology first had to be "buried" before most consumers could drive cars. Among the results are automatic transmissions, electric starters, and diagnostic systems for servicing cars. That transition also required building an infrastructure of service stations, petroleum companies, and highways. Now, 80 years later, we have mass, personalized transportation.

This is analogous to what I believe we will see in information technology. A specific example I am close to is the personal computer.

In the first decade of personal computing, we saw how it was possible to bring computing power to the individual: One person, one computer. This was the era of the "information providers"—a growing legion of people who created and learned to work with tools—like word processing, spreadsheets, and databases—that provide information.

Our goal in the second decade is to bring information to all individuals who need it, not just computing power to those the authors call "IT literate." That is a far more complex systems concept.

To get from the machine-enthusiast stage of personal computers to the stage of mass, personalized information use requires that we make IT invisible to users. We do not have to think about how to drive a car but rather about where to go. Instead of having to think about how to "drive" a computer, we can concentrate instead on what we want to do with it. We will also have to complete the infrastructure in the form of "electronic highways" that connect us to whatever information and entertainment we want, regardless of where that content may reside.

I believe it possible in the 1990s to build desktop computers that will be many times more powerful than mainframe computers are today and do it within the cost domains we have for the high-end personal desktop computers of the 1980s. This is an exciting prospect because it means that we can begin to consider things that have not been considered possible. As an example, we recognize the growing importance of expert systems, yet we have just barely scratched the surface of real artificial intelligence—the ability of the machine to learn. One idea is information technology as an agent, an invisible gnome, transparent to the user, that has the capability of tapping various content sources and, based on its experience with the user, is able to sort out those things that are appropriate for that particular user.

Therefore, by the mid-1990s, we should see mass, personalized knowledge systems. This is much like what has happened with telephones, a far more mature information technology. The telephone is perhaps the most successful personal productivity tool of this century. We are not aware of the technology when we use a telephone nor are we required to conform the way we work to the way a telephone works. I can use the telephone the way I want to and you can use it the way you want to. It is a very individual product, and this could be the paradigm that we look for in newer information technologies that aspire to become pervasive. So our vision of IT use is expanding: one person, one IT device—with the freedom to connect—to become part of a larger system to access a world of other people, content, and IT devices.

I believe that as we redefine the expectations for the individual, we are going to see remarkable gains in productivity from what I call the "connected workgroup." But first we must recognize that what authors call "interoperability" is an extremely important requisite to this vision because it means that a variety of different architectures will be able to coexist. The IT industry has to offer compatibility options so that users are not locked out of specific information and entertainment sources and computing environments. Standards should be the bridges that bring the powerful advantages of information technology down to an intuitive and interactive human dimension. Standards cannot be allowed to become rigid boundaries to innovation.

The vision for individuals, then, is for intuitive interactive access to stored information and entertainment. That is because people buying IT in the 1990s will not be enamored by the technology. Rather, they will be enamored by what IT can do. However complex, IT systems will be transparent to IT users.

This is a new vision that looks at information technology as a transport for the mind, a way of expanding our personal boundary of knowledge, our creativity, and our ability to be more productive, and it will help us learn to communicate, to work, and to entertain ourselves in ways we never before imagined. It is not surprising to find the early explorers of cybernetics concerned with "the human use of human beings." One example is how electronic spreadsheets are evolving into advanced simulation. A simulation makes the individual a proactor, an explorer into knowledge. It makes the individual at the same time skeptical and an active participant in modeling various possibilities. In a way Socrates understood this concept, the role of the proactor, as he focused the learning process on oral discourse as the student gathered under the linden trees.

This poses a formidable challenge to educators—teach the rest of us how to cope with the acceleration of knowledge and especially teach young people (who are going to spend the majority of their lives in the twenty-first century) the process of learning. Information technology can play an important part in all aspects of coursework and learning, not just computer literacy and drill and practice.

I think students would be better served by learning how to use IT devices as lifelong tools to get work done. This is because learning is no longer confined to the structured experience of educational institutions.

Young people today can expect to have multiple career experiences, so learning must become a lifetime process.

Are we preparing today's students correctly for that kind of world? We are beginning to see a lot of progress on university campuses toward this notion. Databases are being tapped in every subject, and we are seeing entire campuses, like Dartmouth, Carnegie-Mellon, Brown, Wooster, and Reed College, being integrated through networks.

Individual use of IT, especially at work, is reshaping the vision of the corporation and its relationship with technology. Companies of the near future will need fewer employees who are skilled at doing repetitive tasks, and many more employees who know instead how to think, create, and make decisions.

At the turn of the century, AT&T was probably the largest and most important technology company. But AT&T now has many competitors for that distinction. As we head toward the year 2000, can anyone confidently predict which will be the greatest technology company?

General Motors no longer talks about being a great automobile company; it now talks about being a technology corporation. Sears, Roebuck no longer talks about just retail merchandising and catalog sales; it talks about being a financial supermarket built upon information networks. Meanwhile, Citicorp talks about information being interchangeable with capital; its goal is to become a great information services corporation. So corporate visions are being redefined through internal strategic redeployments, major mergers, and external alliances.

But the bigger names and headlines do not tell the full story about the IT industry. Our industry is blessed with thousands of smaller, highly entrepreneurial firms. Over half the venture capital in the United States is invested in young IT players; we all will be enriched by the risk takers.

However, these younger companies face tremendous challenges. A brief look at American business history shows that the transition from entrepreneurial start-up to stable mature corporate adulthood is not easy especially for a high-tech business. General Electric, Polaroid, Xerox—even IBM—experienced periods of tumult as they developed. Apple has been no exception.

I recognize that my vision of the IT industry and its impact on individuals, educators, and corporations is not identical to the authors'. Nor should yours be. Information technology is too personal a subject. But the authors have done an exceptional job of establishing a framework and providing the insights that can help each of us shape personalized visions of what IT can do for us and for others.

John Sculley

CHAIRMAN, PRESIDENT, CHIEF EXECUTIVE OFFICER
APPLE COMPUTER, INC.

Preface

This book is dedicated to helping readers anticipate and capitalize on information technology (IT) developments. Therefore, it posits a "unifying theory" of the IT industry that spotlights, links, and interprets the pivotal market forces, technologies, and impacts.

The IT industry encompasses computers, communications, the media, and related businesses. IT is arguably the largest industry in the world. It employs many millions of managers, sales reps, developers, and other professionals. Readers who work within this industry can use this book to tighten their grasp of customer needs, product opportunities, and the strategic maneuvers of IT suppliers, including competitors and allies. In that way, we hope they will be better equipped to plan and execute their professional roles and career paths.

More than a million people working outside the IT industry are dedicated to making IT work within and for their businesses. These include information managers, systems analysts, librarians, and other professionals. As readers, they can learn about new IT tools and technologies that can sharpen their performance.

Beyond IT professionals, we all are touched in many ways by computers, telephones, television, books, and other outputs of the IT industry. As the book describes, information technology is an increasingly pervasive and powerful life force. At times a stimulant, occasionally an irritant, and too frequently a tranquilizer. Whatever and whenever the effect, most people are curious to know what is new, what is next, and from whom to buy IT. This book can help satisfy these curiosities.

Between casual users and IT professionals are travel agents, stock brokers, and engineers, among others, who depend on IT constantly.

Teachers and students increasingly interact using a mix of low-tech (e.g., books) and high-tech (e.g., computers) media. The portfolios of many investors are heavy in IT. Even farmers, factory workers, and soldiers are augmented daily by IT.

Therefore, to paraphrase a familiar commercial, for all that you do (with IT), this book is for you!

Harvey L. Poppel
Bernard Goldstein

Introduction

"Bits," "Bytes," and "Bandwidth" bob up in our everyday banter. Offices, homes, and shopping centers are cluttered with PCs, VCRs, ATMs, and other acronomic paraphernalia. The media arouse our paranoias with spectres of computer illiteracy, fraud, privacy invasion, and electronic eavesdropping.

The common culprit is information technology (IT). We define IT as the use of computers and telecommunications to create, manipulate, and distribute enlightenment and entertainment.

IT has penetrated to the core of our professional and personal lives. IT is at the synapses of our national defense strategy. IT is tilting the balance of international trade, employment levels, and politics.

In and of itself, IT is neither good nor bad. But once shaped into systems, the potential for positive or negative socioeconomic and geopolitical shifts is mindbending.

As IT enables the information society to become a reality, a huge IT industry is evolving to meet the needs of this society.

Simply defined, the information technology industry produces content and the facilities that deliver content to end users. By content, we mean knowledge, wisdom, data, art, and other forms of human and machine-generated information and entertainment. The IT industry then is the fusion of numerous business sectors—entertainment, publishing, office and computer equipment, telecommunications, and consumer electronics, among others—that have been related casually, if at all, until very recently.

IT is firing this fusion. IT is facilitating human access to awesome computer power, megavolumes of information, gigaframes of entertainment, and the cumulative knowledge of millions of other people. All this from wherever people are—at their own workstations, visiting others, at home, or while in transit—24 hours each day.

Spurring the demand side of IT are five dominant forces we call "infotrends." We have labeled each infotrend with single words: content, interoperability, disintermediation, globalization, and convergence. Each represents the turbulent conflux of superpowerful market, environmental, and technology forces. Moreover, they are mutually reinforcing.

As these infotrends intensify, most larger public and private-sector businesses are beginning to grasp just how important IT use is to their success. So are many consumers. Therefore, we have devoted the first part of the book to describing these infotrends in more detail and forecasting their demand-side consequences.

One notable consequence is that businesses and consumers are spending more and more on IT. Indeed, we estimate that as of 1986 gross world IT consumption had surpassed $1 trillion annually. By 1990, IT will reach $2 trillion, with half of that both consumed and produced in North America.

Reinforcing this potential is Simon Ramo, one of the IT industry's pioneers: "If information technology were to be applied to every situation in which it would pay off, it would involve an investment in hardware and software of about a trillion dollars."*

With this surge in demand is an interrelated story of fiercely fought market contests among businesses that develop, produce, and distribute IT. They are the supply siders. Supply siders fall into six categories of IT businesses—each is characterized by groupings of market segments and related products. We call these groupings "clusters."

IT CLUSTERS

Services	Products
Communications	Consumer electronics
Information	Office equipment
Entertainment	Business operations equipment

History amply proves that no IT supplier, no matter in which cluster, how large, or seemingly entrenched, is secure. Today's winners can easily be tomorrow's vanquished. The mid-1980s slowdown in demand for plain vanilla computers and voice equipment has humbled even the most successful and self-confident players.

*Computer Age, January, 1985, p. 4.

In general, all three service clusters will be intruded upon by powerful product suppliers in search of higher returns on equity, greater stability, and more content value added. These product suppliers will elbow their way in by leveraging their new-technology strengths and rigorous management disciplines, qualities often lacking among traditional service suppliers. But, not to worry. Each service cluster has many opportunities both to defend its turf and to expand in its own way.

All three product clusters will continue to experience telescoping product life cycles and technology leap-frogging as well as a much more IT-literate buyer. The cumulative effect will be sharper up-down sales cycles. Product differentiation based on sheer horsepower will be increasingly difficult to assert. Marketing, service, and pricing strategies will often make the difference between prosperity and disaster. Distinctions among product clusters will continue to blur. The quest for content differentiation and control over interoperability will become obsessive and will fuel a shift from traditional NIH (not invented here) to external development activity.

But that is where the similarities among the six clusters end. Each cluster has its own idiosyncratic challenge and success formulae. The second part of this book forecasts the outlook for each cluster, including its share of the trillion-dollar opportunity, and it explains the measures that we believe will separate tomorrow's winners and losers.

Certain common threads to success transcend individual clusters. These critical success attributes and how they are measured and managed apply across the entire range of IT suppliers. These attributes relate directly to four broad categories of management initiatives: (1) strategies, (2) people and culture, (3) product quality and technology, and (4) marketing. Many successful IT suppliers have built their franchise on these initiatives. Just ask H. Ross Perot, John W. Kluge, and David Packard. These three builders of IT companies have been among the four richest people in America, according to *Forbes* magazine. The third and final part of the book describes what readers should do to achieve their own successes with IT.

All three parts of this book are drawn primarily from the authors' combined experience of 50 years in the IT industry. Much of our knowledge base derives from close interactions, research studies, and learning experiences with colleagues and clients of Broadview Associates, a leading IT merger and acquisition firm, and Booz, Allen & Hamilton Inc., one of the premier management consulting firms. In particular, extensive use has been made of concepts, studies, and related materials that were developed while one of the authors was with Booz, Allen & Hamilton Inc. However, the opinions expressed in this book about specific industry and company performances and prospects are strictly those of the authors and are not based on any proprietary or confidential information from Booz-Allen, Broadview, their clients, or other sources.

We especially thank our partners at Broadview—George Grodahl, Ed Metz, and Gil Mintz—for their overall inspiration and support. Also our gratitude to Fran Reich for her sustained and unfailing help. Specific acknowledgements are made within the book to those many other colleagues who contributed directly.

Information Technology

PART 1

Infotrends: Why IT's Happening

1

The Five Infotrends:
Go for IT

Most discourses on information technology (IT) start naturally enough with the technology. They depict plummeting price-performance curves, and show photographs of the incredibly shrinking chip.

We readily concur that the technological accomplishments of the IT era are indeed daunting. Looking ahead to the 1990s, we anticipate still further advances, chief among them the continued technological migration from electro-mechanical to electronic and on to optical products and services.

Nonetheless, our purpose in this book is to explain how users and providers can deal with this technology avalanche rather than being buried by IT. We maintain that, in addition to technology, the governing forces are complex blends of market, environment, and strategic management. These blends have spawned five distinct, yet interrelated phenomena we call "infotrends" that are driving both the use and supply of IT.[1] Each infotrend is described and illustrated in Chapters 2 through 6. The balance of this chapter introduces and interrelates all five (see Figure 1.1).

Content

Content in the form of software, databases, and expert support services is gaining strategic value at the expense of facilities, such as raw computer power, storage, and transmission capacity. McLuhan's assertion to the

[1]The recent sharp up-down cycles in computer and communications hardware acceptance during a period of unrelenting technological achievements lend support to our position that technology in isolation is not a dominant factor. Therefore, we leave a didactic description of technological advances to others, and we do not regard such advances, in and of themselves, as one of the five infotrends.

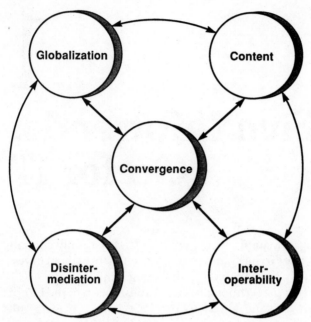

Figure 1.1. The five dominant infotrends are interrelated and mutually reinforcing. *Adapted from concepts developed by Harvey L. Poppel while at Booz, Allen & Hamilton Inc., and copyrighted by them.*

contrary, the importance of the "message" (i.e., content) is transcending that of the "medium" (i.e., facility).

We believe that the message *is* the message. Increasingly IT-literate end users are discovering that appropriate and well-crafted content endures far longer than particular media. These come and go. The opera singer Caruso has been immortalized in various "media": on stage, vinyl records, and audio cassettes. His voice is even being "altered" to perfection by digital technologies on laser discs. So, too, is it for such things as the contents of the *Encyclopedia Britannica* and old films.

The same technologies churning the media are encouraging the creation and distribution of valuable new content. Interactive electronic training and marketing materials inspired by advances in laser discs are among the newest examples, just as previous technology advances spawned packaged computer and entertainment software and electronic databases.

Economics are another reason for content's ascendancy. Technology is shrinking the unit costs of most facilities. Conversely, content is rising in cost. This is due in large part to its costly labor intensity. Knowledge workers or artists who produce content are scarce and expensive resources. Their compensation is inflation driven. So are the artifacts they use such as offices, computer-assisted design workstations, or studio props.

Interoperability

As content grows in relative value, *interoperability* becomes more and more the leading technical challenge for those suppliers and customers seeking to provide the often hyped but rarely achieved "total solution." Interoperability means the ability of two or more parties, machine or human, to make a perfect exchange of content. Perfect means no perceptible distortions or unintended delays between content origin, processing, and use.

Person-to-person exchanges become "perfect" by eliminating intermediaries, either people or IT facilities, that might filter subtleties or slow down communications. Anything other than face-to-face contact is less than perfect if one accounts for the distortions or delays that result. Full-motion videoconferencing, therefore, comes closest to simulating perfect exchanges.

In the world of basic telephone use, interoperability is achieved by providing universal service (or interconnectivity) and low-noise transmissions. What is said at one end is carried through interconnecting paths to come out clearly at the other end. This is so even though we still cannot see the other party. We expect nothing less from a phone call 10,000 miles away than from one a mile away.

In day-to-day computer-room data processing, interoperability is achieved by high-performance systems components, harmonized hardware configurations, high-speed data channels, and automatic error deletion-correction mechanisms.

We have reached a new and challenging stage in interoperability. A 1985 survey by Input, Inc., found that compatibility was the most severe problem faced by users of micro software packages. Indeed, 40 percent of those surveyed felt that compatibility was a serious or severe problem. The sheer complexity is becoming overwhelming as more and more people in dispersed locations want simultaneous hook-ups among themselves and among machines. And they want all this, more and more frequently, while using a variety of media provided by an array of suppliers. No less an expert than James Martin has said, "We are weaving a tapestry with threads of very different colors such as information engineering, personal computing, CAD/CAP for analysts, fourth-generation networks, office-of-the-future, dialog psychology. But these threads are all vital to the overall picture. They have to come together."[2] And Nobel laureate Arno Penzias concludes, "Establishing *physical* links between the nodes of a network is no longer the limiting problem; instead, the challenge is to establish *logical* connections through the network."[3]

A solution requires that all the elements of basic telephony, data processing, all varieties of hardware, and their content formats for input-output, transmission, storage, and processing be in perfect harmony. Once assembled, the end-to-end system's performance has to satisfy the sense of urgency of those who use it. Accordingly, standards for interoperability are essential, and the participation of suppliers and end users in standard-setting movements is becoming a critical success factor.

Disintermediation

As interoperability leads to more perfect exchanges of content, the substantive value of the content deepens and broadens. Where the content exchange is between buyers and sellers, the inevitable consequence is *disintermediation*. The use of new information technologies is leading to more perfect markets. By this we mean markets that minimize the number of intermediary stages between buyer and seller. What took five steps before now takes four and may take three or two tomorrow. All this permits buyers and sellers to conduct transactions more quickly, clearly, and accurately.

In service businesses, agents, tellers, telephone operators, and teachers are among the endangered species of intermediaries. When trading stocks, we might now question why registered representatives are needed to place a buy-sell order if we can do it ourselves electronically. If terminals provide us direct access to travel information, why is a travel agent needed to reserve seats and write tickets? Eventually not only human intermediaries but also such physical intermediary facilities as warehouses, retail stores, outpatient rooms, and theatres can be bypassed.

Disintermediation will also occur within and among enterprises as internal transactions are perfected. New systems—in procurement, development, production, inventory, and sales—are beginning to provoke striking changes in the configuration of manufacturing, distribution, sales, and administration facilities within larger enterprises. One implication is fewer and fewer regional centers. This is already evident as factory

---

[2]James Martin, "The Spring 1985 James Martin Seminar," Technology Transfer Institute, Santa Monica, California, 1985, p. 6.

[3]Arno Penzias, " 'Info Age' Already Here, Nobel Laureate Asserts," *Management Information Systems Week*, March 6, 1985, p. 27.

or warehouse automation allows businesses to close up smaller plant or storage sites. And as integrated office systems proliferate, those managers who served principally as information conduits (and filters) between top strategy makers and front-line implementors will go on the endangered list. Already threatened are MIS/EDP executives who serve only as interpreters and gatekeepers between IT and heretofore IT-illiterate end users.

As a result, disintermediation is a survival issue for those in the middle and strategic IT use has become an essential ingredient to corporate success.

Globalization

Much has been written about the implications of global markets for such industries as primary metals, electronics, automobiles, and package goods. In our context, IT is best understood as both a cause and an effect of globalization. The ability of multinational businesses to globalize successfully is a function of IT. The new technologies enable them to interoperate far flung operations as well as buy and sell more efficiently by leveraging product and market content. "I carry this terminal whenever I'm away," boasts Bill McGowen, MCI's irascible chairman, "and use it."[4]

And as the spectre of disintermediation threatens to restructure global transactions, businesses worldwide are demanding more IT products and services.

Similarly, with the exception of a few culturally bounded entertainment and information services, consumer IT markets are becoming global. This is being driven on one side by universal consumer desires for amusement, knowledge, and other forms of self-fulfillment and on the other by sellers wanting to broaden and leverage new mass merchandising sales channels across national boundaries. Both of these forces are illustrated by a recent deal signed by Ted Turner with Comsat and British Telecom International. Through these carriers' satellite facilities, Turner's Cable News Network is beamed throughout Europe in conjunction with European broadcasters.

Regulatory barriers to free trade of IT products and content are crumbling in the face of mounting user demands and parallel efforts to standardize products and services. Regulators are increasingly frustrated in

[4]Bob Stoffels, "Telecommunications Leader-of-the-Year," *Telephone Engineer & Management*, December 15, 1984, p. 10.

their attempts to stanch transborder content flows, especially of computer software, databases, and entertainment, often directly from author to consumer. Regulatory policy is quickly shifting from restraint to stimulation of IT adoption. Fewer and fewer countries are finding themselves able to cling to protectionist policies that retard the growth of domestic businesses or resist consumer demands despite occasional flurries of well-intentioned but misguided legislative efforts. History clearly shows that protectionism does more to atrophy indigenous IT suppliers than to harm large international competitors.

Convergence

Convergence is the ultimate effect of the four trends described above. Distinctions are blurring between products and services, content and facilities, home and business uses, information and entertainment and among IT modes such as audio, data, and video. Convergence marks the merging of competitive interests among IT suppliers, the players in the IT industry. Those players have their roots in six business clusters that were formerly isolated. But ever-reaching branches of new outputs and markets are increasingly tangling with those of other clusters.

This has strategic competitive implications, not only within the IT industry, but between IT and other industries. The relatively high growth and return on equity (ROE) of the IT industry, detailed in Part 2, is attracting more "outsiders." The IT industry, on the whole, is booming and will continue to surge forward. The largest 10 firms already control $166 billion of the market; the largest 100, over $400 billion (see Table 1.1). The top 300 supply about half of the worldwide market. Companies as diverse as Boeing, Citicorp, General Motors, McKesson, and Sears, deeply rooted in other industries, are publicizing their prospecting of IT oil. Few seem discouraged by the well-known costly dry wells of otherwise competent outsiders, such as Exxon, American Can, and Volkswagen.

Counterattacking are resourceful seasoned industry players, armed with IT-added values, who are invading other industries. This is far more than leveraging cash or management macho. As their IT leads to more perfect markets, IT businesses can end-run the disintermediation process by providing physical distribution and knowledge-based services into other industries. Indeed McDonnell Douglas has started to do this in health care, and Bell & Howell has diversified strongly into education. First Data Resources is already one of the top-ten telemarketing firms. Future in-home integrated market service (IMS) providers are likely to deliver telebought goods to consumers. But these diversifiers should heed the lessons learned over the past 5 to 10 years by such heavies as RCA,

Table 1.1. Top-100 Information Technology Firms as of July 1985

Rank	Prior rank[a]	Company	Headquarters location	IT revs latest FY ($MM)	IT revs prior FY ($MM)	IT revs % change	IT revs % of total	Total revs latest FY ($MM)	ROE	Latest FY end
1	1	IBM	Armonk, NY	45,937	40,180	14	100	45,937	24.8	12/84
2	2	AT&T [b,c]	New York, NY	33,188	32,536	2	100	33,188	10.0	12/84
3	3	Nippon Tel. & Tel.	Tokyo, Japan	18,374	17,533	5	100	18,374	–	3/84
4	4	GTE	Stamford, CT	12,805	11,795	9	88	14,547	13.6	12/84
5	5	Matsushita Electric	Osaka, Japan	10,957	9,309	18	58	19,053	–	11/84
6	6	BellSouth[b]	Atlanta, GA	9,519	8,669	10	100	9,519	13.4	12/84
7	7	NYNEX[b]	New York, NY	9,507	8,664	10	100	9,507	12.6	12/84
8	8	British Telecom	London, UK	8,986	8,382	7	100	8,986	–	3/84
9	9	Eastman Kodak	Rochester, NY	8,380	8,097	3	79	10,600	12.9	12/84
10	10	Ameritech[b]	Chicago, IL	8,347	7,664	9	100	8,347	14.0	12/84
				165,999	152,830	9	93	178,056		
11	11	Bell Atlantic[b]	Philadelphia, PA	8,090	7,289	11	100	8,090	13.0	12/84
12	12	Pacific Telesis[b]	San Francisco, CA	7,824	7,088	10	100	7,824	12.8	12/84
13	13	U S West[b]	Englewood, CO	7,280	6,668	9	100	7,280	13.3	12/84
14	14	Southwestern Bell[b]	St. Louis, MO	7,191	6,434	12	100	7,191	12.6	12/84
15	15	RCA	New York, NY	7,063	6,161	15	70	10,112	16.3	12/84
16	16	Philips	Eindhoven, Netherlands	6,645	6,125	8	42	15,700	–	12/84
17	17	Xerox[d]	Stamford, CT	6,605	5,984	10	100	6,605	7.1	12/84
18	19	Hitachi	Tokyo, Japan	6,369	5,279	21	36	17,626	–	3/84
19	18	ITT	New York, NY	5,680	5,827	(3)	45	12,701	7.4	12/84
20	24	DEC	Maynard, MA	5,584	4,272	31	100	5,584	8.3	6/84

(Continued)

Table 1.1. *(Continued)*

Rank	Prior rank[a]	Company	Headquarters location	IT revs latest FY ($MM)	IT revs prior FY ($MM)	IT revs % change	IT revs % of total	Total revs latest FY ($MM)	ROE	Latest FY end
21	22	NEC	Tokyo, Japan	5,213	4,391	19	73	7,111	–	3/84
22	20	Sony	Tokyo, Japan	5,092	4,484	14	100	5,092	–	10/84
23	23	Burroughs	Detroit, MI	4,876	4,390	11	100	4,876	10.7	12/84
24	21	Siemens	Munich, W. Germany	4,848	4,484	8	32	15,074	–	9/84
25	25	CBS	New York, NY	4,762	4,263	12	97	4,925	13.7	12/84
				259,119	235,968	10	83	313,847		
26	29	Toshiba	Tokyo, Japan	4,189	3,361	25	38	10,925	–	3/84
27	26	Bell Canada[e]	Montreal, Canada	4,084	3,742	9	89	4,613	–	12/84
28	27	NCR	Dayton, OH	4,074	3,731	9	100	4,074	16.5	12/84
29	31	Fujitsu	Tokyo, Japan	3,850	3,123	23	79	4,883	–	3/84
30	28	Control Data	Minneapolis, MN	3,756	3,508	7	75	5,027	1.8	12/84
31	32	ABC[f]	New York, NY	3,708	2,949	26	100	3,708	14.4	12/84
32	36	Sanyo Electric	Osaka, Japan	3,474	2,657	31	60	5,814	–	11/84
33	30	Sperry	New York, NY	3,377	3,215	5	69	4,914	7.7	3/84
34	33	LM Ericsson	Stockholm, Sweden	3,358	2,885	16	100	3,358	–	12/84
35	40	Hewlett-Packard	Palo Alto, CA	3,269	2,476	32	53	6,165	18.8	10/84
36	41	Northern Telecom	Mississauga, Canada	3,227	2,435	33	100	3,227	–	12/84
37	39	Canon	Tokyo, Japan	3,140	2,528	24	94	3,351	–	12/84
38	35	Time	New York, NY	3,067	2,717	13	100	3,067	21.0	12/84
39	34	3M	St. Paul, MN	3,050	2,820	8	40	7,705	19.2	12/84
40	43	Motorola	Schaumburg, IL	2,944	2,365	24	53	5,534	17.0	12/84
41	37	United Telecommunications	Kansas City, MO	2,856	2,559	12	100	2,856	13.7	12/84
42	42	CGE	Paris, France	2,721	2,413	13	34	8,008	–	12/84
43	38	Fuji Photo Film	Tokyo, Japan	2,689	2,557	5	100	2,689	–	10/84

1984 Rank	1983 Rank	Company	Location							
44	44	Times Mirror	Los Angeles, CA	2,569	2,302	12	92	2,805	18.3	12/84
45	48	Dun & Bradstreet	New York, NY	2,397	2,060	16	100	2,397	20.9	12/84
46	56	Olivetti	Ivrea, Italy	2,365	1,930	23	100	2,365	–	12/84
47	45	Thorn EMI	London, UK	2,354	2,247	5	62	3,778	–	3/84
48	53	Bayer (Agfa-Gevaert)	Leverkusen, W. Germany	2,326	1,950	19	17	13,575	–	12/84
49	46	Continental Telecom	Atlanta, GA	2,319	2,142	8	100	2,319	15.1	12/84
50	50	Rank Xerox	London, UK	2,307	2,017	14	100	2,307	–	10/84
				336,589	302,659	11	78	433,310		
51	47	Thomson Group	Paris, France	2,239	2,131	5	36	6,252	–	12/84
52	49	Bertelsmann	Guetersloh, W. Germany	2,210	2,046	8	100	2,210	–	6/84
53	58	Sharp	Osaka, Japan	2,204	1,871	18	54	4,106	–	3/84
54	57	Telefonica	Madrid, Spain	2,196	1,873	17	100	2,196	–	12/84
55	68	Wang Laboratories	Lowell, MA	2,185	1,538	42	100	2,185	16.8	6/84
56	55	Tandy	Forth Worth, TX	2,124	1,933	10	78	2,737	28.5	6/84
57	52	STC	London, UK	2,120	1,980	7	82	2,570	–	12/84
58	51	GE	Fairfield, CT	2,120	2,000	6	8	27,947	(173.6)	12/84
59	60	Warner Communications	New York, NY	2,024	1,723	17	100	2,024	–	12/84
60	59	Moore Corp. Ltd.	Toronto, Canada	2,021	1,814	11	100	2,021	–	12/84
61	54	Advance Publications	New York, NY	2,000	1,940	3	100	2,000	–	**
62	61	Gannett	Arlington, VA	1,960	1,704	15	100	1,960	19.6	12/84
63	69	MCI Communications[g]	Washington, DC	1,959	1,521	29	100	1,959	4.9	12/84
64	66	Ricoh	Tokyo, Japan	1,902	1,573	21	100	1,902	–	3/84
65	62	Honeywell	Minneapolis, MN	1,825	1,666	10	30	6,074	–	12/84
66	67	R.R. Donnelly & Sons	Chicago, IL	1,814	1,546	17	100	1,814	16.8	12/84
67	63	Harris	Melbourne, FL	1,762	1,658	6	88	1,996	9.8	6/84
68	65	TRW	Cleveland, OH	1,750	1,600	9	29	6,062	–	12/84
69	64	Pitney Bowes	Stamford, CT	1,732	1,606	8	100	1,732	19.9	12/84
70	76	Zenith Electronics	Glenview, IL	1,716	1,361	26	100	1,716	14.4	12/84

(Continued)

11

Table 1.1. (Continued)

Rank	Prior rank[a]	Company	Headquarters location	IT revs latest FY ($MM)	IT revs prior FY ($MM)	IT revs % change	IT revs % of total	Total revs latest FY ($MM)	ROE.	Latest FY end
71	71	Hearst	New York, NY	1,700	1,500	13	100	1,700	–	**
72	73	Knight-Ridder Newspapers	Miami, FL	1,665	1,471	13	100	1,665	15.3	12/84
73	70	Dai Nippon Printing	Tokyo, Japan	1,640	1,511	9	60	2,734	–	5/84
74	74	Tribune Co.	Chicago, IL	1,597	1,397	14	89	1,794	12.4	12/84
75	72	Reader's Digest	Pleasantville, NY	1,567	1,500	4	100	1,567	–	**
76	98	Apple Computer	Cupertino, CA	1,516	983	54	100	1,516	13.8	9/84
77	75	Toppan Printing	Tokyo, Japan	1,500	1,378	9	70	2,143	–	5/84
78	78	Gulf & Western Industries	New York, NY	1,492	1,267	18	28	5,356	–	7/84
79	79	Bull	Paris, France	1,468	1,257	17	100	1,468	–	12/84
80	83	Mitsubishi Electric	Tokyo, Japan	1,426	1,192	20	20	7,026	–	3/84
81	77	McGraw-Hill	New York, NY	1,402	1,295	8	100	1,402	20.7	12/84
82	97	Computerland	Oakland, CA	1,400	1,000	40	100	1,400	–	**
83	86	Plessey	Ilford, UK	1,309	1,121	17	82	1,593	–	3/84
84	82	Pioneer Electronic	Tokyo, Japan	1,293	1,246	4	100	1,293	–	9/84
85	84	Konishiroku Photo	Tokyo, Japan	1,282	1,185	8	95	1,350	–	4/84
86	90	Cox Enterprises[h]	Atlanta, GA	1,277	1,071	19	96	1,330	–	**
87	81	GEC	London, UK	1,276	1,248	2	19	6,599	–	3/84
88	85	Southern New England Tel.	New Haven, CT	1,273	1,183	8	100	1,273	13.9	12/84
89	80	Polaroid	Cambridge, MA	1,272	1,255	1	100	1,272	2.8	12/84
90	125	Commodore International	West Chester, PA	1,267	681	86	100	1,267	44.3	6/84

	Prior rank	Company	Location							
91	95	News Corp., Ltd.	Sydney, Australia	1,241	1,005	24	100	1,241	–	6/84
92	88	New York Times	New York, NY	1,230	1,091	13	100	1,230	21.9	12/84
93	92	Fuji Xerox	Tokyo, Japan	1,229	1,065	15	100	1,229	–	10/84
94	87	Centel	Chicago, IL	1,195	1,092	9	87	1,375	15.7	12/84
95	109	Data General	Westboro, MA	1,161	829	40	100	1,161	14.0	9/84
96	99	Hachette	Paris, France	1,156	979	18	100	1,156	–	12/84
97	93	Western Union	Upper Saddle River, NJ	1,134	1,045	9	100	1,134	(8.0)	12/84
98	89	MCA	Universal City, CA	1,131	1,083	4	69	1,651	7.8	12/84
99	94	Reed International	London, UK	1,129	1,044	8	42	2,670	–	12/84
100	100	Nixdorf Computer	Paderborn, W. Germany	1,077	892	21	100	1,077	–	12/84
				416,757	372,608	12	73	574,442		

aPrior rank reflects latest FY83 figures and is not necessarily the rank assigned to a company in the Booz-Allen issued 1984 top-100 list.
bAT&T and RBOC prior year revenues are pro forma estimates based on growth rates from 1Q84 to 1Q85.
cAT&T's reported revenues are net of access charges ($20,633 million in 1984).
dXerox does not include Rank Xerox (50).
eBell Canada does not include Northern Telecom (36).
fABC has agreed to be acquired by Capital Cities Communications (108).
gMCI has agreed to acquire Satellite Business Systems (221) from IBM.
hCox Enterprises includes recently acquired Cox Communications.
*The data are drawn principally from annual reports and supplemented by other published sources. *Advertising Age* is the primary source for private media company data. Recent acquisitions and divestitures are treated on a pro forma basis wherever possible. ROEs are given for U.S. public companies that are 40 percent or more IT. Exchange rates of 7/1/85 are applied to all non-U.S. denominated revenues.
**Revenues are estimated by Booz-Allen & Hamilton Inc. for privately held firms that do not issue financial statements.

SOURCE: Booz Allen & Hamilton Inc.

ITT, Control Data, and Xerox that have been notably unsuccessful in forays outside their IT competency.

Summary

The interrelationship among the five infotrends is deeply rooted and mutually reinforcing. The quest for more perfect content drives interoperability. Interoperability enables disintermediation. Disintermediation leads to globalization and globalization fosters convergence. And to close the loop, convergence stimulates the IT-literacy that drives demand for content. This mutual reinforcement suggests that the strategic importance of those trends will swell exponentially for both IT buyers and sellers. Barriers such as the lack of standardization, IT illiteracy, and regulatory myopia, however intimidating, are being dismantled by those users and suppliers who want to "go for IT."

2
Content:
The Substance of IT

Content, in the form of information, is the source of human knowledge. Ralph Waldo Emerson defined information as "the amassed thought and experience of innumerable minds." Hence the performance of knowledge workers is highly dependent on the substance, accuracy, and timeliness of information flows. And that is what IT is best at—bringing information content to the points of knowledge creation and use. Therefore, our first illustration of the expanding importance of IT-handled content is based on studies of knowledge workers and what makes them tick.

Informational content also serves to enlighten us in our personal lives. Entertainment, a second form of content, amuses us. Together, the quality and availability of information and entertainment content strongly influences our sense of individual self-fulfillment. Therefore, we draw our second illustration from the consumer market.

Knowledge Work: What's in IT for Me?

The Size of IT

Thirty years ago America counted 15 million farm workers. Today the number has shrunk to about 3 million. Not that long ago, manual production line work dominated the statistics. Today, it is down to a small fraction. New jobs are replacing the workers—and proliferating as they go. Social workers, insurance salespeople, IRS auditors, investment bankers, and electronic engineers exemplify the new. Together they share a common dependence on informational content as their raw material and as their principal product. These kinds of white collar tasks now consume over half of domestic business employment and payroll.

15

In the business world, knowledge workers make decisions, design products, market and procure goods and services, and provide the counsel that drives business operations. Indeed, knowledge work is the sole business operation in the rapidly growing professional service business sector, which includes consulting, law, medicine, accounting, and software development. The transactions associated with business operations yield much of the feedback content that knowledge workers ingest. Much of the cerebral processes associated with knowledge work are fueled by content deriving from both internal and external transactions. But historically, these intellectual energy sources have been unreliable and often unwieldy. Experience suggests that most businesses spend too much on content and get too little in the way of knowledge-worker productivity. In the United States some 30 million managers and other professionals—whom we call knowledge workers—cost their businesses well over $1 trillion a year in compensation and direct overheads. Yet businesses only spend a mere $75 billion on the type of IT systems that can make the other expenditures more productive (see Table 2.1). Numerous studies managed by one of the authors, while at Booz-Allen & Hamilton Inc.[1], and others show that 18 to 30 percent of knowledge work is virtually wasted, mainly in the quest for better content.

The need for more substantive, accurate, and timely information is not surprising. In business, as elsewhere, superior information is power (just ask any financial executive). What is surprising is the fatalistic tolerance by businesses of a productive leakage of $200 billion or more, while coming up short in meeting information needs.

Business institutions and ultimately the public are victimized by the consequences of inadequate content: lost buy-sell opportunities, unresponsive service delivery, wasteful spending, and disenchanted workers. The corporate conscience is too often consumed by information thrashing. In 1985, an unfathomable 2.5 trillion pages of printed information inundated U.S. businesses. In just one division of one medium-sized

Table 2.1. The Real Cost of U.S. Knowledge Workers ($ in Billions) – 1985

	Managers		Other professionals		Total	
Compensation and fringes	$380	34%	$440	39%	$820	73%
Clerical and other overheads	130	11	105	9	235	20
IT expenditures	40	4	35	3	75	7
	$550	49%	$580	51%	$1130	100%

[1]Harvey L. Poppel, "Who Needs the Office of the Future," *Harvard Business Review*, November-December 1982, pp. 146–155.

company, Emhart Corporation, some 4 million pieces of computer paper, another 4 million copier pages, and 100,000 lined pads were reported as "consumed."[2]

This trashing enervates the most leverageable business resource—the managerial-professional workforce. Professionals ranging from engineers to senior line executives find themselves frustrated daily by the hidden hand that scrambles content, content handling facilities, and business people so that they fail to work together at the right place and time. Booz-Allen studies[3] show nearly all knowledge workers desire to spend less time thrashing and more time analyzing, planning, participating in decision making, and sharpening their professional skills.

Offices are the nerve centers of businesses. Offices are also business systems with complex flows of content. And like any content-intensive business system they are susceptible to IT-based improvements. Yet, IT penetration among knowledge workers is still spotty. Statistics from 1986 show only one desktop workstation for every six U.S. knowledge workers. Sluggish overall progress can be matched against what leading-edge users have accomplished. As early as 1980, Texas Instruments already claimed to have one electronic device for every three of its employees. And, as of 1985, IBM Canada was approaching a 1 to 1 ratio among its own knowledge workers. (The shoemaker's children have shoes.) But, even in those businesses with a sizable population of workstations, few have designed their office systems to be fully interoperable.

One reason for this somewhat Ludditian state is behavioral. Content use and generation among knowledge workers is often ad hoc. Accordingly, it is common for knowledge workers to make individual decisions to acquire IT systems. Rigorous long-range quantitative cost-benefit analyses are rarely performed. Once acquired, IT use is often driven by events, sometimes random, rather than procedure. The planning of knowledge-work systems, therefore, is not highly deterministic (as are conventional transaction processing systems) since their use is a function of events, individual style, and need, which often shift as enterprises reorganize and professionals change positions.

Nevertheless, the survival of many knowledge workers and their business has become dependent on IT. The balance of this chapter establishes the compelling business case for heavier end-user investments in interoperable office-based technologies. We also explain how the heretofore sluggish pace of user investment in interoperable office systems has begun to accelerate. Our optimism is buoyed by the rapid shifts taking

---

[2]T. M. Ford, chairman, Emhart Corporation as quoted in *The Executive Speaker*, December 1984, p. 7.

[3]Ibid.

place in buyer behavior from resistance and apathy to enthusiastic, albeit cautious acceptance. For example, some 67 percent of European executives feel that white-collar productivity will be a very important business issue in the latter 1980s, up from only 19 percent in the late 1970s. This, according to a 1984 study conducted by Booz, Allen & Hamilton Inc.[4]

Therefore, we forecast that domestic IT spending on and for knowledge workers will surpass $120 billion annually by 1990, representing a 60 percent surge in IT annual outlays per knowledge worker to over $4,000 per year. Indeed by 1990, some 40 percent of all U.S. knowledge workers will have direct IT help at their workstations.

The Business Case for IT

One of the most persistent questions asked by information technology users is, "Will IT save me money?" For many potential users, IT means bringing content to bear at the point at which human knowledge is stored or converted to action. IT means time-saving content-access devices. And, for most businesses, professional time is money.

Personal computers, display terminals, and powerful databases and communications networks have become widely available in the 1980s. Supplier hype runs euphoric on the potential productivity gains. TV and magazine ads abound. But, the availability of technology is not the stumbling block. To date, most decisions makers have been skeptical about what laptop computers, managerial workstations, local area networks, videoconference rooms, and the other newer icons of office automation can do for their businesses. These executives, disenchanted by the results of earlier forays into "management information systems," doubt that knowledge workers will embrace integrated technology, and the executives lack confidence that their organizations can channel and measure the intended benefits. In addition, members of the still IT-illiterate majority are worried about whether, when, and how they personally can cope with these new electronic tools. Some wait for IBM or other leading suppliers to point to a safe and sure route.

The evidence from a growing number of innovative organizations, including several large banks, manufacturers, and government agencies that have made sizable office automation investments, offers irrefutable proof that readily accessible information technology is the professional productivity antidote.

One of the most comprehensive studies of the linkage of knowledge-worker performance and IT was conceived and managed by one of the authors in 1980. The study, conducted by Booz, Allen & Hamilton Inc.,

[4]Sponsored jointly by Booz, Allen & Hamilton Inc., and *The Wall Street Journal/Europe*.

focused on two vital aspects of knowledge-worker performance: (1) how these workers allocated their time toward achieving their business objectives and (2) how likely they were to raise their productivity by using more of IT and hence do a better job of achieving their objectives. Fifteen case studies were completed in varied areas such as marketing, sales, purchasing, finance, design and analysis, and personnel. Each study concerned a different type of manufacturing or service business. Six of the seven manufacturers were among the *Fortune* top-100 industrials. Aetna Life & Casualty and the First National Bank of Chicago typified the size and diversity of the eight service businesses studied. These fifteen businesses together with over twenty-five IT suppliers and Booz, Allen & Hamilton funded the study on a multiclient basis.

Each case was treated as a detailed feasibility study, reinforced where possible by experiential data. During the 10 to 12 weeks of each case study, the team worked with the executives of the particular departments to isolate the critical success factors in their operations and to become thoroughly familiar with the job characteristics, activities, and attitudes of the nine to twenty-five participants.

The participants used a pocket-sized recorder to list and assess their work activities at 20-minute intervals over a 3-to 4-week period, and after the study participants filled out an anonymous questionnaire concerning their receptivity to potential office automation changes. Nearly 300 knowledge workers recorded about 90,000 time samples over 3700 worker days.

The study revealed no work pattern that neatly fit all levels and types of knowledge workers. Knowledge workers acted very differently from the classical model of the highly systematic professional who plans, organizes, coordinates, and controls. This conclusion buttressed the results of previous studies by Mintzberg[5] and others.

Nevertheless, five findings concerning time-use amplify Mintzberg's results and have broad managerial implications:

1. *Many of the subjects spent less than half their work time on activities directly related to their function.* To exemplify this performance leakage, we will look at how the field sales professionals involved in four of the case studies spent their time. Whether called "account executives," "loan officers," "estate planners," or just generically "sales reps," sales professionals are the spigot for the revenue stream of most businesses. Yet they only spent an average of 36 percent of their work time on prospecting and selling—activities directly related to generating incremental revenue (see Figure 2.1). Moreover, they squandered much of this 36 percent on

[5]Henry Mintzberg, "The Manger's Job: Folklore and Fact," *Harvard Business Review*, July-August 1975, p. 49.

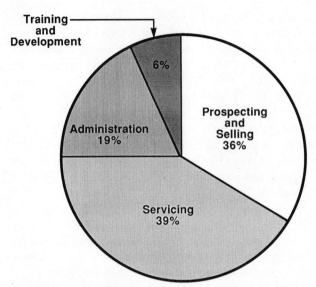

Figure 2.1. How field sales professionals spend their work time—
by function. SOURCE: *Booz, Allen & Hamilton Inc., 1982.*

traveling, calling on low-probability prospects, and working through the
paper-clogged proposal process. Indeed only about half, or 18 percent, of
overall time was attributed to effective prospecting and calling.

Both sales professionals and their managers expressed frustration over
this poor productivity. Furthermore, they were concerned that their
non-revenue-generating chores were keeping them from cultivating a
more lucrative customer base. They had exhausted all the traditional and
quick-fix time management techniques they knew but had failed to improve their use of time.

The gremlin was not time management but the awkwardness and
imprecision of customary content handling and communication processes. It was easy to see how information problems cost most sales
professionals an hour or two a day. More about this later in this chapter.

2. *The subjects spent 25 percent of their work time on "less productive"
activities.* Three "generic" types of activities, by definition chronically
less productive, consumed from 18 to 30 percent of all professionals' time
across all the functions in the fifteen cases:

   a. *Totally unproductive.* Mainly the time spent traveling outside
      or within a building or waiting for meetings to start or a machine
      to become available. On average, each hour spent at an external
      site required an additional 40 minutes of idle travel time.

   b. *Quasi-professional.*   Such activities as seeking information and expediting assigned tasks. These usually required some professional knowledge or interpersonal skills but took more time than necessary because either automated or clerical support systems were unavailable.
   c. *Productive only at a clerical level.*   Professionals who lack adequate support must type, make copies, file, and make reservations and appointments themselves. In one case, highly paid R&D administrators were queuing up at an overloaded word processor to type their own progress reports.

Underscoring the importance of inadequate secretarial and clerical support, the results showed that organizations so handicapped consume more than twice as much time on less productive activities as do offices that are better supported. In one case, professionals misspent 42 percent of their time on such activities. Their communications-intensive mission was to coordinate operational services for an international commercial banking function. Such findings stress the penny-wise and pound-foolish nature of needlessly harsh cutbacks or across-the-board headcount controls of office support staffs.

3. *Meetings, in person and by telephone, are the commonest form of professional activity.*   Meetings range from formal training seminars to bull sessions in the hall. Participants spent nearly half (46 percent) of their working time in meetings, senior managers exceeding 60 percent and nonmanagerial professionals slightly under 40 percent. Overall, they conducted 20 percent of their meetings by telephone. As one might expect, groups with heavy meeting schedules spent less than average time communicating through exchanges of documents.

4. *Professionals spent an average of 21 percent of their work time in document-related activities and only 8 percent on analysis.*   Document preparation and review profiles varied widely, owing in part to differences in the availability and quality of word processing for less senior professionals. Nonmanagerial professionals spent nearly twice as much time composing documents as managers.

Participants understandably felt that "pure" analytical time (time spent contemplating, problem solving, or conceptualizing) was the most precious and self-rewarding professional activity. Yet, they spent only 8 percent of their time in this way.

5. *Most knowledge workers would like to reshape their time profiles.*
Even though most participants and their department heads had distorted perceptions of how they spent their time, many of the managers and professionals interviewed were eager to find ways of improving their productivity and work quality. For example, in interviews before the time

sampling, well over 90 percent underestimated the time spent in meetings. Although a similar percentage overestimated the time they subsequently recorded in analytical tasks, 35 percent felt they needed to spend considerably more time analyzing (even more time than they had mistakenly estimated). They also considered the time spent in planning and in professional development inadequate.

Despite these needs, participants felt blocked by the hours they squandered on the less productive activities. They especially criticized poorly trained and understaffed support systems, unproductive use of telephones and dictation systems, and inefficient means of document production, which often triggered unplanned and disruptive activities. The participants perceived most of the computer-generated management reports as being unwieldy, unfocused, and out of date. As indeed they were.

Clearly, many of these findings have implications beyond the feasibility of interoperable office systems. The time profiles suggest possible useful adjustments in organizational structure, ways of strengthening supervisory effectiveness, and the assignment of new priorities to activities closely linked to critical success factors. Nevertheless, the study teams concluded that knowledge workers could save an average of 15 percent of their time through more IT support. Roughly half the saving would come from reducing time spent in less productive activities. The balance would derive from selective reductions in certain meetings, analytical tasks, and document handling.

In addition to time savings, the study team identified many opportunities in each case to raise the quality of output. Most of the qualitative benefits linked directly to the four critical success factors most commonly identified during interviews with executives and other participants:

1. Direct, timely access to accurate content—product, customer, and internal performance information, primarily through interoperable access from personal workstations to public and in-house data bases

2. Effective intradepartmental coordination, mainly through voice and keyboard electronic mail systems

3. More effective interaction with customers (both external and interdepartmental) through more content-intensive visually attractive documents and faster message systems

4. Adequate, uninterrupted time for work activities, such as analysis, most directly related to functional objectives, by taking the time saved from less productive activities and reinvesting it in high-priority tasks

Because of the promise of both time savings and qualitative benefits, the study team recommended a mix of interdependent applications sufficient to justify a desktop workstation for 80 percent of the knowledge workers studied.

To illustrate how existing information technologies apply to everyday knowledge-worker activities, let us once again consider the plight of a typical field sales rep—just one of several million such knowledge workers.

Tomorrow's Sales Rep: Don't Leave Home without IT

Chuck Coldcall is a traveling sales rep. He works hard and assiduously keeps in contact with his home office. Many of Charlie's days start with a phone call like this one:

> "Dammit, Bobby, I was within 20 minutes of Business Industries yesterday afternoon."
> "Well, Mr. Coldcall, I tried to reach you at the field office. It's lucky that you just called in. A Ms. Buysome at BI said that if you still want to bid on their contract, you've got to see her tomorrow at the latest and your proposal has to be in by Friday."
> "Which proposal? We've talked about four different jobs."
> "She said it was the one with the new drawings."
> "Oh, no! Peter in sales engineering has those at the district office along with the pricing sheets. Please transfer me to Peter. I'll get back to you."
> "Sorry, he's on his line; it's busy."
> "I guess I'll have to hold, but I'm in a phone booth."
> Minutes later. "Pete? This is Chuck. Listen. I need the BI drawings and pricing. Can you get them to the field office by noon tomorrow? I'll make a special trip to pick them up."
> "Those things! Not sure where they are. Also, we've changed some of the specifications and the pricing so I'll have to update them. I'll try to find them, change them and get them to you by tomorrow."
> "Pete, that's not good enough."
> "Sorry, Chuck. I'm already working on five other rush proposals, and I'm expediting three other jobs through some bottlenecks in the factory."
> "Pete, for Chuck's sake, make it happen! Now please transfer me back to Bobby."
> "Bobby, two things: Arrange the delivery with Peter. Then call Joan at the field office. Tell her we're going to have to work late tomorrow night after I come back from my meeting with Buysome. Tell her also to pull the BI files and proposal boilerplates. She's the only one there who knows where everything is, how to work the word processor, and the high-quality copier, and..."
> "Oh, Mr. Coldcall, Joan just called me from O'Hare. Remember, she's off to Acapulco? Chuck...Chuck...are you there?"

Does this sound familiar? Field sales is highly eclectic. It usually embraces most generic activities and content sources and uses of other business functions—meetings, document preparation, analysis, or time scheduling. All of these are time consuming and very often frustratingly inefficient. That is why IT's future seems so clear. For our hypothetical Chuck Coldcall, the future might begin to register savings such as those that follow (see Figure 2.2).

Chuck would be equipped with an easy-to-use portable display microcomputer that would enable him to access information and contact people in a variety of time-saving ways. That is what now is being done in such diverse sales organizations as Nabisco, Wrangler Jeans, and Ciba-Geigy. First, Chuck would scan publicly available databases to select his prospect lists. Next, a "traveling sales rep" algorithm could be used to suggest a minimum-time travel path among prospects and existing customers—a system already used by IT-intensive companies such as Federal Express. Chuck's car would be equipped with a satellite-linked system to help him navigate to his destinations.

Chuck and his office-based assistant, Bobby, would use an electronic mail system operating through Chuck's terminal. Or Bobby might use a portable telephone connection to stay in close touch while scheduling Chuck's appointments to match the minimum-travel path. Naturally, the system would reconfigure the path should any appointments be unavailable or canceled. Bobby would use a personal desk-based communicating computer to send and receive such messages.

Next, Chuck would use his microcomputer while visiting Business Industries to access the BI file, as well as the latest drawings and pricing

Information Technology Aid	Sales Rep Functions				
	Prospecting	Selling	Ordering	Servicing	Reporting
Databases	●	●	●	●	
Mobile Communications	●	●	●	●	●
Electronic Catalogs		●	●	◖	
Sales Engineering		●	◖		
Document Generators		●		◖	◖
Electronic Ordering			●	●	◖
Electronic Messages	◖			●	●

Figure 2.2. Information technology-aided sales calls can be 30 percent (or more) more productive than "conventional" sales calls. SOURCE: *Booz, Allen & Hamilton Inc., 1984 (as published in* High-Tech Marketing, *February 1985).*

information. Thus he could elicit Ms. Buysome's reaction to the main points of his proposal on the spot and adjust it accordingly instead of wasting substantial time and effort preparing a formal proposal. In simpler situations, such as selling personal lines insurance, a sales professional could display and print a complete proposal in front of the prospect, as several large insurers have been doing for years.

In addition to a portable data terminal, Chuck would have a portable telephone that he could use "hands-free" in his automobile to convert idle auto travel to productive time. Not only would this unit enable Chuck to place and receive telephone calls (hands-free) while he was on the move but it would also connect him with a central voice-message computer. Since this type of system can send and receive messages to and from any telephone, it would enable Chuck to communicate with customers and the internal support people who did not have access to a data terminal, as well as to access local traffic bulletins.

In addition, the technology would enable Chuck to send messages with specified delivery times during his early morning commute, during lunch hour, and even late at night. Without having to leave his car, Chuck could check the status of an order, coordinate invoice reconciliation efforts, and arrange proposal preparations or his appointment schedule at any hour.

Video technology would also help Chuck. Full electronic sound and visual demonstrations on an optical disc would be accessed, along with standard pricing and availability, through an inexpensive compact disc player attachment to Chuck's microcomputer. Depending on the type of product, he could view this material with prospects or use it solely to prepare himself. Chuck could also keep current with new product and marketing plans by attending video conferences available periodically at a nearby motel.

The "new Chuck" is far from being a pipe dream. Rather, research demonstrates that information technology can provide extraordinary productivity opportunities for marketers with direct salesforces. (For some IT suppliers, this should prove a double blessing. Not only can they enhance their own marketing and sales performance, but they might also capitalize on the similar needs of their business customers if they can marshal the appropriate products and services.)

As mentioned earlier, field sales professionals spend, on average, only 36 percent of their time prospecting and selling, and less than half of that is typically productive. The rest is frittered away calling on low-probability prospects because of inadequate preparation or making unnecessary return visits due to a lack of product, pricing, or availability information at the point of sale. The direct costs of a typical sales call can run $120 to $200 and double that when burdened with out-of-pocket expenses and field administration overhead. Based on studies as well as the mounting experiences of IT-equipped salesforces, effective selling time often can be doubled (see Figure 2.3). This translates into direct savings of $10,000 or more per salesperson per year to cover a fixed territory. More likely, most businesses would reallocate and reconfigure their salesforces to deepen account penetration. Strategically, marketshare gains are usually more important to marketing organizations than are cost savings.

To date, no organization we know has capitalized on all the relevant IT aids. Indeed, many of the techniques are quite new to the selling profession. Yet, most of the tools are in use somewhere generating demonstrable benefits. It is simply a matter of integrating what is currently available.

Putting IT to Work

A handful of companies have demonstrated striking progress. One example of IT at work is at IBM's North-Central Marketing Division (NCMD). It is a keyboard display system that enables marketing reps to assemble complex proposals, retrieve sales data, update product knowledge, and analyze competitive offerings on-line. Standard electronically stored product information is tailored and merged with system configurations

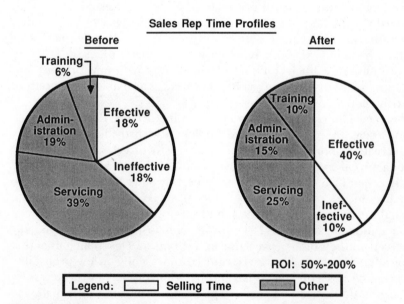

Figure 2.3. A comprehensive performance improvement program leveraging from information technology can make a big difference. SOURCE: *Booz, Allen & Hamilton Inc., 1983.*

and financial analysis information. The completed document is then printed locally on a high-speed quality printer. This system has helped pare the time taken by IBM marketing reps to prepare complex customer proposals.

IBM sales offices house videodisc-based demonstrations and can access an area wide voice message system. IBM managers track expenses and related business measurements, exchange electronic messages on a real-time basis, and maintain their schedules all through a single information system. By the early 1980s, IBM had extended the reach of these systems to customer locations and, where appropriate, to the homes of IBM employees. Even selected direct customer access to certain IBM databases has been facilitated.

At GTE Sylvania, sales reps have, for many years, used portable data terminals to do industrial lighting sales and engineering proposals at customer sites. For Satellite Business Systems, Connecticut Mutual, and other firms with similar sales engineering functions portable microcomputers are sent into the field. And in Japan, Daiwa Bank has supplied its agents with suitcase terminals to handle field transactions.

Wescar, a rail carrier, allows selected high-volume customers to trace shipments simply by dialing Wescar's computer. This and other real-time customer service and sales support systems have enabled Wescar to reward their sales reps with added commissions and bonuses attainable because of their much higher productivity.

These scattered experiences point to at least six industry segments whose marketing productivity is most likely to benefit from IT. These are industrial hard goods and supplies, consumer package goods and pharmaceuticals, commercial and personal line insurance, commercial banking and trust, wholesaling, and professional business services.

But, despite this high potential, marketing and sales functions lag other knowledge work segments in terms of IT use. A 1983 estimate by Dun & Bradstreet[6] showed that microcomputer usage for sales substantially lagged uses in financial-accounting, data processing, production, and planning, regardless of the size of the business. Yet, we do estimate that collectively applied, IT could boost effective prospecting-selling time for at least 2 million professional salespeople domestically. This translates into a gross market potential of several billions of dollars for those IT-suppliers who can develop and market interoperable field sales systems. Among the early leaders are Hewlett-Packard and a handful of systems developers, including Sales Technologies and Envoy Systems.

---

[6]*Dun & Bradstreet Looks at Business*, July/Aug 1983, vol. 1, no. 2.

Home: Can't Get Away From IT All

IT's Growing

Even the most cursory look into an American home tells us that the content business is prospering. TV series, videotape rentals, radio programs, records, videogames, words, and images in books, newspapers, or magazines are all part of an $85 billion (1985) U.S. consumer-content business. Including hardware and networking facilities that deliver consumer content, domestic consumer expenditures for IT now exceeds those for automobiles. Indeed, the consumer segment accounts for nearly 40 percent of all domestic IT revenues.

Content consumes a surprisingly large portion of our leisure time as well as our budget. The average household watches TV nearly 7 hours a day. Seventy percent of all households read a daily paper. Sixty-nine percent of all drive time is spent listening to the radio. One billion movie tickets are sold every year. Billions of coins are put into video arcade games. The cumulative total of TV programs watched by all Americans is an unfathomable 300 billion.

Consider that American adults absorb 20 trillion minutes per year of IT products and services. What if a mere additional penny per minute could be collected? Let's see, 20 trillion pennies equals...

Or consider that every household in America already has an average of over four IT devices—televisions, stereos, telephones, radios, and computer-videogame devices. That means 400 million in place. What are the supply-side implications as the number of conduits inexorably swells to five, six, or more?

But despite the overwhelming commercial and sociological significance, consumer content businesses notoriously tend to avoid the strategic analysis well-proven in other types of IT businesses. To provoke this kind of worthwhile analysis, this chapter describes our perspective of the major trends influencing strategic decisions.

The content business serves two major needs. It provides consumers with amusement and enlightenment, and it allows advertisers to reach both mass and target markets. It can be segmented by method of physical distribution: printed materials, broadcast and cable television, radio, prerecorded audio and video, or box offices. But that puts too much emphasis on the media: too little on the message. History clearly tells us that while much content is enduring and some is timeless, media wax and wane in popularity.

Electronic media were born barely a century ago and have churned ever since. For the past 30 years, entertainment flows have diverted toward broadcast TV and away from radio and box office. Broadcast TV siphoned some news content away from general purpose magazines and newspapers. Audiotapes overtook vinyl records as the most popular medium for prerecorded music.

Looking ahead to the early 1990s, newer media will further change distribution patterns. Electronic information systems, delivered by wideband telecommunications and compact digital discs, will narrow the market for printed newspapers and reference books. Cable TV increasingly will eat into broadcast TV market share. One can already see videotape and pay cable dampening the appeal of movie box office (and of each other). Similarly, teledelivery could subsume the physical distribution of floppies for home computer software. But we think that read-only and write-once compact discs will eventually overtake audiotape, records, floppies, and even teledelivery for prerecorded music, information, and software.

IT's a System[7]

Physical distribution is important and costly, but it is only the third of three value-added stages that characterize a complete content system. The first two stages are "development" and "synthesis." For example, some 10,000 domestic television series are created annually during the initial *development* stage (see Figure 2.4). Out of these, one out of a hundred may survive to go into production. The broadcast networks *synthesize* their prime-time schedules after screening available series and programming the sequence. Finally, the prerecorded tape, film or live signal, is *distributed* electronically. Households receive TV programming through the tandeming of nationwide TV networks using satellite or long-haul terrestrial facilities and a local affiliated station "broadcasting" the signal over the air via an assigned VHF or UHF band. In some cases, this final stage of physical distribution is through a coaxial cable that carries a number of TV signals.

Eight fundamental types of content go through this three stage system:

News	Transactions
Documentaries	Games
Knowledge and opinion	Fiction and drama
Data and Facts	Music and humor

Certain distribution media—audiotape, newspapers, and box office—are each focused mainly on one type of content, while broadcast media

[7]Adapted from concepts first advanced by Jennifer Bater, "Consumer Content," *Information Industry Insights*, Booz, Allen & Hamilton Inc. issue 9, pp. 9–12.

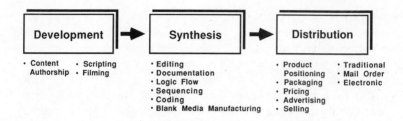

Development	Synthesis	Distribution

• Content   • Scripting
  Authorship   • Filming
	• Editing
	• Documentation
	• Logic Flow
	• Sequencing
	• Coding
	• Blank Media Manufacturing
		• Product • Traditional
		  Positioning • Mail Order
		• Packaging • Electronic
		• Pricing
		• Advertising
		• Selling

Broadcast Television Example

1. Universal TV develops a concept about a Vietnam veteran now working as a private eye in Hawaii.

3. Universal makes the pilot.

7. Universal produces the series.

2. CBS sees a prime time slot for such a concept and orders a pilot, suggesting further enhancements.

4. CBS schedules the pilot.

6. Based on Nielsen results, CBS orders a series, suggesting enhancements and modifications.

8. CBS schedules the series on Thursday night.

5. CBS distributes the pilot to its broadcast affiliates who broadcast it in their markets (or carried by cable systems).

9. CBS distributes the series to its affiliates who clear it for Thursday night.

10. Following a successful run, Universal sells the series in syndication to stations.

Figure 2.4. Value-added steps in the content business. SOURCE: *Jennifer Bater, "Consumer Content,"* Information Industry Insights, *Booz, Allen & Hamilton Inc., Issue 9, p. 10.*

and, potentially, videotex and compact discs are able to channel diverse types of content. Because of that breadth, multicontent media can adapt more readily to the changing environment. Radio could not compete with TV for fiction and drama, so it successfully fell back into news, music, and talk-show formats. If music video, 24-hour cable news, custom tailored news services, or autoteleconferencing were to become universally accessible, radio could again be forced to reshuffle its repertory.

In addition to allocating time or space to different content types, the media are being challenged by the emergence of new hybrid content forms. Docudrama, edutainment, data-driven news (e.g., financial markets) are only a few of the possibilities. Ultimately, these content forms compete for two finite measurable consumer resources: time and money. And consumers place somewhat different measurable values on their content consumption.

The content business is unique. The *marketplace* is one of its distinguishing characteristics. The content business strives, with some exceptions, to serve its two principal masters—consumers and advertisers. Roughly 50 percent of all consumer content revenues come from advertisers. Broadcast TV networks compete ferociously to demonstrate high audience levels to mass-market advertisers. Ad-supported cable, radio, magazines, newspapers, and home information systems also seek greater circulation or audiences, although often in more focused segments. Advertisers actively are seeking new advertising channels, including pay TV and even videotape and electronic databases. Only books, software, and prerecorded music remain relatively free of advertising.

Another unique content characteristic is the implicit power associated with *franchise territories*. In the electronic media, spectrum scarcity led to local TV and radio licensing. Cable television also is rewarded on a local franchise basis, albeit for different reasons related to "natural monopolies."

Even without technical or legal allocations, content enterprises have built their own market franchises. Most medium-sized and smaller cities have only one local newspaper or telephone directory. Early on, the domestic TV networks established a triopoly by affiliating with most local stations. Certain prerecorded music and book suppliers have used "clubs" as a territorializing mechanism while magazines and pay TV services have established subscriptions.

Indeed, the opinion-molding power of certain market franchises has led to FCC cross-ownership rules severely limiting newspaper-TV station or TV station-cable system combines in the same markets and cable system ownership by the broadcast networks.

Finally, *content can be leveraged across multiple media*. Companies with newspaper roots, such as Gannett, Knight-Ridder, Times Mirror, and The New York Times, have become owners of broadcast stations, and Knight-Ridder and Times Mirror were videotex pioneers. The parents of three major broadcast networks also own major-market TV and radio stations, record companies, and magazines and have deepened their involvement in TV production. Film companies, such as Warner, Fox, and Columbia, have sought ownership of pay TV networks, although often unsuccessfully. Content companies with a variety of roots have large positions in cable TV. Examples include Time, Cox, and Times Mirror. Many have sought consumer software positions (e.g., Macmillan, Warner, and CBS), albeit with mixed success. These content companies diversify not only for growth but also to balance popularity shifts among media. In addition, they participate broadly to capture a greater share of the value added.

Where IT's Going

Overriding all this is an evolution—indeed a crucial technology path—toward active digital-based electronic media that blend both information and entertainment.

We describe the new media as *"infotainment."* Traditionally passive media are giving way to interactive forms yielding greater physical or mental stimulation and control for consumers. Examples include consumer-controlled time-shifting of TV programs using programmable VCRs, simulation software such as *The Business Strategist* and new telephone-based information retrieval systems, such as DowPhone and Dial-A-Date.

At the same time, distinctions between entertainment and information values, delivery systems, and content are blurring for consumers and their suppliers. This is spawning new hybrid media forms of content such as interactive disc-based games that also instruct.

With the emergence of infotainment superimposed on the secular growth of mass-market content consumption, we forecast that the domestic consumer content business will remain a growth segment with an overall compounded annual growth rate of 10 percent through the early 1990s. Of particular note, the video segment will outpace the others, with a 14 percent growth rate. Furthermore, certain interactive media, such as videotex, will grow rapidly but still be only comparatively small revenue generators until the 1990s. The only segment shrinking in absolute terms is the video arcade business.

Product distribution options will continue to multiply. Video entertainment will flow not only through broadcast, cable, and box office and prerecorded videotape but, to a lesser degree, through such other, more arcane broadcasting technologies as Satellite Master Antenna Television, Low Power Television, Multichannel Multipoint Distribution System, and Direct Broadcast Satellite. New intelligent modular in-home "playstations" will increasingly enable consumers to manage their own media and its content mix. Home computers will proliferate, albeit under a variety of guises ranging from smart telephones, already omnipresent in France, to portable intelligent channel selectors. Through these new interactive control devices, information will move beyond passive paper and video formats. Interactive systems will expand to encompass randomly accessible compact discs and consumer-editable videophotography.

Despite the continuing churn in distribution technologies, the development of quality content will grow in importance relative to the syntheses and distribution stages of value added. This continuing shift in relative values will accelerate as IT makes synthesis and distribution more efficient and larger players rationalize their positions in these stages. Rights owners will continue to demand and probably get spiraling prices for compelling entertainment and information content as multiple media compete for content distribution. Talent—programmers, authors, directors, actors, and musicians—will gain a larger share of the revenues generated by their creative talents.

As a result, the competitive interests of traditional collaborators across the three value-added stages—development, syntheses, and distribution—will converge. Certain participants who heretofore focused mainly on only one value-added stage such as distribution will seek to enhance returns by carving turf from other participants. As an example, the TV networks are striving to participate more fully in the development of prime-time TV products as well as in the distribution of that product in the syndication market.

Synthesizers, such as Home Box Office and most book publishers, will be squeezed from both ends by the strengthening of content developers and the consolidation and outreach of distributors. As of this writing, both broadcast networks and pay services are experiencing mounting difficulty managing program suppliers and affiliates. Until recently, pay-per-view, a service with benefits to consumers, movie studios, and cable operators had been stymied. Why? In part because content providers could not agree on how to share the value added with any network operator. But by the early 1990s, pay-per-view will become a very big business and will contribute to the rebalancing of power among consumer content providers and distributors. Already, such powerhouses as AT&T are introducing products (Star 85) that enable consumers to order pay-by-view services from any TouchTone phone.

3
Interoperability: Making IT Happen

A state of interoperability exists when perfect exchanges of content can take place within an information system. This is a simple definition, but it is an awesome challenge to both users and suppliers.

Perfect exchanges must, by definition, transcend differences or incompatibilities among physical and logical elements of a system. In more complex systems, the physical elements include various terminals (interfaced to both end users and other systems), linked to a far-reaching network which may have several subnetworks (such as metropolitan and local area networks). In turn, the subnetworks may contain computers and database storage units and may interface to yet other systems.

Enabling all these *physical elements*, which may number in the tens of thousands, to interconnect is challenging enough. Telecommunications suppliers have focused on the interconnectivity issue for over 100 years (see Figure 3.1). But that is nowhere near as difficult as achieving content and compatibility among *logical elements*. These logical elements begin and end with the various information modes—voice, data, and image—and the three human senses they reach—hearing, touch, and sight. In between these input and output elements are various layers of electronic content—operating systems, database managers, applications software, and the information itself. Such information or the software and other elements with which it is collected, manipulated, and distributed often are not available at precisely the same time. So the ability to time-shift is another necessary characteristic of most interoperable systems.

A further dimension of complexity is that the physical and logical elements in a large-scale system typically evolve at different times. Moreover, they often are provided by multiple suppliers, both internal and external to the enterprise. Not only does each supplier's system have its own architectural concepts but few suppliers have achieved total interoperability within their own product lines much less with others.

Though immense, the hurdles to interoperability are being surmounted.

Despite the formidable complexity, interoperability is both the cause and effect of new technological devices (both data and voice), applications, and standards-setting processes. The relationship between devices and interoperability is illustrated by a 1983 International Data Corporation survey[1] which found that the single most-mentioned reason for network implementation was personal computer (PC) communications. Seventy-one percent of respondents identified PC communications as their primary networking goal.

The emergence of new software, hardware, display, database, and network standards is one of the principal facilitators of interoperability. Therefore, the processes for setting such standards become critical paths to interoperability. In this section we will probe the requirements for interoperability by examining one major interoperability-related application—the IT-integrated factory. Then we will describe one example of standards-setting processes—Initial Graphics Exchange Specifications.

The IT-Integrated Factory—
IT Don't Mean a Thing, If...

An article in *Electronic Business*[2] forecasts a domestic manufacturing automation market of over $50 billion in 1990, double the 1986 level. Past

[1]*Communications & Distributed Resources Report*, November 1984, p. 8.

[2]John Kerr, "Galvanizing the Rust Bowl: New Electronic Horizons", *Electronic Business*, November 15, 1985, p. 73.

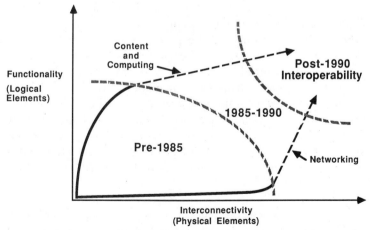

Figure 3.1. Only now are content and networking vectoring on convergent paths.
SOURCE: *Modified from Booz, Allen & Hamilton Inc., 1984.*

forecasts have been even more optimistic. Yet, for all its touted technological wizardry, the actual market for sophisticated automated equipment in
manufacturing has been disappointing. Even though a few highly publicized examples of automated factories—in Japan and the United States—
presage major IT opportunities in manufacturing, to date they remain
exceptions and not the rule.

For traditional "smokestack" industries, the prospects for IT integration still seem more smoke than fire. Scared away by questionable economics, germinal technologies, and ingrained labor and management
practices, executives in these industries have not seized on the promised
benefits. For IT suppliers, self-hyped into expecting major profits from
new hardware, software, and services, the concept is still a mirage. Donald
K. Grierson, senior vice president for the industrial electronics business
group of General Electric is blunt about the challenge,

> Buying a robot or two . . . or a laser . . . or a CAD station . . . *a cappella* may
> leave you feeling warm and automated . . . but unless you are at least *thinking*
> ahead . . . you'll be doing the same kind of incremental ratcheting that caught
> up with the dinosaurs and the hat makers. I like Woody Hayes as much as
> anyone . . . but three yards and a cloud of dust doesn't cut it any more. Step
> back and throw the bomb.[3]

But what some see as a fizzle, we see as a sizzle. The IT-integrated
future is the right—and only—road for most discrete manufacturers.
One primary driver is a need for U.S. and European manufacturing
sectors to become more competitive with Asian suppliers in global markets.

One of the most outspoken advocates of the new technologies is James
A. Baker, another senior vice president of General Electric. He likes to
provoke listeners by asking whether they would spend several hundred
million dollars on an aging locomotive plant. As though confirming the
seemingly obvious negative answer, he points out that 5000 to 6000
locomotives are sitting idle throughout the country. Who needs to invest?

"I sometimes wonder where I got the nerve," he says, "but I did invest.
The [$316 million] automated investment we made at Erie, Pennsylvania,
is permitting us to build, at a competitive price, the world's most reliable
and efficient locomotive." Baker then discloses that the automation clearly
visible to visiting buyers has led to several multimillion domestic and
foreign orders. "The People's Republic of China came over. They took a
long look and dropped the other shoe. They ordered 220 locomotives.
Dreary Erie is now cheery."[4]

[3]Donald K. Grierson in a speech for the Automation Executive Seminar, April 5, 1984.
[4]James A. Baker in a speech for Alex Brown, February 15, 1984.

The GE case confirms our belief. Those potential IT customers who do not ante up for advanced productivity-oriented technologies will be disintermediated. The winners will be those who focus their manufacturing, technology, and competitive strategies on key success factors in narrowly defined market segments. This is as true for IT suppliers as it is for their discrete manufacturing customers.

Market Evolution and Dynamics

In addition to global market forces, new technologies are a principal driver. A few key components—microprocessors, local area networks, robotics, professionals workstations, sensors, and programmable controllers—have changed the automated factory from a concept to a reality. But for the present, technology is also an inhibitor. The lack of interoperability makes implementation unwieldy. Moreover, IT also creates operational problems that give old-line factory managers and labor a plausible excuse for not buying in. New integration technologies are needed.

IT suppliers also need to recognize a fundamental shift in their customers' focus. Manufacturing will no longer be driven by the simple function of the end-product such as a plumbing part, an auto part, or an electronics part but rather by a combination of both the manufacturing and market characteristics of the product such as high-volume molded plastics or customized milled metal parts. John Nichols, president of Illinois Tool Works, Inc., states that, "We are in the midst of a fundamental shift from those not so long ago days when manufacturing plants made a product that the marketing and sales force had to sell. We are making a 180 degree turn to a new world where customer *needs* define the manufacturing activity."[5]

The efficiencies of the IT-integrated factory are accelerating the shift. They offer lower manufacturing costs, achieved at less scale with more product variety, and major cost savings in support and indirect areas. This will strikingly alter value-added relationships. In turn this will shift the primary basis of competition from the production functions to marketing and physical distribution. Once this shift takes place, new, more direct supplier, distributor, and customer relationships will be forced, fulfilling the prophesy of the third infotrend—disintermediation, which we discuss in more detail in the next chapter.

---

[5]John D. Nichols in a speech for the American Marketing Association Marketing Conference, "The Impact on Marketing of the Factory of the Future," March 24, 1984.

Dollars and cents, likewise, are driving and inhibiting the change. Few executives would challenge that heavy long-term factory automation investments are essential for world-scale survival. For the short term, however, many question the return on investment because they myopically view intelligent manufacturing systems only as interconnects to the conventional equipment the systems supercede. More enlightened manufacturers take a broader view of the new market opportunities to be unleashed by these systems, the heightened flexibility they offer, and the lower overhead costs that will accompany them.

Organization and Structure[6]

The factory is driven by three functional areas of management: enterprise planning, engineering design, and manufacturing planning and control. The factory itself performs a fourth function—physical manufacturing. These four functions overlap, and enabling their integration through interoperable exchanges of content can be viewed as a fifth function (see Figure 3.2).

Manufacturing market opportunities within the top three functional areas are important but relatively mature. They require mostly generic IT hardware such as variously sized computers, workstations, and communications networks. These hardware products are virtually interchangeable among discrete parts manufacturers once the application software is suitably tailored.

Differentiation[7]

However, within the physical manufacturing area real hardware-product differentiation occurs—both in terms of the actual manufactured goods and the interoperable, intelligent devices used to control and make them. The flexible manufacturing systems that produce jet turbines are different from those that produce microchips—and this industry specificity accounts for a marked value-added factor in supplier products.

This level of specialization generates the need for a large number and variety of industry-intelligent products: sensors, programmable control-

---

[6]Adapted from concepts first advanced by Robert J. Mayer, "I^2 Opportunities in the Factory-of-the-Future Arena," *Information Industry Insights*, Booz-Allen & Hamilton Inc., issue 6, pp 1–3.

[7]*Ibid.*

lers, and process controllers for machine tools, robotics, automated materials handling, and test and inspection systems. These products and related services will be needed to support all the physical manufacturing functions. Examples include hardware for machinery, materials handling and testing, software applications, and services such as maintenance, training, and interoperability engineering. No supplier can unilaterally do IT all. Therefore, product-market segmentation is a "must" for any aspiring IT supplier.

To turn the fizzle into sizzle, IT suppliers will need to provide increasingly receptive customers with interoperable solutions to their needs. Therefore, in addition to selecting the right segments, strategic alliances will be a critical success factor.

Computer and communications hardware and software suppliers will want to seek out partners with complementary and potentially interoperable product skills from within and outside the IT industry. Outside candidates include manufacturers of factory equipment such as machine tools and materials handlers.

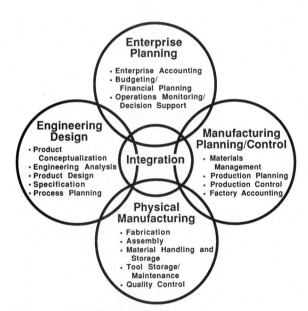

Figure 3.2. IT-integrated factory logical structure. SOURCE: *Robert J. Mayer, "I^2 Opportunities in the Factory-of-the-Future Arena,"* Information Industry Insights, *Booz, Allen & Hamilton Inc., Issue 6, p. 2.*

Standardizing IT

As attractive as interoperability sounds in concept, it is terribly difficult to achieve in reality. The obstacles are both technological and competitive. Technology efforts are built around specifications, and specifications are drawn based on standards. So, once we have standards, then we are well on the way to interoperability. But, we cannot achieve the interoperable factory unless all five functions are linked. And we cannot link them effectively until each is individually interoperable. But that is where competitive obstacles enter the scene.

Few IT issues are as controversial as standards. Some suppliers who have pioneered markets and invested heavily to establish defensible leadership justifiably see their proprietary positions threatened by standardization efforts. Conversely, trailing suppliers and most end users seek standards as a means of reducing supplier dominance or dependencies. For example, computer marketshare leader IBM currently faces the challenge of protecting its investment in its own network architecture standard (SNA) in the face of a major international drive to establish Open Systems Interconnection (OSI) as a standard.

Only a few end users have the resources and influence to drive a standards-setting process. General Motors is one who has taken the lead. They have fostered an interoperability concept called manufacturing applications protocol (MAP) and mobilized a snowballing number of suppliers to support MAP. MAP cuts across some, although not all, of the five functions that fully define the scope of the IT-integrated factory. The MAP story is still unfolding so we will look at an earlier chapter in the standards-setting process that has to do with only one function. How tough is it to set standards for just one function—in this case computer-aided design (CAD)?

Engineering design supply-siders fall into three broad categories: (1) newer specialized companies (e.g., Computervision, Apollo, and Mentor Graphics), (2) divisions of traditional IT suppliers (e.g., IBM and Control Data), and (3) divisions of diversified manufacturers (e.g., GE's Calma and McDonnell Douglas' Information Systems Group). Yet despite strong marketplace growth, CAD has had its share of problems, namely:

- Difficulty in capturing all product definition data needed for manufacturing
- Inconsistency in format of design information
- Incompatibility of CAD systems from different manufacturers

Failure to address these issues helped precipitate a dramatic marketplace shakeout which began in 1984.

User Concerns

Interoperability among multisupplier systems is becoming vitally important to many CAD buyers. A commitment to a single supplier puts the buyer at risk since the supplier may not survive or at a minimum may not be able to keep pace with the price and/or performance of competing suppliers. In that case, the user is faced with a dilemma: stick with the obsolete capabilities of the original supplier or reinvest in recreating databases and interfaces developed over several years. Also, a multiplicity of supplier systems may be required to address all the needs of a diverse organization (e.g., one that has many different business units or is highly vertically integrated). Without full interoperability, the user is forced to select either the best integration or the best task performance.

Interoperability is also a major concern for nonvertically integrated manufacturers who buy components designed on dissimilar CAD systems. Manufacturers of these components must be able to download their design information to the assembler's CAD system and vice versa—which is possible only if both CAD systems are the same or are made interoperable through both compatible networking and a common language such as Initial Graphics Exchange Specification (IGES).

The marketplace is demanding standards, such as IGES, to support multisupplier systems environments. Recognition of the need for interoperability is reflected by extensive participation in user-supplier standardization coalitions. Major manufacturers, such as General Motors, have accepted IGES in their product design and are insisting on it for subcontracted parts design as well as within the context of their larger MAP standardization initiative. Others are following suit.

The U.S. government is also playing a lead role in CAD standards R&D. In 1980, the National Bureau of Standards released IGES as a common representation for CAD information. The Department of Defense has stipulated that IGES be utilized in the design of its new weapons and communications systems.

IGES Study

In 1983, the Air Force funded a study, conducted by Booz, Allen & Hamilton Inc., to evaluate the degree of compatibility among dissimilar CAD systems as part of an overall analysis of the quality level of implementation of CAD standards. Specifically, the study assessed the success of the IGES standard from the standpoints of both suppliers and users.

The study found that all participating suppliers—representing more than 35 percent of the market—were utilizing the standard to some extent. But problems existed both with IGES itself and with IGES translators developed by CAD suppliers. The market was demanding better and more thorough implementation of standards. CAD suppliers who ignored this trend might well find their equipment isolated and their marketshares diminished.

Many of the problems found were site specific. Nevertheless, several IGES-related problems were identified that warranted further industry-wide work. For example, current implementations were most successful when dealing with simple geometry and less successful with complex surfaces.

In addition, the IGES approach was found not to be truly "neutral." At the time of the study, IGES had been based on first generation commercial CAD systems representation. Systems that differed from IGES had markedly more difficulty in processing some IGES entities.

Overall, the study showed that IGES was a workable approach for exchanging product definition data in a CAD-to-CAD environment. It could provide the basis for a product definition data interface. Despite these early IGES shortcomings, its utilization across the CAD market was already widespread. And most users and suppliers had a positive attitude concerning IGES.

As CAD evolves, more suppliers are adopting different representations. Some will also strive to improve their own internal representation and will keep those advancements confidential for fear of compromising a marketing edge, especially since technology often evolves faster than a standard can be issued. Apollo Computer, Inc., for one, stresses the IGES compatibility of its Domain network.

This situation is not unique to IGES or CAD but rather is generic to standards and, indeed, to the entire issue of interoperability. A firm position on standards is an essential element of a successful IT market strategy. As users become increasingly sophisticated, so will their buying habits. They will demand interoperability across ever-expanding systems.

Continuing with the CAD example, strong market incentives will mount for new users to buy the same CAD system as their component suppliers or at least one that can interoperate with a different system. Users are less likely to accept blanket supplier assertions of IGES support and will be scrutinizing the level and quality of IGES implementation.

Beyond CAD, a mix of other formal industrywide agreements and ad hoc supplier collaboration are settling into place. For the broader IT-integrated factory, there is MAP. In the office, Boeing has been spearheading another set of interoperability standards (TOP). In 1986, a similar effort aimed at hospitals (Medical Information Bus—MIB) was launched. Some of these initiatives are now being integrated although a universally accepted "standard of standards" may not ever be accomplished.

Also, numerous nonapplications specific standard efforts are well along. In data transmission there is Open Systems Interconnection (OSI); for operating systems, one example is UNIX; video standards include NAPLPS and VHS; and standards are developing for exchanging content across industries (X.12) using Electronic Data Interexchange networks. Other major ongoing standards initiatives are focused on database management software (the "relational model"), public Integrated Services Digital Network (ISDN), and electronic mail (X.400). Together with numerous other active standards developments, they provide the preliminary frameworks for interoperability.

What is interoperability worth? The Navy recently introduced an office systems standard for document exchange (DIF) that they claim will save $1 billion in rekeying and interface programming costs—just within the Navy. The Department of Defense, overall, seems intent on establishing Ada as a standard programming language. The benefits of interoperability on the battlefield are obvious.

Systems Integration

Where standards are lacking, suppliers often step in with software, hardware, and service that convert from one protocol, format, or speed to another. This is visible in a stream of "compatibility" products and services that enable IBM equipment to exchange data with equipment produced by other suppliers and among different protocols. Even IBM itself has introduced several such compatible products and features over the past 2 years as well as supporting certain aspects of the OSI and UNIX movements. This quest for interoperability is causing IT suppliers to shift more and more R&D monies to systems integration. One effect is a move away from basic components. This is leading to an explosion of firms specializing in systems integration while fundamental component suppliers consolidate in number.

We define systems integrators as those who enable and ensure interoperability among multiple elements within a system such as:

Hardware

Software

Network

Information

Human

These systems may be disparate in terms of their:

Suppliers

Protocols

Locations

Availabilities

They may interface with other systems within the same entity, and/or across different entities throughout the system's life cycle:

Conceptualization

Design

Implementation

Operation

Enhancement

Renewal

Figure 3.3 depicts the many roles that systems integrators perform. Some firms, like EDS, Computer Science, and Planning Research, often play all of these roles. Others specialize in the development, operational or enhancement-renewal stages of a systems lifecycle.

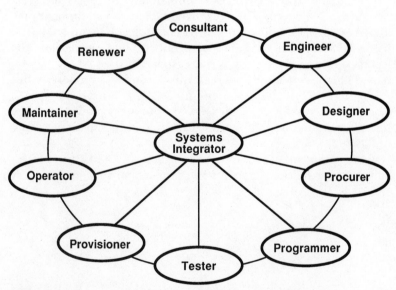

Figure 3.3. Systems integrators play and can link together multiple roles.

Summary

Unfortunately, like the mythical Hydra monster, technology threatens to grow incompatible heads faster than systems integrators, other suppliers, or standards setters can slay them. This will delay the principal impact of certain highly publicized megatechnologies. For example, the new Japanese-sponsored "fifth-generation" computer program is hampered because the new software architectures do not yet interoperate with present artificial intelligence centers, new protocols do not mesh with older communications systems, and new languages do not fit old operating systems. In contrast to the fifth generation project, another more imminent megasystem, the Integrated Services Digital Network (ISDN), is well along its development path worldwide. It is driving, rather than being driven by, interoperability. Yet, even the strong ISDN movement could bog down if certain standards issues are not resolved rapidly.

4
Disintermediation: IT Power

As IT becomes more and more embedded in the business operations of customers, IT is shifting the values upon which business competition is based. Inevitably, this has begun to trigger fundamental restructurings of other industries, a dramatic effect we call "disintermediation." Very simply, it means eliminating steps involving parties interposed between consumers and producers. In banking, financial disintermediation that is unrelated to technology has existed for some time. Many of us contribute to it when we bypass savings banks to lend our money directly to the government by buying Treasury bills.

As information systems become more interoperable and deliver more content from end to end, new forms of disintermediation are emerging. Some are taken for granted. We bypass telephone operators every time we direct-dial a credit card call. In every day banking, over 40 percent of banking customers now use an automated teller rather than transact with a human teller. Outside of banking, we disintermediate when we order a product through a telemarketing operation instead of going to a store or meet face to face with a sales rep.

For those businesses and individuals that are bypassed, disintermediation is a disaster. But, in some rare cases, cutting out intermediaries can take unexpectedly humorous turns. Diaper makers, for example, are under constant pressure to improve their products. This means constant effort to redesign and alter their diapers. Traditionally large and small babies would be brought to design labs as mannequins. New diapers would be tested for good fit and comfort. But technology has disintermediated the babies. As a GE executive likes to put it, "Now scores of babies' behinds are stored in computer software. And the diapers can actually be tested for fit and load factors with our computer-aided engineering software." Also on a lighter note, Washlet, a microcomputerized bidet manufactured by Japan's Toto, is threatening to disintermediate toilet paper in Japan.

Connecting to IT

IT is already generating the power to disintermediate roles within companies and between them. Telemarketing and computer-to-computer order entry, for example, are displacing field sales organizations. Consumers with access to public terminals (i.e., "electronic kiosks") are ordering merchandise on-line and are receiving electronic coupons. Cable channels increasingly are running successful merchandising programs which trigger strong in-bound WATS ordering responses from certain segments of consumers. Travelers staying overnight in hotels are accessing tourist directories, airline schedules, stock market results, and even their own hotel bill without leaving their room. Some systems now allow consumers to make their own travel arrangements or to initiate stock trades without calling in a "live" agent or broker.

Indeed, Gregory Parsons states, "By introducing a new competitive weapon into various settings, IT sparks outbreaks of firm warfare."[8] He cites specific examples in airline reservations, securities brokerage, and banking, all of which demonstrate disintermediation within service industries. Disintermediation of stock brokers, in particular, is well under way. Charles Schwab & Co., among others, now offers several information services direct to investors via TouchTone phones and personal computers including quotes, portfolio analysis, market commentary, and electronic mail.

Why has IT become such a potent force? The key reason is that information is often the principal product exchanged in a transaction—such as the purchase of a training program or the contracting of consultant services. This is true within businesses (e.g., manufacturing to logistics), between two businesses (e.g., buyer to seller), and between a business and a consumer (see Figure 4.1). This disintermediation is linked to new technologies which add value to information by converting, storing, processing, and transporting it into more highly usable and immediately accessible forms.

Out of all this come striking IT benefits. One is *wider reach*. More people can be linked with electronic networks and a host of new tele-based applications such as telemarketing, teletraining, teledelivery, telediagnostics, telegaming, and telemusic, to name just a few.

There is *greater convenience*. Terminals are getting easier and easier to use as software that selects and formats information to individual needs is perfected. Building on artificial intelligence and image-display technologies allows sellers to offer *richer content* on a more timely basis from a

[8]Gregory Parsons, "Information Technology: a New Competitive Weapon" *Sloan Management Review* Fall 1983 p. 6.

	Business-to-Business	Business-to-Consumer
Goods	Distributor	Retailer
Services	Financier-operator	Agent-broker

Figure 4.1. Disintermediation will result from the outreach of trading networks which have begun to proliferate. SOURCE: *Booz, Allen & Hamilton 1983*.

from a broader selection of sources. And best of all, it means *lower costs* as the unit costs of technology undercut traditional people- paper- and travel-intensive alternatives.

Business to Business

IT is affecting relations between buyers and sellers. Distributors, financiers, brokers, and agents are threatened. In business-to-business transactions, some manufacturers are able to bypass wholesalers and jobbers through electronic data interexchange networks, especially when the information values added exceed the physical distribution values added by distributors. A 1985 survey by the National Mass Retailing Institute claimed that over 50 percent of major retailers would have electronic supplier data exchange within two years.[9] In some instances, powerful distributors have defended themselves against this type of bypass by seizing the initiative in developing such new networks. American Hospital Supply, McKesson, and Anixter Brothers have been among the pioneers in this area. Not only has each succeeded defensively, but each has gained marketshare at the expense of smaller less-aggressive intermediaries.

Indeed, McKesson has even "reintermediated" by taking share from manufacturers. McKesson's Economost service has been particularly successful. The company, which invested some $125 million on IT, achieved an annual growth rate of 16 to 17 percent in both sales and profits from 1980 to 1985. Together with Bergen Brunswig and other successful IT-driven distributors, wholesalers now account for 65 percent of all

[9]David L. Anderson, "LDI: Why Data Communications Managers Should Be More Interested," *Data Communications*, January 1986, p. 157.

domestic pharmaceuticals up from 45 percent in 1970. Sterling Software and other information service firms report growing interest in their EDI services among both large and small manufacturers and distributors.

Natural resource-based industries such as oil and chemicals are another fertile bed for disintermediation. In mid-1985, Citicorp and McGraw-Hill joined forces to establish GEMCo as a test vehicle for facilitating trade between buyers and sellers of such commodities. We expect many more such powerful collaborations, although not all will be successful. Another type of direct business-to-business link is illustrated by Burlington Industries' Denim Division. They are now sending their customers free communications software that enables customers to locate and order the right bolts of fabric from Burlington's mainframe computer. These customers, primarily apparel makers, are now able to reduce their inventories as a result of the shortened and more accurate order-placement cycle. More importantly, Burlington is in a strong position to boost its share of market.

In the services sector, where inventory management is not a consideration, service suppliers (such as transportation companies and commercial insurers) are beginning, albeit cautiously, to bypass brokers and agents. The love-hate relationship between airlines and travel agents, which has long smoldered beneath the surface of airline advertising programs, is likely to flare publicly soon.

Within Businesses

Within companies, IT is rebalancing and in some cases eliminating value-added stages. Production facilities are being reconfigured. Links in the supply chain are already being eliminated. Numerous manufacturers are achieving just-in-time inventory systems by establishing interoperable inventory management networks with their suppliers. General Motors has been streamlining its engineering and purchasing transactions with original parts suppliers by encouraging them to install interoperable CAD systems.

In the office, integrated systems will inevitably lead to sizable displacements of middle managers, although not until the 1990s. Also as suggested earlier, field sales and service organizations are endangered species in many firms.

In addition, we find that the organizational structure of firms can be altered. Flatter hierarchies and broader spans of control are enabling hair-trigger organizational responsiveness to electronic stimuli. Internal electronic mail and teleconferencing networks are unleashing opportunities for interdisciplinary problem solving heretofore stymied by time and distance barriers. IBM has been using over forty slow-scan video reference rooms worldwide mainly to integrate physically dispersed product and market development teams. Digital Equipment Corporation employees worldwide are now linked in a system that allows graphics, data, and word information to flow interactively among over 30,000 terminals.

Business to Consumer

As highlighted in Chapter 2, the home is already a huge IT market. In 1986, the average U.S. household spent $1600 a year for telephone, broadcast, and music systems as well as for printed publications and other IT outputs. And the IT industry garnered an additional $900 per household from businesses in consumer-directed advertising revenues and telephone subsidies.

Integrated Market Services (IMS) promise to restructure and disintermediate several other industries as they raise IT's take. According to Robert J. Buckley, chairman and chief executive officer of Alleghany International, Inc., ". . . electronic shopping will have a major impact on the businesses of both the manufacturer and retailer and on print and broadcast advertising. I think that impact is likely to come sooner—rather than later—as the pace of technology steps up. It becomes irresistible."[10]

A new consumer IMS concept termed "automated replenishment" threatens to bypass traditional retail channels. The notion is that certain consumer segments would prefer to have their package-goods stocks replenished through automated reorder systems rather than be inconvenienced by routine trips to local supermarkets and pharmacies. Consumer goods manufacturers see it as a way to avoid the brand switching that occurs when consumers are drawn, either by coupons or necessity, to retail stores.

What is IMS?   IMS is a network linking consumers and producers. IMS providers are themselves a new form of intermediary that facilitates commercial transactions between buyers and sellers. Until recently, most providers have performed only one of the three roles (see Figure 4.2) that an integrated intermediary can perform. Also those roles have been played with relatively low-tech vehicles such as printed directories and catalogs, telemarketing, and narrowcast advertising. Nevertheless, under the rubric of direct marketing such low-tech domestic providers of information, marketing, and fulfillment services are racking up over $50 billion, growing at 15 to 20 percent annually. Comp-U-Card, Home

---

[10]Robert J. Buckley in a speech for the Touche Ross & Co. Conference on Electronic Shopping—the Coming Revolution in Retail Marketing, "Marketing Revolution #4321: The Electronic Phenomenon of the 1980s and 90s" June 12, 1984.

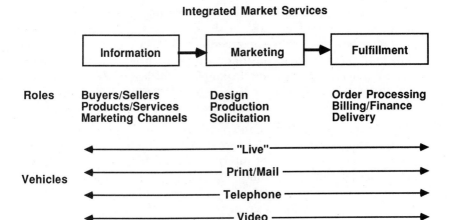

Figure 4.2. Integrated market services (IMS) is spawning huge new market opportunities.

Shopping Network, and Safecard are among the most successful independent IMS players to date.

Looking ahead, IMS is what every consumer has been led to believe high-tech could do. IT enables consumers to purchase products, manage financial affairs, communicate with businesses and personal acquaintances, work, and learn—all through an interactive device. Depending on the beholder (and the motivations of the IT supplier), access to IT is through a versatile home computer, an intelligent audiovisual playstation, a display telephone, or an electronic kiosk in a public place.

Regardless of how the access device is configured or positioned, the results of extensive market studies clearly point up the four sets of attributes a successful mass-market IMS will need to have:

- The system will have the ability to display normal TV-quality images. Computer text and graphics (such as ASCII, videotex, and teletext), while adequate for some services such as banking and electronic mail, simply will not do for enough others to provide sustainable profitability across a mass market. "Still" video pictures and even some full motion will be required to attract most business advertisers and to impress the substantial amount of product information consumers require as they teleshop. Wide bandwidth telecommunications and interactive compact discs are the two IT vehicles capable of delivering video-quality images.

- The scope of services offered will be broad and diverse. They should include, at a minimum, shopping, banking, reservations, investments, electronic mail, as well as home budgeting and tax preparation, home security, and learning. Most of these services are based on existing content to be delivered by a new medium. But, the medium will stimulate the development of new consumer content such as proactive investment portfolio management and telegambling. (Telegambling is already an established practice in Hong Kong where 300,000 telebettors wager by telephone.) The most innovative uses probably remain to be conceived.

- Services, marketing, and technology will be thoroughly integrated into a simple interoperable system—simple in its technology (so the consumer need learn only one way of interfacing with the system), simple in its marketing (pricing and promotion), and simple in the information flows among services (e.g., the shopping service would interface directly with the consumer's banking accounts).

- Beyond their own integration, access and pricing mechanisms for such information systems should dovetail with those relating to entertainment. The established socioeconomic value of entertainment is the flywheel that is driving the earlier stages of IMS growth. Searching through an electronic catalog should be fun, not work. Interactive advertising should be intellectually as well as economically rewarding. Cable television, VCRs, and compact disc players initially acquired as entertainment conduits can be the infrastructural elements of IMS home delivery when they are linked to interactive controllers.

Market Acceptance.   The smashing acceptance of cable-TV shopping in the mid-1980s, while not very high-tech, attests to the latent demand. Other supporting evidence includes the impressive growth of home-based information systems in France. By mid-1986, over 1.5 million Minitel terminals were in use an average of 80 to 85 minutes per month.

In a massive market study conducted by Booz, Allen & Hamilton in 1982 (its methodology follows), almost 60 percent of the households surveyed showed a "high propensity" to subscribe to a system displaying many of the characteristics described above. (Booz-Allen termed this concept Home Information Systems (HIS)). Conservatively interpreting both the results of this extensive study and other empirical results, we forecast that more than 30 million households will be regularly using some form of high-tech IMS either at home or at kiosks by the latter 1990s.

HIS Study Methodology

The primary objective of this $2.5 million study was to assess the willingness of consumers to make the behavioral changes required by HIS. The study probed some 700 demographically balanced households in communities in which some form of HIS technology already existed—in New York, Ohio,

Colorado, and California. The relationship between consumer acceptance and business sponsorship and restructuring was then interpreted by five teams of senior Booz-Allen experts.

The majority of consumers surveyed were representative of heads of households with income at or above the U.S. median. A sample of these consumers had already been exposed to first-generation HIS systems (such as QUBE), and some of the others were early adopters of advanced non-HIS consumer electronics.

To expose respondents to a system that would most closely resemble the technology that would be available by 1990, Booz-Allen, with MIT's assistance, developed an HIS simulator with features including:

- Touch-sensitive TV monitor used for display, user response, and data entry
- Three levels of interactive display: computer-generated graphics, TV-quality still pictures, and full sound-and-motion video
- A menu of fourteen transactional and/or information-oriented services: banking bill paying, entertainment tickets, household budget, personal calendar, home monitor, vacation travel, learning, games, news, shopping, electronic mail, classified ads, insurance, and investments

Participants (screened and recruited by telephone) were initially interviewed for several hours in their homes. Each family was then invited to a special demonstration center where they interacted for an hour or so with the HIS in use. Some respondents who expressed a strong interest in HIS were exposed to the simulator again and questioned 1 to 2 weeks later, while others were interviewed in depth in their homes.

Consumer reactions were analyzed, as were other economic-demographic data, to identify the likely level and timing of consumer acceptance and the implications on the pace, structure, and substance of the market place. "Best" and "worst" case market outlooks were developed reflecting the HIS market evolution.

The consumer results were then analyzed from a strategic perspective by five teams of senior Booz-Allen partners and associates: financial services, retailing, broadcasting and publishing, electronics and telecommunications, and travel-reservations. Each of these teams considered the competitive dynamics, technologies, and fundamental economics of HIS versus existing consumer products and services. Based on these analyses, the teams formulated recommendations for market positioning and investment.

As might be expected, interest was very strong for those under the age of 45. Those in the 45- to 55-year-old age bracket showed strong interest in individual services but were less certain of the overall offering. Curiously, the over-55 age group displayed a relatively higher propensity than the 45 to 55 age group, reflecting perhaps the attractiveness of electronic delivery to those less mobile.

Overall interest in HIS did not vary measurably with education, occupation, and family household income, although demographic differences did show up in individual service preferences. Consumers perceived home computer-based security and learning services and the network-based banking and shopping services to have the greatest value. Consumers' interest in specific HIS services ranged from nearly 75 percent for banking and bill paying to around 35 percent for insurance and investment services (see Figure 4.3)—these percentages were based on those stating they "definitely would use" or be "very likely to" use such services.

Consumers cited five content-driven reasons for their HIS enthusiasm:

- *Substantial time savings and convenience.*   Such services as shopping and banking would allow consumers to perform these activities 24 hours a day without the burden of travel.

- *Tightened control over personal lives.*   This would occur through such HIS services as home security and home management software.

- *Expanded experience and knowledge base.*   Through interactive learning and shopping services and through such business support services as insurance and investment "advisors" and interactive advertising, consumers could learn more at home.

- *Some economic advantages.*   They would be provided in electronic-based shopping and banking services and through better management of household finances.

- *Self-enhancement.*   This would occur not only through on-line learning services but also through videogames (i.e., parents see an opportunity to interact with their children and, thus, build the parent-child relationship).

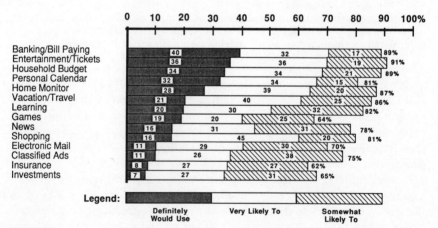

Figure 4.3. Demand is strong across a wide variety of services. SOURCE: *Booz, Allen & Hamilton Inc., HIS study, 1982.*

Going beyond the results of the Booz-Allen study and whether IMS is delivered in the home, automobile, or public places, consumer enthusiasm for it is a function of deepening IT literacy. Beyond acculturation, changes in the environment have heightened the need for potential IMS benefits. The growth in two-wage-earner households argues for more time savings and convenience. Mounting concern about serious crime in the United States is spurring the demand for home security systems. With aftertax inflation-adjusted real household income having been flat to slightly down over the past 15 to 20 years and with fewer government hand-outs, demand is swelling for more efficient retailing channels and more effective management of household assets. And widely publicized problems with public education are convincing many families to seek home-based computer-aided learning.

Revenue Potential.   We see the total annual value of high-tech IMS services exceeding $30 billion annually by the latter 1990s. Even at that level, high-tech IMS will only represent a modest fraction of total low-tech plus high-tech IMS revenues, which should be well in excess of $200 billion by then.

Consumers will not be the principal source of IMS revenues. Over 60 percent—or an annual amount equal to about $700 to $800 per household (in constant dollars)—of high-tech IMS revenues will be funded by the business community. Beyond these direct outlays, we see enlightened businesses contributing to the total IMS opportunity in seven important areas: advertising, shopping (product presentation and transaction handling), home management education (how-to-do-it), reservations, the merchant side of bill paying, insurance (as a prospecting and educational tool), and brokerage services.

In addition to these direct and indirect content contributions from businesses, we anticipate an incremental $5 to 10 billion IMS facilities market for related telecommunications services, mainframe computer hardware and systems software, and consumer electronics.

Clearly then, the major high-tech IMS revenue streams will not come from cannibalizing traditional IT businesses, such as broadcasting and publishing. Rather, IMS will continue to carve most of its incremental revenues from such other industries as banking, retailing, education, and travel by helping to disintermediate less efficient stages of their marketing and delivery systems to consumers. Households already spend thousands of dollars annually within each of these other industries, and IT suppliers will eventually take a share.

But, a potential bottleneck is the reluctance of other industries, such as banking and retailing, to streamline their value-added structures to bypass low value-added intermediaries. The strategic implications of high-tech IMS for the marketing and physical distribution stages of these and other consumer-oriented businesses, are daunting.

Paying for IT Now

A major consequence of IT disintermediation is a rethinking of business strategy for most industries. "Technology is the driving force," says James J. Howard, president of Ameritech. "My company is in the business of helping people send and receive information. Anytime. Anyplace. In any form. And that puts us in the business of information handling."[11] in a joint 1984 Booz-Allen/*Wall Street Journal* survey of European CEOs, communicating and handling information better was cited as their number one IT need (see Figure 4.4).

The basis of competition in many industries is shifting away from personal relationships and sheer size (in facilities and other fixed-cost assets). The "old boys club" approach is rapidly disappearing. No longer can larger insurance companies or banks be assured of first-tier positions with their brokers or corporate customers simply because of personal ties between managers. More important now is the ability to fine-tune superior-value customer content in narrowly targeted market segments

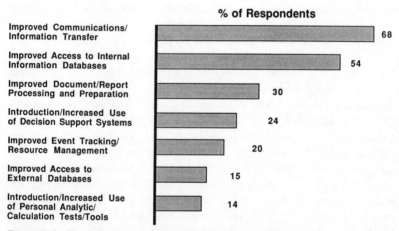

Figure 4.4. Top executives perceive multiple information technology benefits over the next 5 years. SOURCE: *1984 Survey of European CEOs sponsored jointly by Booz, Allen & Hamilton Inc., and* The Wall Street Journal/Europe.

[11]James J. Howard in a speech, "Mene, Mene, Tekel, Upharsin—The Telecommunications Industry Needs a Daniel," April 2 and 3, 1984.

and to flesh out new trading and distribution channels with electronic backbones.

In many cases pricing strategies are growing more vital to success as IT leads to more perfect markets. More intense and volatile pricing competition results. In other cases, to tailor customer value, sellers are linking buyers electronically so that marketplace needs are better and faster understood. Many new electronic data interchange networks record transaction activity so that it can later be analyzed for market trends and in some cases resold as a derived database. This may eventually disintermediate market information brokers, such as mass-market research firms.

Because the effect on corporations is becoming not only pervasive but also necessary as a means of survival, IT investments have begun to rival other capital investments in size and attractiveness. Rowland C. Frazee, CEO of The Royal Bank of Canada, states that his organization's IT expenditure "totals 20 percent of noninterest expenses. Twenty years ago, the percentage was negligible; ten years ago, it was still under 10 percent. The best internal estimate is that these costs as a percentage of noninterest expenses will climb by at least 1 percent annually for the balance of this century."[12]

Therefore, *"pay now* for IT, *or pay later* in lost marketshare and profits," is the new dictum. This presents problems especially for smaller firms. Many IT investments, such as factory automation, retailing point-of-sale, and high-tech IMS are costly up front. Therefore, these firms need an IT resource allocation methodology to engender the confidence necessary to pull out their checkbooks.

How to Allocate IT

For private sector IT customers, the strategic deployment of information technology is driven by two critical success factors. One is *product differentiation in targeted markets* leading to greater customer value, price recovery and profits; the other is *least cost production* through ongoing productivity gains leading to wider margins and/or greater competitive pricing flexibility. Competitors with visibly superior products and least cost are in a position to be the disintermediators rather than the disintermediatees (see Figure 4-5).

However, not all IT customers should place the same amount of importance on each of these factors. The relative importance of critical success factors is derived from the strategic positioning of a business. At one extreme, strong product-market differentiation is primary to fashion

---

[12]Rowland C. Frazee in a speech for the Brookings Institution, "Traded Computer Services: A Bilateral Beginning," April 10, 1984.

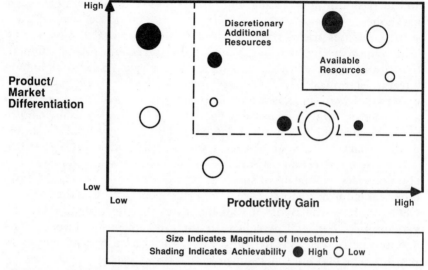

Figure 4.5. Strategic prioritization grid for information technology projects. SOURCE: *Harvey L. Poppel, "The Strategic Management of Information Technology—Challenging the I² Customer," Information Industry Insights, Booz, Allen & Hamilton Inc. Issue 6, p. 8.*

apparel. Conversely, productivity is pivotal to success in commodity businesses in which product-market differentiation may be unachievable. Other businesses have varying degrees of dependence on these success factors. For example, the luxury auto business may have about the same productivity needs as the economy auto business, but its success is more dependent on customer perceptions of product features, hence product-market differentiation.

Once derived, the critical success factors generate the strategic technology imperatives. For example, in a financial business whose strategy targets high-net-worth consumers, strong product-market differentiation is the dominant critical success factor. Strategic imperatives, therefore, will be focused on providing a high-quality, flexible customer service capability. One resultant technology imperative will be to have an integrated customer-oriented database which is readily accessible.

On the other hand, a mass-market targeted financial business will be characterized by high-volume transactions and tight margins. The applied technologies need far less flexibility but must have a high productivity quotient if the business is to be profitable. In fact, multiple "systems solutions" may be needed within the same organization that is striving to serve multiple product-market segments.

This thinking leads to a six-step program whereby a potential user can develop an IT strategy:

1. Define the value-added structure of the industry and the firm's position in it.

2. Determine IT's existing contribution to the operations and management processes of each internal value-added stage. Also determine the extent to which IT is leading to more perfect markets externally.

3. Assess competitors' progress and plans. Identify where the combined actions of suppliers and customers could result in fundamental shifts in the value-added structure, such as external or internal disintermediation.

4. Ascertain the firm's future strategic leverage points and the potential value that applying IT can add to each. Concomitantly determine where IT implementation may be a gating factor in accomplishing certain strategies.

5. Define and set priorities for specific improvement actions based on relative value added, investment, interdependency, and achievability.

6. Formulate the IT development strategy and reach agreement on how IT should alter the industry's value-added structure and the firm's competitive positioning in that structure.

Ironically, those who might be responsible for formulating IT strategies to deal with disintermediation—the traditional MIS/EDP departments—are themselves being disintermediated by IT. Increasingly IT-literate end users find they do not need MIS/EDP professionals to interpret and gatekeep IT. Anticipating this, savvy MIS/EDP executives are repositioning themselves into "information technology managers."

Information Technology Management

Information Technology Management (ITM) has evolved from *three waves of management processes* aimed at exploiting computer and communications developments (see Figure 4.6).

The first wave, which peaked in the mid-60s, was narrowly focused on harnessing new data processing hardware and software to reduce clerical and administrative staff requirements. The second wave, Management Information Systems (MIS), focused on reshaping and elevating the transaction data captured in the first wave to provide accurate and timely business information indicators to managers.

Then, as business managers began to realize the limits of historical transactional information, they sought the value of a wider range of business information. This fostered the Information Resource Management concept—the ability to enhance decision making through the retrieval and manipulation of a variety of internal and external informa-

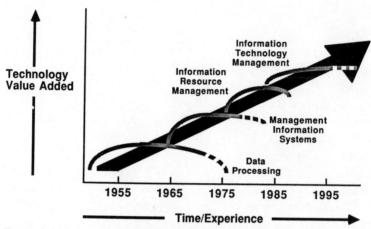

Figure 4.6. Driven by the potential strategic benefits of newer information technologies, a fourth wave of management change is now upon us. SOURCE: *Harvey L. Poppel, "The Strategic Management of Information Technology—Changing the I² Customer,"* Information Industry Insights, *Booz, Allen & Hamilton Inc., Issue 6, p. 8.*

tion. This concept explicitly calls for these content sources and the facilities associated with content production to be managed through a coordinated process.

However, even before Information Resource Management has gained a substantial strategic management foothold, the three infotrends described thus far have triggered the need for a much more powerful management process—ITM.

ITM involves a positioning of key experts in a user organization so that at least six vital activities take place.

1. *Educating executives and end users.* This allows people to become aware of how the overall strategic position of the business will change as the result of technology and of how their role will (or will not) change with it. This is especially important relative to the automated office environment, i.e., how new productivity tools can facilitate tasks and the quality of worklife.

2. *Energizing the organization.* To encourage senior managers to pursue IT opportunities.

3. *Facilitating the acquisition of resources.* A process that enables individual users to marshal the technologies, human resources, and related funding yet encourages the sharing of IT resources with other end users who have similar needs if development lead times can be telescoped and budgets conserved.

4. *Guiding end-user planning and implementation processes.* Accomplished by demonstrating how applications can differentiate products and boost productivity and by transferring proven methodologies already successfully used by others.

5. *Integrating the implementation efforts and systems architectures of multiple end-user groups.* Develops a framework within which compatible technology modules can interoperate with each other and new ones can be added and later upgraded without costly systems conversion.

6. *Setting priorities for investments at the strategic business unit or corporate level.* Assisting those with responsibility for system cost and service to set priorities for installation schedules driven by that function's critical success factors.

Organizationally, the ITM process provides a great deal of flexibility. It can be established centrally, within strategic business units, and even within individual departments. In a larger enterprise, it works best when all levels are involved and committed. Those companies that decide to establish an ITM function will probably opt to customize it so that it integrates easily into existing functions and blends with organization structure, culture, and other management processes.

The strategic management of information technology is the major challenge facing business customers today. Shouldn't IT suppliers be doing more to help their customers face this challenge?

Exploiting IT

IT-supplier executives can capitalize on disintermediation (and avoid being disintermediated) by recognizing emerging market characteristics.

"The first step," according to Bill McGowan, chairman of MCI, "has to be to get top management thinking about these technologies not as an expense item, but as a competitive tool—a profit tool."[13] Beyond this simple truth, it is clear that IT-buying decisions are becoming more complex. Consumers have to trade off their time against cost. More and more, business decisions involve higher-level executives and interdisciplinary task forces. And for systems that disintermediate externally, at least two sets of parties, buyers and sellers, must agree to do business with IT.

Because IT uses are becoming so complicated, many customers plan cautious pilot programs that can postpone big ticket sales for IT suppliers.

---

[13]William G. McGowan in a speech for The Research Board, September 12, 1984.

In part, this complexity has contributed to the slowdown in IT-hardware growth during the mid-1980s. All this puts more pressure on IT suppliers to understand specific industry applications, competitive dynamics, and the customer's critical success factors. Correspondingly, knowledge of industry-specific information content, in the form of databases and software, becomes pivotal. This is true whether the content is provided by the supplier, its customers, or the industry.

An example is the MAP project spearheaded by General Motors and the automotive industry. The goal of this program is to establish standards that will make the diverse computer integrated manufacturing (CIM) elements interoperable. Local area networks specifically oriented to factory requirements are at the core of this effort. And the MAP program also embraces many other industry-specific elements such as robots and data recorders.

Although MAP is still under development, GM has already committed to IT-integrated factories. A recently opened plant in Hamtramck, Michigan, was designed to assemble a car a minute using such systems as driverless carts, fully automated welding paint, and car-door installation stations and machine-vision inspection all under the real-time control of an integrated manufacturing database.

At about the time that Hamtramck was opened, GM forecast that over half of their 200,000 programmable devices would interoperate by 1990. (Programmable devices include not only robots but controllers, machine-vision systems, and the like.) This compares with only about 15 percent of 40,000 such GM-installed devices in 1984. Despite some subsequent glitches at Hamtramck that could downsize GM's forecasts, IT-integrated factories are becoming a reality throughout the automotive industry.

Not to be outdone, Toyota is marketing a value-added network service to customers in Japan, partnering to establish a second Japan telephone company, and distributing Computervision's CAD products (through their trading company affiliate).

Summary

By the 1990s, the potential for IT disintermediation strongly suggests that many traditional barriers between established non-IT and IT businesses will erode. For example, firms providing information services to hospitals, insurers, or banks may well find themselves advantageously positioned to enter the hospital management, employee benefits, or financing businesses. Other "natural" diversification plays for IT suppliers include education, insurance, wholesaling, commercial transportation, and professional services.

Conversely, certain aggressive aerospace, automotive, transportation, financial services, and retailing firms have already invaded the IT industry. Although many outsiders have been unsuccessful to date, the few winners have been leveraging the disintermediation opportunity (whether or not they call it that).

Where does this lead us? For the moment, the current wave of disintermediation among IT customers will beget considerable disintermediation within IT suppliers. And there is one type of IT disintermediation—common carrier bypass—that is not waiting. It is happening now and it is happening fast. Private electronic networking being put in place by Merrill Lynch, Ford, and others for both internal and external communications are effectively bypassing (i.e., disintermediating) certain local and interexchange telecommunications carriers. This contest merely is the beachhead in the war for vaster territorial realignments between current and emerging warriors across blurring industry borders.

5
Globalization: Thinking the World of IT

Global consumption of IT products and services is roughly twice that of North America. In general, the North American share of free-world consumption ranges from about 40 percent in most telecommunications products and service categories to well above 60 percent in software and microcomputers. Precise shares are difficult to compute since comprehensive market-product segment data are not readily available for Eastern-bloc, other less IT-developed countries, and even for government-monopolized market segments in certain developed countries outside North America.

Japan, the second largest country market, consumes 12 to 18 percent of the noncommunist world's IT output. Western Europe in total consumes 25 to 30 percent, with the United Kingdom, France, and Germany each accounting for roughly 20 percent of that total. The balance of Asia and the other continents in aggregate amount to 5 to 10 percent.

Which companies from which countries are best positioned to cash in on this world market? Will IBM gain world share? Will AT&T succeed internationally? Will Japan continue its onslaught? Will Europe be able to catch up to the runaway U.S. and Japanese front-runners?

North America and Japan: Racing for IT

Supply Side

The top-100 private sector IT providers (see Table 1.1) account for close to half of the world's supply. Of the leading 100 firms in 1984, 70 percent

64

of their combined sales ($416 billion) was controlled by North American-headquartered companies. Japanese-based firms accounted for 18 percent and Europe and Australia, the balance. The remainder of world sales was claimed by smaller private-sector firms and by national post, telephone, and telegraph operations such as the U.S. Postal Service and Germany's Bundespost.

As a front runner, North America is slipping, despite its dominance of the top 100. The entire roster of North American IT companies, both large and small, supply surprisingly no more than the same proportion, 50 percent, of the global market as North Americans consume. Actually, in most service and product clusters the once higher North American supply share has shrunk to less then 50 percent. The result is that North America is headed toward being a net IT importer. This seems so despite two striking exceptions: the IBM-led U.S. dominance of computer equipment, supplying a 75 percent share of global markets, and computer software with a 65 percent share of the world total.

Two trends account for the overall North American marketshare erosion. First, many large maturing service markets, such as telephony, entertainment, printing, and publishing, have traditionally been dominated by native suppliers for both policy and cultural reasons. Because the U.S. and Canadian markets for these services blossomed first, North American supply-side revenue growth, and hence worldwide share, outpaced other country suppliers. But now the momentum has shifted. The current period of more rapid growth for non-North American service markets has spurred non-North American service supplier world shares upward over the past 10 to 15 years and will continue to do so, although more slowly as these markets approach maturity as well.

Second are the constant gains by the Japanese in global product domains at the expense of North American (and European) manufacturers, especially in consumer electronics and low-end office equipment. Eighteen of the top-100 IT suppliers are now based in Japan. Also, global competition has begun to emerge from Australia (Rupert Murdoch's News Corp., Ltd., Storage Research) Korea, Taiwan and other Asian-Oceanic, and Caribbean Basin countries. Singapore, in particular, has established the goal of becoming the focal point for delivery of software and other information services throughout Asia.

Since the late 1970s, Japan has manufactured about 50 percent of the free world's consumer electronics, and more recently such other Asian producers as Korea's Goldstar and Samsung have begun to push heavily as well. And in the office equipment domain, Japanese manufacturers now account for over 40 percent of the copier market and close to 100 percent of the calculator and facsimile markets within North America itself.

A recent analysis by the American Electronics Association shows that Japan racked up a $15 billion surplus in IT trade with the U.S. in 1985, up from $12 billion in 1984. Not satiated, Japanese producers have most recently been taking aim at other worldwide consumer and office IT markets they do not yet dominate, notably film supplies, home computers, printers, and typewriters.

Can Japan Cut IT?

Nonetheless, the Japanese have had considerable difficulty and suffered many embarrassments in the more complex global equipment markets, such as mainframe computers and PBXs. Mostly, these failures can be attributed to three factors which are harbingers of troubling faults that will dampen all Japan's IT export market opportunities. First, Japan has too many fast-followers, i.e., Japanese firms who crowd one another in world markets, such as consumer electronics, in which Japanese leaders have been successful. The effect is an intensifying internecine competition among Japanese heavyweights, as well as with numerous high-powered Japanese niche players, such as Ricoh and Oki.

Second, Japanese firms lack either the content development know-how or the service business base that is increasingly helping to distinguish otherwise similar hardware and media products. As content and interoperability gain in relative value, the weakness of Japanese suppliers in these areas will be damaging. Few Japanese-developed application software, databases, or telecommunications network service offerings to date have had North American or European utility. And cultural barriers will continue to thwart most Japanese initiatives in these areas.

"We see no evidence that America is losing its hegemony in systems design and advanced software development, and that is what really counts."[1]

Third, and potentially most devastating to Japanese ambitions, is their heretofore dependence on stable non-Japanese distribution channels. Up until recently, the Japanese have successfully leveraged well-established general merchandise retailers for consumer electronics and independent and "interconnect" dealers for low-end office equipment. Only NEC has had some sustained success at establishing major captive channels in other countries. But, driven by the infotrends, traditional distribution channels have begun to change and in some cases are being disintermediated. Computer stores and value-added resellers, among others, have grown to be major channels, and the Japanese have not penetrated them success-

---

[1]Ulric Weil, "Computer Research Note," Morgan Stanley, February 25, 1985.

fully. Partly, this is due to the physical and cultural distances between Japanese headquarters executives and dynamic, and often unforeseen, developments in other countries. Indeed, many hitherto successful Japanese suppliers are likely to "hit the wall" during the later 1980s and early 1990s.

Sensing the wall's imminence, some Japanese suppliers have begun to acquire equity positions in Western-world supplier firms, such as Mitsubishi has with Britton Lee and Atari-Tel, or to Americanize their captive manufacturing and marketing functions. Other acquirors include Sanyo, who acquired Fisher, a well-known U.S. consumer electronics firm; Fujitsu, who acquired the Imaging Systems Division of Burroughs Corporation; and Konishroku, who has made several deals including taking a partial position in Fotomat and making an outright acquisition of Scripto. Not to be outdone, at least one Korean firm, Dawoo International Corporation, has acquired Corona Data Systems, a producer of IBM-compatible personal computers.

Joint venturing is the other solution sought by many Japanese firms. The variety of strategic rationales for Japanese-American joint ventures is illustrated by these examples:

Japanese	American	Purpose
Toshiba	Westinghouse	Joint manufacturing of CRTs.
Canon	Kodak	Canon manufactures, Kodak distributes.
Sony	RCA	Sony markets RCA satellites in Japan.
NEC	GE	Interconnecting packet networks.
Ricoh	DEC	Ricoh supplies laser printer for DEC distribution.
NEC	Honeywell	NEC builds large mainframes for Honeywell.
Consortium	Microsoft	Microsoft is developing MSX software standard for Consortium.
MITI	IBM	IBM lends support to $120 million software automation—Sigma project.

Of course, the Japanese are not alone in seeking these ventures, especially given the growing attractiveness of Japan's domestic market. One indicator of this reverse demand is that within 9 months of opening a Tokyo office, the American Electronics Association fielded inquiries from over 500 high-tech companies wishing to penetrate the Japanese market. These joint ventures may help overcome some endemic Japanese problems, but only if Japanese IT suppliers can keep up with the accelerating global demand-side changes taking place.

Demand Side

One reason for intensified global competition is the diffusion of similar IT demands worldwide. Despite local market differences, products demanded in America are increasingly the same as those in demand in Japan and in Europe. Six reasons explain this growing, broadly based similarity.

Different *IT-literacy* levels lead to varied rates of business and consumer diffusion across countries. Stimulated by their high-tech proclivity, the Japanese population enjoys the highest per-capita use of advanced consumer electronics, such as VCRs and compact discs, as well as of factory automation devices, such as robots. Conversely, the relative conservatism of Europeans has slowed the penetration rate of computers in comparison to that either in North America or Japan. Overall, however, IT-literacy gaps among countries are shrinking rapidly.

A second diffusion variable is the *IT cost-benefit* relationship. The user cost of emerging technology, such as high-powered computers and communications networks, has differed across countries by a factor of 3 or 4 during the initial market-product life cycle stages (covered in Chapter 17). This is ameliorated by a more rapid worldwide availability of new products which reduces the cost variant. But many important economic and social benefit differences will persist. In the business environment, labor displacement savings are more difficult to achieve in socialized countries, and labor and interest rates fluctuate widely across countries. Also the age and utility of potentially displaceable assets, such as factories, vary across countries. Differences in consumer benefit values, however, will narrow somewhat as worldwide IT-literacy levels rise.

Government support is a third variable. As discussed later in this chapter, the French have invested heavily in videotex and currently have the highest penetration rates in the world. The French government has anticipated that IT export market opportunities have much in common with other successful French export products, namely perfume and champagne. The packaging often yields more revenue than the contents. As of mid-1986, well over one million terminals were in operation in France, or one for every fifty people. And, many U.S. information providers are taking a close look at French-made terminals.

During the 1970s, several European countries with government support, most notably in Scandinavia and Switzerland, pioneered on-line banking networks. Norway gained an early lead in mobile communications penetration that was due to regulatory encouragement. Driven in part by diffusion objectives, the Japanese government is making sustained IT commitments, the most visible of which is the current fifth-generation computer development effort.

Nevertheless, some government programs have been ineffectual. The Canadian Development Corporation, for one, has experienced a string of failures in its IT investments and probably has not stimulated Canadian IT usage measurably. Perhaps the highly restrictive Foreign Investment Review Act, which initially discouraged U.S. participation, contributed to these failures. Pioneering efforts by the United Kingdom to lead world-wide in videotex produced the Prestel technology. This now appears to have been equaled or surpassed by French and North American developments.

Restrictive government policies can slow diffusion. Business computer penetration started lagging in Brazil during the mid to late 1970s because of government import restrictions on the leading U.S. manufacturers. Despite this, Brazilian authorities intensified import constraints as well as foreign ownership rules and extended protection into the telecommunication equipment sector as well. Similarly, both broadcast and cable television penetration in the United Kingdom has suffered from restrictive government policies, although many politicians staunchly defend those policies as having avoided the cultural deterioration they then saw in the U.S. In Washington, the FCC's procrastination in setting aside spectrum and establishing other ground rules delayed the emergence of newer mobile telephone technologies in the U.S. by at least 5 years, even while the Norwegian market using the same technologies was burgeoning.

But, despite these travails, restrictions are on the wane. "We simply must understand that regulators and regulation are no longer the wave of the future. In the information distribution business, which is our business, regulation is the dying exception to the national rule which favors competition," according to Laurence DeMuth, Jr., EVP, general counsel and secretary, U S West.

The FCC example also illustrates a fourth variable which governments often influence—*standardization*. Simple differences in electrical or frequency standards have discouraged many product manufacturers from globalizing their markets rapidly because of the added product development and certification costs. More complex variations in emerging ISDN, data communications protocols, systems software, and media format standards will undoubtedly continue to mire diffusion in those countries either lacking indigenous suppliers capable of unilaterally setting de facto standards or clinging to restrictive IT policies. But, as stated earlier, most governments are bending toward more encouragement and less restraint. For example, European and Japanese governments are encouraging the interoperability of indigenous packet switching data networks with those of such private-sector suppliers as GE Information Systems Company, Computer Science, and MCI. These activities will temper future diffusion rate differences.

The relative merits of *technology cross-substitution* is yet another diffusion variable. In Canada, cable systems penetrated rapidly because of their clear-cut advantages over terrestrially broadcast TV in countries with low population density. Conversely, in both the United States and Canada, VCR penetration and tape rentals lagged other countries in which consumers had far fewer real-time TV channel choices to enjoy. In Japan, word processing was slow to develop because typewriters were not as widely used, while facsimile flourished early because of the heavy use of image-laden documents. And, in banking, the United States has lagged many European countries in cross-substitutable electronics funds transfer (EFT) applications because of the ingrained use of paper checks and cash.

Many of these variations in cross-substitution will persist to some extent because of entrenched infrastructure differences. But *technology availability*, the sixth variable, will slowly mitigate them. Technology availability also is a bridge between IT demand and supply sides. Cross-country diffusion variations appear during the initial market-product life cycle stages when suppliers of emerging technology typically are hard pressed to serve native country demands. Foreign import restrictions or export subsidies do not wield much influence during these stages. Because their suppliers have dominated both content and facilities innovations to date, the United States, Canada, and Japan have usually led in demand-side penetration. This is best illustrated in the software segment. The United States currently accounts for 65 to 70 percent of world software consumption primarily because of the strong lead established by U.S. software suppliers, most of whom are fully occupied trying to keep up with domestic market demands.

Consumer VCRs are another graphic example of supplier influence. Throughout the early to mid-1980s, penetration rates in Japan were double that of either the United States or Europe, owing heavily to Japanese supplier innovation of consumer VCR products (first introduced in the Japanese market) and an ongoing 80+ percent share of worldwide VCR production. Compact disc players, robotics, and office imaging products are three other leading-edge examples of mutually reinforcing supply and demand in Japan. But some Asian countries are exceptions to supply-driven consumption. Korean and Taiwanese suppliers aim directly for the large export rather than the limited native markets, and IT-penetration rates within these countries are much more modest than their supplier successes would imply.

Technology availability and hence diffusion rates will continue to vary as new market-product segments go through their first and second stages. But on average, life cycles are telescoping and, therefore, diffusion differences will shrink.

Europe: Lagging IT

West European suppliers could be the principal beneficiaries of any share loss by North American and Japanese firms. Indeed because Europeans are heavy net IT importers, indigenous suppliers could grow markedly if they could only fully satisfy domestic demands.

However, as seen through one set of eyes, the prognosis is pessimistic. European IT companies, with the notable exception of several world-class providers, are viewed as completely—and perhaps permanently—relegated to the sidelines when it comes to world-scale IT competition. This fatalistic conclusion can easily be drawn from the tone of public opinion. Even senior European executives are pessimistic. In a survey conducted by Booz, Allen & Hamilton Inc., and jointly sponsored by *The Wall Street Journal/Europe*[2], respondents in three countries, with a combined participation in sixty-two IT sectors, believed world-level competition possible in only fourteen sectors.

Why the widespread gloom? Some of it derives from the sharp demand disparities between the European and U.S. IT industries. Western Europe consumes only 25 to 30 percent of the world supply and that proportion may be shrinking. By contrast, nearly half of world demand comes from the U.S.

Further, European companies collectively have captured only 30 to 40 percent shares of their own markets. On a worldwide basis, the supply picture gets worse. Europeans supply no more than 10 to 15 percent of the global market. Only 19 European companies appear among the top-100 private-sector suppliers. All European countries are net IT importers, and Europe's high-tech trade deficit is growing.

That is the bad news. There is another side to the story. This one is more optimistic. What current performance statistics mask are three key indicators. First, not only does Europe have a long history of technological innovation, but some European companies are seriously contending for world leadership. A few are even setting the pace in several very important IT segments. Optical disc technology developed by Philips is one example. Second, European IT initiatives are backed and encouraged by stronger public support than in the U.S. Indeed, public IT R&D spending has swelled by factors of 3 to 5 in recent years.

Third, latent demand within Europe is enormous. Europe's GNP is of the same order of magnitude as that of the U.S. Its population include nearly 300 million educated people in the Common Market and some 500 million for all of Europe (excluding the USSR).

---

[2]George Anders, "European Panel—Companies that Seek to Diversify Find It's Not Always That Easy," *The Wall Street Journal/Europe*, November 30, 1984.

How IT's Going

A 1983 study conducted by Booz, Allen & Hamilton Inc., and Digital Equipment Corporation[3] points up that European companies had at least adequate capabilities in most of the twenty-five IT segments studied. Moreover, the study showed that European players were contending at the world-class level in eleven of the twenty-five areas. More recently, home videotex is an area in which Europeans have aggressively and successfully pursued a leading-edge position. Europe leads the U.S. in network experience by 1 year, although technical capabilities are roughly comparable. Furthermore, a Europeanwide videotex standard has been proposed. France's ambitious videotex program in particular currently stands in stark contrast to the scattered and, to date, relatively unsuccessful initial American ventures into in-home videotex, many of which have lacked long-term strategic direction or sustained commitment.

Beyond videotex, European manufacturers are making big strides in *telecommunications services*. European telecommunications agencies are promoting the rapid implementation of integrated services digital networks (ISDN). Since these agencies rely heavily on indigenous telecommunications manufacturers, their large procurements and funding of major R&D efforts are enabling European suppliers to develop state-of-the-art technology. These communications suppliers are now mobilizing to compete outside their traditional home markets. Officials from twenty-six nations agreed in 1984 to begin harmonizing their standards for telecommunications technology—a move that will help break the technical and protectionist barriers that have kept European telecom markets confined within national borders. Big European customer-premise equipment suppliers have already committed the necessary R&D to state-of-the-art PBX technologies, targeting the interoperable office systems market. One very exciting new product is an ISDN compatible modular PBX from Siemens called HICOM that might trigger the fifth generation of PBXs.

Germany stands out as a potential world-class competitor in *robotics and related CAD/CAM technologies*. This is particularly true with optical and acoustical pattern recognition, tactile sensors for next-generation robotic systems, and CAD/CAM for mechanical applications. German institutes and suppliers are doing extensive work on the application of flexible manufacturing systems, recently focusing on the difficulties of assembly operations.

Germany's work in *ergonomics* also stands out. Its achievements are a direct result of a Ministry of Research and Technology program which

---

[3]Robert Boers and Hanns G. K. Schwimann, "I² Technology in Europe," *Information Industry Insights*, Booz, Allen & Hamilton Inc., issue 9, pp. 1, 3–6.

devoted approximately 700 million DMs to the "humanization of work-stations." The program created standards for word processing equipment and terminals that are now applied around the world.

Applications software is a well-established traditional European strength. Each of the three largest European countries outperforms Japan in software sales. France, in particular, is second only to the U.S. in software exports, and some European-controlled software and systems houses, such as CAP Gemini, are already competing successfully in the U.S. One caveat: As software content value added grows, further European success will be linked to packaging capabilities and competence in international distribution—both physical and marketing.

Sustained investments in *computation theory, artificial intelligence (AI), processor architectures, distributed systems, and consumer computing devices* are being made throughout Europe. As a result, software research is emerging as an important scientific discipline. The English have demonstrated impressive skills and world-class capabilities. This was clearly a reason behind Japanese attempts to gain input from British AI technologists for their fifth-generation effort.

Certain European efforts in *microelectronics* deserve recognition—for example, French capabilities in the growing Gallium Arsenide technology and both British and French research in VLSI and hardened components. But, these achievements aside, Europe materially lags Japan and the U.S. in microelectronics. Recognizing their weaknesses, European component manufacturers and telecommunications laboratories are planning to spend billions of European currency units (roughly equivalent to one U.S. dollar) in coming years to secure at least adequate market positions for their indigenous component companies. But this is unlikely to threaten U.S. and Japanese world-scale dominance.

Government Roles

Despite strong skepticism among European business executives about government efforts to develop technology, European governments are spurring the recovery of their IT industry. They have begun to take aggressive action, helping locally based companies not only to reconquer large parts of their home markets but also to export technology across Europe, to the United States, and even to the Pacific.

Some of the tactics governments have initiated have long-term implications for IT thinkers and planners. In France the socialist government undertook a dramatic restructuring of the IT industry. In what looked like a game of high-tech musical chairs, the telecommunications network equipment business was transferred from the Thomson-CSF Group to CIT-Alcatel in exchange for CGE's semiconductor interests; Bull received

Transac's terminal business from CGE and SEMS minicomputer business from Thomson-CSF. Subsequent changes in France's governing party philosophies could scramble the players and their owners once again.

On another front, governments are stimulating IT growth by creating the needed *national infrastructure*. Some are using their mammoth state-owned telecommunications carrier organizations to "fiber" and "cable" their countries for videotex. The three largest such carriers would rank among the world's top-twenty-five private-sector firms. These state-owned enterprises can afford to invest on the basis of long-range considerations because they are free of shareholder pressure. In Germany, the Bundespost plans to have 1 million households blanketed by Bildschirmtext by the late 1980s.

Government *investment in R&D* appears sensitive to the views of local business leaders. According to a survey conducted by Booz, Allen & Hamilton Inc., which they jointly sponsored with *The Wall Street Journal/Europe*[4], European executives cite improvements in factory operations as by far their most important technology objective. European governments rank advanced manufacturing processes, robotics, and other factory technology among their own R&D priorities. In fact, the Mitterand administration in 1983 declared these technologies as the most important focus for state-funded IT R&D in France.

And money buys more than policies or good intentions. Taken together, France, Germany, and the United Kingdom currently allocate well in excess of 5 billion European currency units in annual public funding to electronics and IT-related R&D. Each is spending roughly equal sums on R&D programs to enhance the competitive capabilities of its indigenous IT industry.

Yet, while the amounts are equivalent, each is managed differently. France has a centrally planned program, directed and controlled by the French Ministry of Research. The United Kingdom, on the other hand, had until recently only minimal IT planning at the national level. One example is the Alvey initiative whose government support falls into the diffused, highly decentralized, and loosely coordinated category. Germany's approach falls midway. It is a well-coordinated cooperative effort between the public and private sectors. The German government, moving away from direct grants for projects, uses more indirect incentives such as tax advantages to encourage R&D. Substantial R&D work is being done throughout the academic community and in more than 200 R&D institutes.

In addition to the national government focus, IT R&D has attracted the attention of the European Community, which is sponsoring an ambitious

---

[4]George Anders, "European Executives Consider U.S. Prime Area for Expansion Abroad, Journal Poll Shows," *The Wall Street Journal*, December 5, 1984.

program for resource pooling. The European Community believes that fragmented national approaches to R&D result in duplicated efforts and do not allow for cross-fertilization. Therefore, it has been vigorously prosecuting a 5-year Europewide research program called the European Strategic Program for Research in Information Technology. (ESPRIT).

ESPRIT is designed to foster Pan-European cooperation and give European IT suppliers a better chance to compete more effectively world-wide by sharing front-end research costs. The European Community believes ESPRIT will help create bigger and better research teams and promote standards throughout Europe. One major ESPRIT program involves precompetitive research with planners of twelve major European IT companies in areas of advanced microelectronics, software technology, advanced information processing, and IT-integrated manufacturing.

The first pilot projects were begun in 1983 and the early results are encouraging. The costs (1.5 billion European Currency Units) are being shared equally between the European Community and industry participants. Over the life of the program, hundreds of companies are expected to participate in a work plan designed by the European Community Commission. A 1985 independent review of ESPRIT found the program "highly successful in promoting trans-European cooperation between industry, academia, and research institutes." Work on standards was judged particularly valuable, allowing "Europe to speak with one voice" for the first time in standard-setting forums.

European Community proponents have also defined another program called RACE (Research And Development in Europe). RACE's objectives are to specify and develop interoperable network technologies. When completed, the program could cost the European Community and other sponsors $1 billion.

To gain maximum leverage in global markets, joint ventures among European companies and among European and non-European companies are common. One case is a 1985 decision by Bull, Siemens, and ICL to create a shared research center in Munich. More meaningful, however, is that many business leaders acknowledge the unlikelihood of Europe's technological survival if European countries act in isolation. International companies such as DEC, IBM, and American Microsystems, through their capabilities and willingness to transfer technology into their European development centers, have already had a substantial impact on Europe's knowledge base. They are comfortably entrenched in the European scene. Americans have led this move. The Japanese appear to be following suit.

Multinational European-based companies, such as ICL and Siemens, have tapped the best of U.S. and Japanese innovation by buying technology from both countries. Olivetti and Philips have teamed up with AT&T in office automation and telephone exchange switches, respectively. Ericsson and Honeywell are cooperating in PBXs, and Siemens and GTE are working together in telecommunications network equipment.

To gain a bigger share of the U.S. market and access to U.S. technology, European companies have become involved in minority participations and venture-capital investments in start-up technology-oriented companies. For example, Olivetti has teamed up with dozens of U.S. companies since the late 1970s. Such approaches are often welcomed by small and medium-sized high-tech U.S. companies that need to grow outside their initial product or market niches. But not all of the investments work. One example is the Docutel-Olivetti venture which ran into serious problems in the early 1980s.

As one looks upon the European economy from outside, several conclusions can be made about Europe's inability to meet its full IT potential. The introduction and acceptance of technology management as a discipline has been slow. Expertise in commercialization has been lacking. And, marketing skills remain to be proven outside Europe. Nevertheless, these problems are surmountable. Given the number and variety of IT strengths Europe is nurturing, one may well expect to see European companies capturing a much larger share of the global market. Their goal: a "natural" 25 to 30 percent share of the market, in line with their own demand. But their demand is declining in proportion to the world market and this formidable challenge is perhaps best summarized by Christian Fayard, head of CIT Alcatel's public telecommunications division: "We have . . . great difficulty compensating for the reduction in our home market through international sales."[5]

Summary

Globalization is but one dimension of the fifth infotrend—convergence. In addition to geographic confluxes, suppliers from different IT and non-IT roots within each country are discovering the interoperable potential among hitherto disparate physical and logical systems elements. They also are recognizing the commonality of interests shared by consumers and producers that are increasingly doing business via interoperable networks.

[5]Guy de Jonquieres and Paul Betts, "The Euphoria Is Over," *Financial Times,* February 2, 1985.

6

Convergence:
Homing in on IT

Product businesses and service businesses used to be easy to define and to isolate. But the four infotrends described previously are scrambling business definitions. True, some product and service categories are clear cut. Typewriters and calculators are products; telex and broadcasting are services. Yet, certain products, such as telex machines and TV sets, depend interoperably on the two aforementioned services to give them value. Some systems even combine devices and services. Examples include brokerage quotations, automated tellers, and energy control systems.

Increasingly though, certain categories of products and services are competing as cross-substitutes for each other. The following is a table of functions that could be provided by either a product *or* a service:

Desired Function	Product	Service
Computer power	Personal computer	Time sharing
Bibliography	CD-ROM	On-line database
TV program	Videotape	Broadcasting
Security alert	Smoke detector or alarm	Remote sensing
Speech message	Minicomputer	Store-forward network
Computer program	Floppy disc	Downloading
Game	Home computer	Video arcade

As a result, some computer and information service operators, such as McDonnell Douglas and ADP, have become equipment distributors, while some equipment suppliers, such as IBM and Wang, have become information and telecommunications service providers. And these only hint at the encroachments and overlaps which necessitate a technique—we call the "IT Grid"—for analyzing the structure and scope of IT businesses.

IT Grid

This grid, developed by one of the authors while at Booz, Allen & Hamilton Inc.,[1] (see Figure 6.1) is structured to relate IT elements of products and service to marketplace segments. Once having done that, we can then map the principal domains or spheres of influence for each set of IT businesses as a cluster of adjacent cells. Once each of our six clusters are so depicted, we can then visually analyze the degree to which they have or will overlap or converge.

We will start by defining each of the two dimensions of the IT grid.

The Product Service Dimension

Like the ninety-two "natural" atomic elements, which in various molecular combinations form everyday objects, the columns represent six IT elements which are the building blocks of all IT businesses.

Transport. Physical flow of information and entertainment by either electronic (e.g., telecommunications) or nonelectronic (e.g, postal) means.

Media conversion. Human-human (e.g., speech), human-machine (e.g., video display), keyboard, and machine-machine translations (e.g., analog sensor to digital computer).

[1]"Strategic Mapping of the Information Industry," *Information Industry Insights*, Booz, Allen & Hamilton Inc., issue 8, pp. 2–4.

Value-Added Elements

Marketplace Arenas	Facilities				Content	
	Transport	Media Conversion	Storage	Processing	Information	Entertainment
Consumer						
Interarena						
Business Operations						
Knowledge Work						

Figure 6.1. For analytical purposes, we map the IT industry in terms of value-added elements and marketplace arenas.   SOURCE: *Booz, Allen & Hamilton Inc., 1984.*

Storage.   Content preservation either in electronic (e.g, magnetic or optical disk) or nonelectronic (e.g., paper, film) media.

Processing.   Transformation of content substance (does not include format changes purely for media conversation or transport purposes).

Information.   Data and knowledge content or software which manipulates that content whose primary purpose is to enlighten.

Entertainment.   Creative content whose primary purpose is to amuse and please human senses.

The first four elements fall under the heading of *hardware and facilities,* and the latter two, into the softer definition of *content.* Postal services, telephone circuits, and copy machines are examples of pure facilities or hardware. Encyclopedias, television programs, applications software, and databanks are examples of pure content.

Convergence is catalyzing facilities and content elements into new molecular combinations of businesses. Increasingly, IT suppliers and IT users alike are offering products that bridge the content and facilities boundary. As one example of how content can be leveraged across multiple facilities, Buick Motor Division of General Motors has been developing a system called EPIC to help market its cars. Based on interactive videodisc and videotex technologies, EPIC can visually demonstrate feature options, calculate finance terms and charges, compare Buicks to similar models (through a tie-in with Compuserve), and even locate the nearest in-stock car matching with the customer's desired options. As of this writing, EPIC is being installed in Buick showrooms and public access terminals and is slated to be available at home to consumers as well.

EPIC and certain other outputs, such as turnkey computer systems, value-added networks, or computer retail stores, plot midway on the grid because they are facilities with embedded informational content. Bridging the facilities-content boundaries is expressed by a euphemism—*systems solution.* It is now a cliché. Nevertheless, the complexity of integrated content-facility systems, such as videotex, public transaction stations, electronic data interexchange networks, and IT-integrated factories, has spawned a seventh new man-made element we call *systems integration.* As defined in Chapter 3, this combines the required resources, often procured from others, for end-to-end assembling, interoperating, and marketing various software, database, input-output, processing, storage, and telecommunications components (see Figure 6.2). For example, Home Box Office has been a quintessential systems integrator to consumers, while Computer Sciences Corporation and Planning Research Corporation conceptually play the same role with esoteric defense information systems.

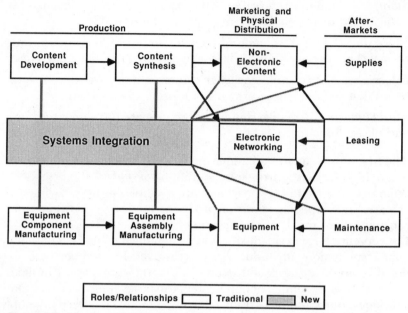

Figure 6.2. IT value-added structure is shifting. SOURCE: *Booz, Allen & Hamilton Inc., 1984.*

   This trend has spurred the convergence of both the competitive and collaborative interests of historically unrelated content and facilities producers. Some of the newer content-facilities bedfellows include publishers with communications network operators, educators with personal computer manufacturers, direct marketers with cable TV operators, and software developers with hardware manufacturers. Also there is a growing tendency for even the largest businesses to collaborate both with one another (e.g., IBM-Sears-CBS) and with smaller entities (ATT-Omnicad). Other surprising-to-some recent examples of collaboration include Time and CBS with respect to video production, and AT&T and MITI, a Japanese development cooperative, working together on UNIX.
   Thus, suppliers face a fundamental positioning issue: *which mix* of product-service elements *aimed at what* marketplaces? This leads us into the second dimension of the grid—the marketplace.

Arenas

We term the principal segments of the marketplace "arenas" because they are the turf upon which the wars of IT convergence are being waged.

The *consumer* arena encompasses communications and consumption of information and entertainment by individuals as opposed to enterprises. This consumption can take place in one's home, one's auto, a familiar shopping mall, or a hotel room. Many individual IT buying decisions, such as placing toll calls, can also be made by business employees from their workstations without organizational approvals.

Business operations includes consumption of IT products and services in business procurement, production-servicing, marketing, physical distribution, and other value-added stages. IT use is commonly high volume, repetitive, procedurally driven. Procurement of IT is normally based on quantitative cost-benefit analysis.

Knowledge work applies to information consumption and communications among managers and other professionals. Although often mistakenly lumped with business operations, knowledge work implies something very different. As Francis Bacon once said: "Knowledge and human power are synonymous." Consumption is more ad hoc, lower in volume, and is driven by events rather than procedures. Moreover, despite available quantitative analysis techniques (such as described in Chapter 11), most buyers are motivated by qualitative criteria and intuition. Life cycles of knowledge-work systems are relatively short.

Knowledge work and business operations, therefore, are distinctly different IT market segments. IT use in business operations is typically high volume, repetitive, and highly systematic. Increasingly, decisions to acquire information technology in business operations are driven by long-range quantitative cost versus benefits analyses. And once installed most business systems last for 8 to 12 years, albeit with ongoing modifications because they are embedded deeply in the value-added flow of the business which tends to be relatively stable.

Although each of these three primary arenas present distinct challenges to IT suppliers, areas of convergence among the three are redefining the competitive equation. All three arenas consume the same six product-service elements—transport, media conversion, storage, processing facilities, information, and entertainment content. Therefore, patents and proprietary technology and content and product-service skills are often transferrable among the arenas. For example, videotex, electronic mail, and personal computing appeal to all three arenas. Most of the physical and electronic distribution channels—retail stores, value-added networks, etc.—can deliver to more than one arena with some economies of scale. Some investments in content such as software and databases can be amortized across arenas, especially with respect to finance, travel, and vocational training.

Soon, electronic channels will be capable of transporting billions of transactions daily among and within the three arenas. And this facet of convergence defines a fourth arena we call the interarena. Many examples of interarena businesses already exist, including most businesses and consumer directories, commercial television, and telemarketing services. Newer examples include automatic teller machines, which can also be thought of as part of the business operations arena because they perform an operating function for banks as well as interfacing with consumers.

Convergence of the three arenas and emergence of new electronic interarena applications strongly suggest that IT business customers should focus their information technology analysis on: (1) how to develop, produce, and physically distribute products and services; (2) how to market them; and (3) how to reallocate their fixed financial and human assets accordingly. Therefore, the relationships among arenas are synergistic from both the demand side and the supply side. User resistance is eroded by constant exposure and interaction with IT systems at home, at work, while traveling. Meanwhile suppliers accelerate their experience curve progress by participating in and enabling interoperability among multiple arenas.

A Practical Construct

The IT grid is a useful mechanism for positioning customer needs and circumscribing socioeconomic and regulatory impacts. More importantly, the grid has enabled us to plot and analyze alternative vectors for emerging technologies as well as for corporate diversifications and encroachments.

And most important, it enables us to define graphically the six primary sets or clusters of IT businesses. Three are *service* businesses defined by their function: communications, information, and entertainment. The other three are *product* businesses defined by their market focus: consumer electronics, office equipment, and business operations equipment. The definitions are:

Communications services. Public telephone, data, and audio-video network operations and nonelectronic information delivery such as by postal services

Information services. Nonfiction print and electronic publishing, packaged and custom applications software and computer processing services, and advertising and other professional services

Entertainment services. Production of music, drama, humor, and game content, and distribution by prerecorded and/or print media, broadcast and cable channels, and theaters

Consumer Electronics. Standard household and automobile information and entertainment devices, such as TV-audio components and telephone instruments and newer systems (e.g., home computers and laserdisc players) that process and store infotainment media

Office equipment. Ranging from simple stand-alone media-conversion devices (e.g., copiers and typewriters) to networked personal computers, telephones, and other workstation configurations that store, process, and transport information

Business operations equipment. Generic processing, storage, and transport products such as most mainframe computer configurations and accounting software and industry-specific products such as communications switches sold to common carriers; factory data collectors, robots, avionics, CAT scanners, and process controllers; and public transaction stations such as ATMs, electronic kiosks, and automated gasoline dispensing controllers

Table 6.1 shows our analysis of the size and growth of each cluster. Sizing of the three product clusters also includes systems software and their principal aftermarkets of supplies, leasing, and installation and maintenance.

Over 40 percent of the total U.S. IT market is consumed by the IT industry itself. For example, over $20 billion of telecommunications network equipment, one of the industry-specific segments of business operations equipment, is consumed annually by communications service firms. A major chunk of local telephone company revenues are derived from access charges to long-haul carriers. In turn, communications services

Table 6.1. U.S. Cluster Shares ($ in billions, assuming overlaps are allocated)

Services	1985 ($)	Share (%)	1990 ($)	Share (%)	Compound Annual Growth Rate (%)
Services:					
Communications	115	21	160	17	6
Information	131	24	230	24	12
Entertainment	64	12	100	10	10
Subtotal	310	57	490	51	10
Products:					
Consumer electronics	37	7	60	6	10
Office equipment	55	10	110	11	15
Business operations equipment	143	26	300	32	16
Subtotal	235	43	470	49	15
Grand total	545	100	960	100	12

and business data processing equipment are the two major direct-cost categories for most computer service firms.

As the three service clusters migrate towards high-tech, they are consuming proportionately greater amounts of output from the three product clusters. This is just one factor contributing to the more rapid overall growth of the product clusters, especially those serving the business market.

Indeed the three product clusters cumulatively will nearly match the three service clusters in sheer size by 1990. Later on, however, we will show that this growth will not automatically translate to higher profits.

But the seemingly neat and orderly arithmetic presented in Table 6.1 belies the fact that the clusters overlap extensively, as shown in Figure 6.3. And in sizing the relevant market potential for each cluster, these overlaps lead us to count most cells in the grid more than once as we move from cluster to cluster.

With these market and product-service overlaps, we derive a total of $3 trillion by adding up the relevant potential 1990 U.S. markets for each cluster. Clearly this far exceeds our "real" IT market forecast of $960 billion. At first blush this bloated total seemed meaningless. But, upon deeper analysis, the roughly 3 to 1 ratio between this number and the core total represents an important indicator of competitive expectations, con-

Output Elements

Marketplace Arenas	Facilities				Content	
	Transport	Media Conversion	Storage	Processing	Information	Entertainment
Consumers						
Interarena						
Business Operations						
Knowledge Work						

Legend	Primary Product Clusters	Primarily Service Clusters
	▬▬▬ Consumer Electronics	■ ■■ ■■ ▪ Communications
	\\\\\\\ Office Equipment	////////// Information
	▨▨▨ Business Op. Equipment	▪ ■ ▪ ■ ▪▪ Entertainment

Figure 6.3. Within the IT grid, we depict the six primary businesses as overlapping clusters of output elements and market arenas within which competitive battles are waged. SOURCE: *Derived from "Strategic Mapping of the Information Industry,"* Information Industry Insights, *Booz, Allen & Hamilton Inc., Issue 8, pp. 2–4.*

vergence, and intensity. In effect, each market is being *contested an average of three times over.*

Similarly for each cluster, the ratio between the more broadly scoped potential market and the real market forecast is meaningful. The larger the ratio for a given cluster, the greater will be the competition from business interests rooted in other clusters. This means a smaller share of the full potential to be garnered by the cluster's businesses. Using this measure, office equipment and information services show intensifying cluster competition; for entertainment services the pressures from other clusters will be relatively weaker. There is more about specific cluster winners and losers in Part 2.

Getting IT On

One effect of convergence is a rapidly growing tendency of IT players to forge strategic affiliations with others, through outright acquisitions or lesser levels of corporate ownership. Within the past 3 years, once-iconoclastic IBM has affiliated with such diverse partners as Sankyo-Seiko, Sears, Agridata Resources, Merrill Lynch, MCI, CBS, Rolm, Intel, and Stratus. AT&T has struck partnerships with Quotron, N. V. Philips, EDS, Convergent Technologies, Olivetti, Ricoh, and Japan ENS (among many others).

Since 1980, we have counted over 2000 acquisitions, and over the past 2 years the number of IT acquisitions show a 25 to 30 percent year-to-year growth. As Joseph Dionne, CEO of McGraw-Hill reminisces: ". . . we tracked our company's evolution. It has been the result of one acquisition after another, all based on the recognition of new technology, its impact on society and the need to anticipate and interpret that impact."[2]

By the early 1990s, we see the infotrends driving the annual number of IT industry mergers and acquisitions close to 1000 with some $5 to $10 billion changing hands. The three services clusters will continue to be the most active, but the product clusters will see a faster growth in deal making.

Clearly, going IT alone is "out"; getting IT on is "in." But this is not just another fad. IT strategic planners are seeking sustainably higher returns of their shareholders' equity (ROE). They have come to realize that the underlying trade-offs to growing ROE have tilted away from internal development and towards external development. True, internal development still has its advantages. Most important of these is control. R&D

---

[2]"Information Technology and Management," *Outlook*, Booz, Allen & Hamilton Inc., issue 8, p. 41.

teams can be focused on specific targets, and funding spigots can be opened up or closed down.

In many instances, internal developers can control the pace of commercialization and the degree of standardization. The resultant product and service can be highly proprietary or open for others to share and leverage. Moreover, internal developers are bred from the same corporate culture, and they pool the benefits of cumulative experience for their corporations.

But, many companies that have relied solely on internal development have been frustrated by their inability to keep up with, much less exploit, the accelerating pace of change.

I Want to Make IT with You

This section describes how each of the five infotrends is spurring the mounting level of external development activity. As emphasis swings from the mass marketing of generic facilities to the specialized and often vertical marketing of *content*-differentiated products, the available R&D dollars and talents can be spread too thin to satisfy all (or any) development imperatives. As a result, hardware and telecommunications firms, previously vertically and horizontally integrated, are seeking content-laden partners. For example, Wang has begun to take positions in databases that relate to document preparation (including exclusive publishing rights to the *Random House Dictionary* and *Roget's Thesaurus*). Apple, Tandem, AT&T, and most other computer manufacturers are increasingly cultivating value-added resellers with differentiative applications through comarketing arrangements and even in some cases through financial and technical support. Local telephone companies and value-added network carriers are encouraging interconnections and joint marketing of audiotex and other electronic databases.

The quest for *interoperability* has led some content companies to enter the networking business to facilitate electronic distribution of their databases, software and applications processing. Dun & Bradstreet, for example, has Dunsnet, Lotus has Dataspeed, and GE Information Systems Company has Marknet. Also numerous computer, office, and telecommunications equipment companies have coventured with other suppliers in the following areas:

- The physical interconnection of their products; for instance, Northern Telecom, Inc.'s computer-to-private branch exchange interface
- Electronic mail; for example, X.400, the Consultant Committee on International Telephone and Telegraph's Message Handling System
- Meshing industry-specific content expertise with a sizable facilities base; illustrated by two 1985 minority equity deals: (1) IBM's investment in

Agridata Resources, Inc., aimed at the agricultural information service market and (2) Convergent Technologies' purchase of 40 percent of Baron Data, provider of software to the legal market

- The compatibility of their operating systems; for example, the recent European supplier agreements involving AT&T's UNIX

- The interface between systems and applications software; for example, the Japanese-Microsoft Extended Basic (MSX) project to standardize low-end home computer operating systems

- Content for new storage media; exemplified by an agreement between Digital Audio Disk Corporation (a Sony subsidiary) and KnowledgeSet Corporation (formerly Activenture Corporation)

- A broader set of industry-specific interoperability standards; for example, GM's proposed Manufacturing Automation Protocol

- Shared tenant services; for example, a joint venture of Wang, InteCom, MCI, and GE Information Systems Company

More than simple agreements and coventures, however, some players involved in communications hardware are aggressively acquiring others who have interconnecting components. Among the products that fit together in an interoperable system are terminals, codecs, modems, LANS, multiplexers, switchers, concentrators, private wide-area networks, and network management devices. And external developments among suppliers of these and other related products is spreading rapidly. For example, Micom, an office system company, acquired Interlan, an LAN supplier ostensibly to help their customers achieve interoperability. More recently, Contel and Comsat have proposed to merge. Also Italtel, CIT Alcatel, Plessey, and Siemens are engaged in a research project to standardize ISDN network components.

As interoperability becomes more universal, so will high-tech integrated market services (IMS) electronically linking buyers and sellers. This can be business to business, such as with industrial products, or business to consumer.

Some information service companies, such as Control Data Corp. with Redinet, General Electric Co. with Dealertalk, and McDonnell Douglas with EDI-Net, are targeting certain business-to-business IMS segments. Others, like CoVidea (a joint venture of Bank of America, Chemical Bank, Time Inc., and AT&T), appear to be focusing mainly on the broadly based business-to-consumer segment.

As briefly mentioned earlier, the spectre of *disintermediation* is spurring businesses with deep roots in other industries to enter the IT industry. Several banks and aerospace firms have been among the leading computer servicers since the 1960s. But now they are being joined by other financial institutions (e.g., CIGNA and Merrill Lynch) and other types of manufacturers (e.g., General Motors and Toyota). Moreover, leading players in other industries are joining the fray including retailing (e.g, Sears and J.C. Penney), distribution (McKesson), transportation (American Airlines and Norfolk Southern Railway), and professional services (Arthur Andersen). Some like Coca Cola, who acquired Columbia Pictures, and Gulf + Western, who acquired Prentice Hall, may simply be diversifying into what they perceive to be a more robust industry. But most of the others are impelled primarily by the need to control the restructuring of their core businesses and only secondarily by the diversification opportunity.

Globalization is a very powerful rationale for external development. One goal is to gain economies of scale by spreading fixed and semifixed costs over a broader geographical base. But even the largest firms are finding it increasingly difficult to deepen penetration in foreign markets unilaterally. As a result, they have established collaborative relationships with strong indigenous players. Xerox (Rank Xerox and Fuji Xerox), Honeywell (Honeywell Bull), and Fujitsu (Siemens, TRW, and Amdahl) were among the first to go this route during the 1960s and 1970s. Some of these partnerships no longer exist, and there were relatively few followers until recently. Now such diverse entities as AT&T Technologies, Dun & Bradstreet, MCI, GE, GTE, and Ameritech are leveraging their products and services, in part through joint ventures and other collaborative agreements with foreign firms.

A second goal related to globalization is to gain access to leading-edge markets and technologies. And this is the principal rationale for the intensifying invasion of North America by European and Asian firms, most often through external development. U.S. print and electronic publishing has become a hot-bed of external development activity for British, Dutch, and Australian publishers.

Japanese firms, until recently, have opted for collaborative arrangements in the U.S. rather than outright acquisitions. In many cases, these are OEM arrangements, for example, Toshiba manufacturing image equipment for 3M to market domestically. Some are joint development efforts, such as Sharp and RCA in CMOS. Other collaborations leverage Japanese manufacturing and technology experience. One example is NEC which is developing integrated circuits for Corvus. However, such collaborations can be fragile. RCA recently has backed away from certain joint efforts with Sharp, and Corvus' financial difficulties imperil NEC's yield as an OEM.

Other examples are smaller in scale. Late in 1985, Esprit Systems, a producer of display devices received $2.5 million in equity investment from its principal supplier, Advanced Datum of Taiwan.

Europeans are especially interested in the U.S. A late 1984 survey of

European CEOs conducted by Booz, Allen & Hamilton Inc.,[3] showed that 45 percent picked the U.S. as the first choice for foreign investment (see Figure 6.4). Only 37 percent picked other European countries. Olivetti, AT&T's partner in certain European segments, also has cultivated several dozen equity positions in U.S. companies. Siemens, Plessey, and Racal Electronics are among the more acquisitive European hardware firms, while Nixdorf, Ericsson, CIT Alcatel, and Nokia seem to favor joint ventures and other such vehicles. Indeed, an example of both European-American and content-facilities convergences is Reuters' 1985 acquisition of Rich, Inc. Reuters, a well-known U.K. supplier of financial content acquired Rich, a U.S. manufacturer of communications systems that display financial content.

[3]George Anders, "European Panel—Companies That Seek to Diversify Find It's Not Always That Easy," *The Wall Street Journal/Europe*, November 30, 1984.

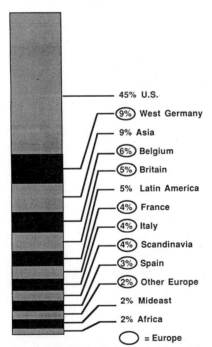

45% U.S.

9% West Germany

9% Asia

6% Belgium

5% Britain

5% Latin America

4% France

4% Italy

4% Scandinavia

3% Spain

2% Other Europe

2% Mideast

2% Africa

◯ = Europe

Figure 6.4. West European executives' first choice for foreign investment. SOURCE: *"European Executives Consider U.S. Prime Area for Expansion Abroad, Journal Poll Shows,"* The Wall Street Journal, *December 5, 1984, p. 34.*

The first four infotrends are fomenting a *convergence* of IT interests among the leading players that is driving them to high levels of external development activity. In the mid-1980s, IBM proudly asserted its intentions to have $100 billion in sales by 1990 and $185 billion by 1994. Few question its internal R&D competency, but the goal of achieving and then surpassing a 5 percent share of the swelling world's IT market undoubtedly will lead the company to expand external development in the years ahead.

Other publicly held firms, smaller than IBM and lacking R&D critical mass, will rely even more on external development in the years ahead. Many are severely limited by current profit and cash-flow pressures in expanding their R&D budgets but can leverage their stock value or debt-equity position in acquiring other firms.

Some smaller, privately held firms are in an even tighter bind. Venture capitalists, until recently the primary funding source for emerging firms, are stretched thin, and the initial public offerings market opens and closes cyclically. During the halcyon days of 1983, some 75 percent of $3 to $4 billion in venture capital went into the IT industry, while some 120 IT companies went public for the first time raising another $3 billion. By 1985, those funding sources had dropped by 40 percent, and they are unlikely to rescale the 1983 heights fully for some time. The data for just one IT sector—Electronic Information Services—show how rapidly venture capital and IPO spigots constricted from 1983 to 1985 (see Figure 6.5).

Worse yet, if all companies financed by venture capital in 1983 alone had been initially successful, they would have required an additional

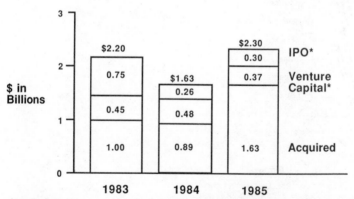

Figure 6.5. The real picture for small electronic information service firms. SOURCE: *Broadview Associates estimates based on Broadview and Venture Capital Journal data. Calculation assumes that 13 to 15 percent of small company IPO and venture capital money goes to information service firms.*

$9 billion over the ensuing 2 to 4 years to keep going, shutting out subsequent start-ups.

And even where available, R&D monies do not go as far as in the past. Good R&D talent is hard to find, motivate, control, and retain. R&D facilities are growing more asset intensive. Information technologies are becoming more specialized and the failure rate of new product introduction is high. Hence the motivation to grow via acquisition.

R&D is not the only area in which scale and scope is critical. Many manufacturing companies find that they lack distribution leverage. The leverage they seek may be geographic or horizontal in scale or it may relate to boosting sales productivity or tightening account control. As a result, larger IT firms with substantial marketing, maintenance, and physical distribution capabilities can often readily acquire or collaborate with the manufacturers and developers of their choosing, especially those who bring vertical market expertise to the table.

Computer Service and Software: The Cutting Edge

The computer service and software sector of the IT industry was the first to come to grips with these external development drives, and other IT companies, confronted with them for the first time, would do well to heed the lessons learned by this sector.

First, we will look at the trend in computer services and software. Since 1970, the number of annual U.S. acquisitions has swelled from 25 to over 200 (see Figure 6.6). Initially limited to raw facilities firms—mainly batch

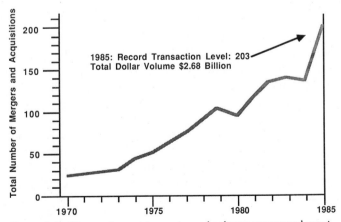

Figure 6.6. History of computer service and software merger and acquisition activity. SOURCE: *Broadview Associates.*

data processing centers, contract programming, and time-sharing—the majority of deals now are in content-related areas—software, value-added reselling, and remote transaction processing. Many of the early deals were stock swaps and other easily valued transactions. Nearly 75 percent of today's acquisitions involve cash, and more than 60 percent involve contingency valuations, such as earnouts (the amount of money that is paid is contingent on how well the company does after it is acquired).

Automatic Data Processing (ADP) was one of the pioneers in growth by external development. By 1973, ADP had already made more than 40 acquisitions and by year-end 1984, it had passed 100.

The ADP success story is especially compelling. Nearly all of ADP's acquisitions have been by two strategic objectives: (1) expanding existing business and (2) entering related new markets. ADP is commited to an ongoing program with an established team that seeks out, rather than simply responding to, acquisition opportunities. Generally, ADP expects that 75 percent of their acquisitions will be successful, and they are not shy about divesting those that do not meet objectives after a reasonable period. And who can quarrel with this strategy thus far. ADP stands alone among all publicly held firms (IT and all other) in recording over 25 unbroken years of growth in revenues and profits.

Many other information service firms have been relatively successful in external development. D&B's 1983 acquisition of McCormick & Dodge and 1984 acquisition of A.C. Nielsen stand out in retrospect as particularly shrewd deals for all three parties. Freed from the obligation to justify quarterly performance, M&D executives say they have more time to concentrate on long-range planning and other business concerns. "This has been a lot more fun," Robert K. Weiler, head of McCormick & Dodge recently admitted. "I sleep nights."[4]

Indeed, there is a growing affinity among content-based information service, hardware, and telecommunications firms. Younger software suppliers, transaction processors, and database developers find that they cannot afford to develop national, much less international, distribution power by themselves. Microcomputer retailers are highly selective in stocking software and hardware from smaller, unproven firms. Specializing database providers and transaction processors lack end-user visibility unless promoted by a strong marketer.

Besides distribution, emerging players lack the wherewithal to develop next-generation products because they are stretched out fully trying to make the current generation successful. Meanwhile, larger hardware, telecommunications, publishing, and non-IT companies know that they cannot marshal enough talent, vertical-market knowledge, and, hence,

---

[4]David Olmos, "Firms Find Union Blissful," *Computerworld*, February 11, 1985, p. 124.

product internally to satisfy their growth objectives and market strategies. They need those smaller content-based firms. And that is why the computer services and software sector has been an early hotbed of convergence.

Outright acquisitions of publicly held firms are expensive. Since 1980, the price/earnings ratios of publicly held IT industry players have ranged from double to triple the Value Line 950 all-industry average. On top of that, the acquisition premium (the amount paid over the trading price 2 months before the acquisition announcement) has averaged 20 percent more than in other industries. This means that the more successful of the acquired publicly held companies typically are being capitalized at 25 to 40 times earnings. Strategic rationale notwithstanding, this places a tremendous onus on the acquiror of a publicly held firm to pay back its external development investment. Effectively, an acquiror of a public company is marked up twice: first by the higher P/E and second by the higher premium over the then public price.

To reduce the risk of not recovering their investment, IT firms are increasingly pursuing other options. These include acquiring privately held firms with more modest capitalization ratios, often ranging between 8 and 15 times earnings, rather than 25 to 40.

In computer services and software, where deal making is a way of life, the median transaction has been between $3 million and $5 million. And 75 percent of acquired companies have been lower profile, privately held businesses. In fact, only 6 percent of acquired information services companies have been stand-alone and publicly held, the balance being divestitures of parts of publicly held firms.

Clearly, the bigger IT deals, like Burroughs/Sperry, GM/EDS, MCI/SBS, McDonnell Douglas/Tymshare, IBM/Rolm, D&B/A. C. Nielsen, and Digital Switch/Granger, may grab the headlines, but they are just the "tip of the chip" when it comes to IT external development.

Stopping short of outright acquisitions, some firms favor joint ventures with no equity exchanges. Nevertheless, such arrangements, especially joint ventures, have often proven unstable since the strategic interests of the parties, even when congruent at the outset, typically diverge over time. Also, jointly owned new entities tend to have schizophrenic cultures, especially when peopled from both owning organizations. And, as we discuss in Chapter 15, people and culture are the single most critical attribute of successful IT companies. Witness Honeywell/Bull—a marriage that was eventually annulled; Satellite Business Systems, Inc.—where all three of the original owners have reduced or sold their position; Fujitsu/TRW—a mismatch of intentions and contributions; Texas Peripherals—a joint venture of Tandon and Tandy, which was disbanded in early 1986; and Anaconda-Ericsson, Inc.—unquestionably a naive vehicle for U.S. entry by L. M. Ericsson.

One of the relatively few long-standing successful joint ventures is Sony/Tektronix Corp. Formed in 1964 to give Tektronix access to the Japan market, the partnership now does over $100 million annually and also facilitates much technology transfer between the two firms.

One less risky vehicle for IT firms is to invest in venture capital pools directed at areas of possible strategic leverage. Tektronix, GE, Xerox, and Raytheon are among the growing legion of firms investing strategically-directed venture capital. Some firms believe in commingling their monies with others. Another approach is for an IT firm to establish its own dedicated pool, typically $10 million or more to be effective, with clear-cut strategic objectives relating to specific areas of technology, market, or product development. This "strategic capital" fund can then be invested in multiple situations, thereby spreading the financial risk while maintaining a clear strategic rationale. These investments, which can be managed internally or by an outside agent, can take many forms—minority equity purchases, loans, OEM discounts, or R&D resources—with the ultimate objective of jointly leveraging the portfolio companies' capabilities once they mature. Even here, recent studies by McKinsey & Company and others show that only a small percentage of such large-small affiliations succeed.

Regardless of the external development vehicle, from outright acquisition to strategic capital funding, external development has four critical success factors:

■ Staying close to and leveraging experience and expertise—what we call the "strategic core." One often quoted survey of the Fortune 100 showed that only 27 percent of unrelated acquisitions had been successful, while 64 percent of those related to an existing internal product, market, or technology had been successful.

■ Relatedness is not enough; companies should go for strong longer-term marketplace-driven opportunities. They are the cake, synergies are the icing.

■ IT companies should select affiliations strategically; they are not deal making. Not all acquisitions and joint ventures can be directed or preplanned. But when unexpected candidates surface, as they frequently do, successful acquirors will have the benefit of an explicit external development strategy, or at least guidelines, against which to evaluate the candidate situation.

■ Once a strategic partner is in sight, IT suppliers should anticipate how the partnership will best function before the transaction is structured. Potential conflicts abound. Most of those acquireds wish to retain some or all of their autonomy and culture, yet they are seeking some sort of strategic assistance. Acquirors have learned that they need to invigorate, not smother or homogenize acquired firms.

Yet, corporate leadership will want more than an addition to the balance sheet or a new bubble on the corporate portfolio grid. Therefore, to overcome the potential for conflict, we have learned that issues of governance, compensation, reporting, mutual assistance, and cultural independence should be agreed upon before the deal is struck.

Summary

Convergence, then, is a multidimensional phenomenon triggered by the other four infotrends. The Integrated Market Services (IMS) concept, introduced in Chapter 4, is a robust example of the ascendency of *content* value, delivered through *interoperable* systems, thereby *disintermediating* traditional distribution channels, contributing to a *globalization* of markets. The inevitable consequence is a convergence of competitive interests. In the case of IMS, the IT players include information providers (e.g., McGraw-Hill), direct marketers (e.g., Comp-U-Card), data processors (e.g., First Data Resources), and network operators (e.g., Compuserve). American Express and Sears are but two of the heavyweight non-IT players converging on IMS.

Clearly, not all the players will be successful. The infotrends are already at work changing the bases of competition in the IT industry. For some IT suppliers, it is already too late. It takes as long as 10 to 12 years to develop and commercialize a new interoperability architecture or next generation intracity public switched network standard. Even IT companies with easier-to-develop products have great difficulty making 180 degree shifts in their organizational or distribution strategies in less than 5 years.

Nevertheless, "tomorrow is the first day of the rest of your company's life" and adroitly managed IT firms can materially raise their probability of success by monitoring the infotrends and anticipating (rather than just reacting to) the fundamental marketplace shifts and competitive dynamics sparked by these infotrends.

Although many of these infotrends, shifts, and dynamics will affect all IT suppliers, some are more critical to certain clusters. In Part 2, we forecast those product and market thrusts most vital to success in each of the six services and products clusters.

PART 2

Clusters: The Winners and Losers of IT

7

Communications Services: Going IT Alone

The frenetic level of new competitive activity in the communications services cluster is one of the aftershocks of the AT&T divestiture. But do not look for those aftershocks to subside soon. The rush of start-ups and entrants from other clusters (such as IBM, Eastman Kodak, and McDonnell Douglas) into a mature and only moderately growing and diversifying market has begun to induce substantial price erosion in some segments, notably interexchange transport.

Surviving the Aftershocks of Divestiture

Therefore, having been faced with the double whammy of more intense competition and less revenue growth than other IT clusters, communications carriers surviving into the 1990s will have differentiated themselves in several ways. One is by having expanded the content value added in some cases by successfully invading the information or entertainment services clusters. An example of the quest for content is SBS's offering to its customers of Dow Jones' DowPhone quote service.

A second way will have been through superior price and/or performance by selectively deploying new distributed intelligent all-digital switched networks. A third will have been by marketing their services not as raw facilities but as part of applications, such as IMS and teledelivery. Like computer service and software firms, winning communications carriers will cultivate the interarena electronic flow of interest among buyers and sellers by leveraging from their natural role as intermediaries.

To secure these elements of differentiation, successful carriers will have convinced regulators to allow them freedom of choice, i.e., deregulation, especially of artificial limitations on the provisions of enhanced services and market and cost-based pricing. (But, despite their newfound freedom, shrewd carriers will have avoided all-out price wars lest they inadvertently mastectomize their cash-cow carriage businesses.)

Many of these new elements of differentiation will have been achieved through external development since most carriers have historically lacked their own R&D capabilities. Nevertheless, to reap the full benefits of new collaborations, winning carriers will have materially beefed up in-house technology talents and learned how to manage R&D. And this will have been only one element of a new culture stressing more individual accomplishments, less hierarchical management, and more top-level intellectual rather than symbolic leadership. The new emerging 1990s generation of carrier CEOs, therefore, will be coming more from product-market development than from operations and finance backgrounds.

As recently as 1982, communications services was the largest domestic cluster, accounting for 25 percent of the IT industry. It has since been surpassed domestically by both information services and business equipment, although it still leads in most other countries except Japan.

Nonetheless, the domestic communications market is quite large and, even as prices erode, user demand continues to mount. Local telecommunications, sometimes called the "last mile" business, will account for slightly above 25 percent of this cluster's $160 billion in 1990. Longer haul telecommunications including telephone toll, data, and video will be about 45 percent, and the balance will accrue to nonelectronic content carriers such as the U.S. postal service and Federal Express.

Nevertheless, size alone does not ensure success. Indeed, on the IT grid (see Figure 6.3) the communication services cluster is completely subsumed by information services. In other words, other clusters are sucking the electronic value added of communications into their businesses, leaving most telecommunications carriers to scramble for a piece of a limited growth, hard-to-differentiate market. As Larry Kappel, former vice president of strategic planning at U S West, puts it: "Competitors are going to overlap and conflict as old distinctions between obvious products and services change and become less clear. What we used to think of as a customer is becoming increasingly a competitor, and competitors in turn, become customers or collaborative partners in our new business."

Therefore, survival, rather than size and growth, is the issue. Participants with a traditionally sheltered marketshare position have been thrust into an intensely competitive and potentially bruising contest. Moreover, the U.S. situation is not unique. More subtle but similar "games" are taking place within and among all developed countries. Larry Geller, manager of Asian network operations for General Electric was only half kidding when he said, "You'll walk down a back street in Tokyo and someone will jump out of the shadows and say, 'You want to buy a network?' "[1]

Investors and other stakeholders are eagerly watching the scoreboard, ready to cheer, hiss, or worse yet, exit the arena. At stake are several hundred billion dollars of assets and revenues, growing at only a modest 6 to 7 percent annually to the early 1990s. The major players are the telecommunications carriers (both local and "interexchange"), the network equipment suppliers, and the industry's consumer and business customers. Setting the rules and monitoring certain aspects of the games are regulators and other policymakers.

Five Strategic Challenges[2]

Telecommunications carriers face five sets of strategic challenges, all interrelated and crucial to survival, in both this decade and the next (see Figure 7.1).

[1]E. S. Browning "IBM and Others Maneuver for Position as Japan Nears Deregulation of Its Telecommunications," *The Wall Street Journal*, December 31, 1984.

[2]Derived from concepts initially advanced by Robert J. Cymbala, Steven P. Nowick, and Harvey L. Poppel, "The Trials and Tribulations of the Telecommunications Industry," *Information Industry Insights*, Booz, Allen & Hamilton Inc., issue 8, pp. 1, 8–9.

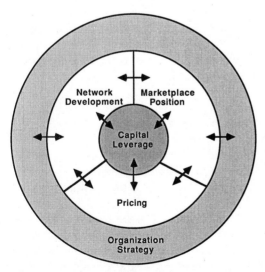

Figure 7.1. Common carriers face five interrelated sets of strategic challenges. SOURCE: *Booz, Allen & Hamilton Inc.*

The first is the question of how to position themselves in the market-place. Carriers must balance larger on-going core businesses with other incipient opportunities. This means that within each new business area selected careful end-user analysis must select out segments worth aggressive pursuit. This requires realistic evaluations of how well customer "account control" can be maintained. Some of the new, yet highly related businesses we think have the greatest potential are:

- Systems and applications turnkey systems for telecommunications-intensive customer functions (e.g., marketing)
- Office equipment, supplies, and maintenance
- Broadly based electronics retailing
- International information and entertainment services
- Paging, message, and navigational networks
- Systems integration and operations management of customer-owned facilities
- Integrated Market Services (IMS)
- Cable television

With respect to cable television, both local and long-haul carriers are beginning to recognize the potential in pooling the two revenue streams from consumers associated with both entertainment and communications. Moreover, consumer-derived revenue will swell as in-home IMS and other information services mature. This large pool could make "residential service" highly profitable without unpopular rate increases. But, this will happen only if a single entity controls all electronic conduits to the home, and we expect to see many joint ventures and acquisitions relating to this market strategy.

Other critical marketplace positioning issues include dealing with other interconnecting but potentially competitive carriers or courier services. And positioning also means rethinking the proper balance between internally generated value added and value added that is contracted out or coventured. The latter might include marketing, systems engineering, construction, software and database content, operations, maintenance, billing, finance, or technology R&D.

A second challenge is knowing how best to migrate network capabilities into new markets. An array of related strategic objectives need to be achieved. Marketshare must be defended, new service revenues must be generated, premium services must be bridged to the next generation, operating costs and labor must be reduced, and new pricing must be rationalized. In addition future networks will need to be sufficiently modular to enable them to be deregulated, condominiumized, and geographically expanded.

To achieve these strategic goals, we see several viable strategic directions for carriers. One is to integrate voice, data, and video switching. Another is to achieve ISDN-compatible interoperability spanning both on-premise and off-premise networks, all under centralized control of network signaling, operations, maintenance, and administration. Similar improvements must be made in plant quality by introducing new transmission technologies such as Ku- and Ka-band satellites (for long-haul only), monomode fiber optics, and digital cellular and digital FM communications. Also vital are new gateways to enhanced services, carriers, or end-user networks such as LANs (local area networks). Throughout, migration phases must be disciplined and rapid.

In addition to migrating existing network architectures and services, we see some very exciting new technologies and services. Among the most important are multimedia combined (voice, data, and image) electronic mail and very high-speed voice-data packet switching. Also, mobile services that enable people on the move to not only place telephone calls but to send and/or receive data and to receive navigational instructions will mushroom.

But to deploy such services successfully, carriers, especially local telephone companies, need to resolve a fundamental architectural issue. Awkwardly termed, Comparably Efficient Interconnection (CEI) is a bold concept promulgated by the FCC and others. Its objective is to establish a clear separation between basic information transport and value-added information services related to that transport. As of this writing, such players as Pacific Telesis, Tymnet, and IBM are collaborating to define the performance and technical interface specifications which would comprise the open network architecture (ONA) needed to ensure separation. If CEI becomes a reality, local carriers will be allowed to compete on a level footing with information service suppliers, subject only to remaining restrictions of the modified final judgment.

Pricing is a third challenge. Subsidies must be removed that might undermine competitive positioning and deregulated pricing should continue to be sought. Pricing tactics should be dynamic, reflecting both the relative service value to certain customer segments and the difference in value of some customers to the carrier. The relationship among installation, fixed, and use charges should be restructured and accompanied by more creative bundling and unbundling.

The fourth challenge is how to exert maximum capital leverage. It should be clear, first, that the carrier is in a core business that should at maturity yield and not consume cash. Maximum return should then be sought from discretionary capital investments, acquisitions, divestitures, or swaps. All such growths should be founded on leveraging the core business strengths and, in turn, most new thrusts should help perpetuate the core business cash-generating capacity. And as carriers become more fiscally aggressive, they will reduce dividend ratios, accelerate capital recovery, and engage in creative financing. Sources of creative financing

Applications Management

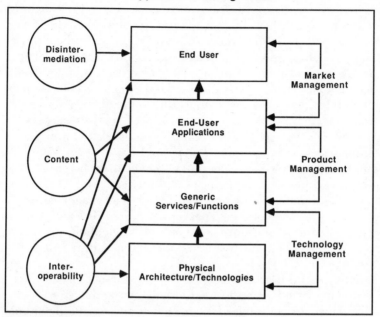

Figure 7.2. The infotrends drive the need for a new integrative function— applications management. SOURCE: *Booz, Allen & Hamilton Inc., 1984.*

include leasing equipment from suppliers and selling ownership of certain network elements to customers.

Organizational strategy must be aligned with the new business directions as a fifth challenge. This means completing the transition from a sheltered organization to one that is competitively exposed. An entrepreneurial spirit must be established and sustained with the attendant risks and rewards. But, carriers should not forget to balance their attempts to delegate authority with retaining the full leverage of their shared network and customer franchises.

Also, we have conceptualized "applications management" as a new management system that subsumes and integrates the traditional functions of network design, product, and market management. The need for this derives from the rapid rise of content-intensive interoperable networks (see Figure 7.2). All of this will put new pressures on the recruitment and training of people and will require fresh attitudes, new skills, and outside perspectives.

8

Information Services: Getting with IT

Information services will experience competition from both broadly based and specialized new entrants (including non-IT firms) who see this cluster and its intrinsically high ROE potential (see Chapter 13) as a prime target for diversification. Some of the principal attackers include financial institutions, business and office equipment manufacturers, telecommunications carriers, and large retailers.

No one will have an outright "win" by the early 1990s. Despite an onrush of external development on the heels of the EDS, Quotron, A. C. Nielsen, Prentice Hall, Informatics, and Applied Data Research acquisitions, the rate of start-ups will keep pace with acquisitions and failures, and the overall level of concentration will remain in ecological balance.

The information services cluster will continue to experience the superior returns and shareholder rewards it has had in the past. The underlying reason for sustainable high returns is that information services subsumes the technological values added by at least three other clusters—office equipment, business operations, and communications services—and then adds its own incremental value in the form of content.

The more successful information service companies of the 1990s will have focused on IMS opportunities and helped to foment disintermediation. Interactive business-to-business electronic data interexchange and integrated business-to-consumer transaction systems will be the hottest areas.

Rather than deal only with disintermediating transactions, winning electronic information service firms will integrate "backward" to the pretransaction marketing and purchasing activities and meld advertising-related services into their product line, much as successful print publishers have historically done. To accomplish this, they will have begun to master the electronic handling of photographs, other images, and sounds and voices as well as data. This will lead to a new generation of integrated software and services. Systems and communications software, environmental software, horizontal applications, and vertical applications will have been synthesized by successful suppliers into interoperable information services. These services will manage as well as deliver the content end users need, when and how they want it, because of embedded artificial intelligence.

Meanwhile, the next successful generation of publishers will be leveraging their bibliographic, knowledge-based editorial and advertising content through multiple distribution channels with the media mix tilting toward telecommunications and optical-storage devices. Accordingly, the domestic market for electronic databases will exceed $5 billion by the early 1990s. Surviving printers and photofinishers likewise will have aggressively migrated toward more electronic means. The passive losers will find that it would have been far better to control the pace of electronic cannibalization proactively rather than to be consumed by IT.

Successful information servicers also will have expanded their technology skills base and investments. This may mean more asset intensity for such artifacts as R&D facilities. Therefore, to maintain their customary high returns, winning information service businesses will have gone global to build scale. Much of this will have been accomplished the same way successful information servicers have always expanded—through acquisition. But the multinational losers will naively ignore the idiosyncrasies of each foreign country in their obsessive quest for new turf.

Information services will reach $230 billion in 1990. While in aggregate pacing the overall 12 percent rate of the remainder of the IT industry, individual product segments will experience markedly different rates of growth. Publishing, although still accounting for 40 percent of information services in 1990, will only be growing at about 6 to 7 percent, despite the rapid maturation of electronic publishing. Printing and advertising will also be growing only modestly and will be about 25 percent of information services in 1990.

The star will continue to be computer-based services and software, the third major segment, growing at about 20 percent. But even this rate masks the even more striking growth of certain subsegments such as high-tech IMS. Given the previously discussed potential to disintermediate other industries as well as cross-substitute for other IT outputs, the foreshocks of their rapid evolution on other IT businesses will be more notable than their sheer size.

In particular, software will be at the vortex of growing IT services. On the systems software front, fourth-generation end-user languages, teamed with relational databases will, by the early 1990s, yield hundred-fold improvements in systems development productivity. This will make end-user programming of medium-complexity systems a reality, rather than just a premise.

Artificial intelligence technologies embedded in applications software will lead to a new self-teaching, self-adapting generation of packages by the early 1990s. As these packages become available on new interoperable office networking systems, the long-promised integrated office will also become a reality for mainstream knowledge workers and support staffs.

And, finally, the mounting ability of software to manage, transport, and display multimedia databases will make integrated voice-data-display hardware truly attractive.

Integrated software and hardware is what most of today's "value-added resellers" are all about. But many are experiencing profit-margin squeezes which are likely to intensify unless they restructure their economic models and reposition their added values.

Specifically we suggest that these firms consider a four-pronged strategy to ensure sustained success:

- Expand value added by integrating external databases and additional function modules—for example, a firm selling an integrated hardware-software text preparation, accounts receivable, and billing system to the legal market would also integrate (and market) LEXIS or similar information service as well as add a software module to help legal firms track their inquiries and new business prospects.

- Boost direct selling effectiveness by blending in targeted telemarketing, direct mail, and promotional vehicles.

- Gain flexibility to select the best price and/or performance hardware by utilizing transportable software languages such as C and widely accepted operating systems such as UNIX.

- Stanch profit leakage through better internal management systems.

The success of value-added resellers epitomizes the increasingly tight linkage between software, other information services, and hardware. Indeed, technological and marketing advances in software are gating factors to the continued double-digit growth of both the office and business equipment clusters.

Similarly, developments in other information service technologies are pivotal to growth in the other hardware cluster, consumer electronics. Delivering high-quality, easy-to-use services to consumers requires a sophisticated architecture. Generally, "providers" of business-supported services, including shopping, advertising, news, and reservations, will place the toughest demands on the architecture. These demands, and the revenues behind them, will make the market for integrated media hardware and software dramatically different from today's consumer-supported home computer market.

More specifically, each IMS service exerts unique demands on the architecture. Advertising, shopping, and learning requires TV-quality displays. Videogames and security services have simple communications requirements but will need special peripherals. Pay-per-view entertainment services require addressability and a software-controlled electronic tuner. Printed output is needed for certain applications, such as couponing.

However, neither the facilities nor the content required to tap the in-home IMS market at a mass-market price is yet available. Facilities include a data communications network capable of supporting millions of on-line households; "still" picture and interactive full motion video production and delivery systems and in-home store-frame capabilities. Also needed are microcomputer operating systems that can retrieve "virtual" pages from the communications system and integration software to allow several discrete services (for example, banking and insurance) and data-bases (such as dictionary and thesaurus) to appear as one interoperable offering. Operators will also require systems that monitor service quality and usage and perform accounting and billing of integrated infotainment offerings.

High-Tech IMS
Market Evolution

As these facilitating technologies evolve, the U.S. IMS market will move through two stages beyond its traditional low-tech stage. During the first new stage, already nearing completion, a limited number of consumers are experiencing the first commercial high-tech IMS offerings. These services range from omnibus, relatively low-tech communications services, such as H&R Block's Compuserve, to more focused, higher-tech graphics services, such as Keycom. Almost all first-generation systems are targeted at families that have home computers or specially designed limited purpose terminals.

Lacking the technology required to deliver the full range of IMS services consumers need (see Chapter 4), none will achieve both mass-market penetration and strong profitability. They will, however, serve as important learning experiences. As this initial stage draws to a close, the media will undoubtedly continue to point to lack of mass-market acceptance as proof that in-home videotex will never be a reality.

But we think it will be a reality and not that far off. Several firms are rapidly delivering a more powerful set of services using more sophisticated information technologies. Both businesses and consumers will find this second generation attractive, and, under a new economic model, high-tech IMS will soon enter a period of extremely high growth. This high growth phase is likely to last at least 5 to 10 years.

IMS Competitive Structure

Market acceptance and technology evolution notwithstanding, the gut question is, "Can we make money in this business?" The answer is probably yes, depending on strategy, timing, and willingness to accept risk (see Figure 8.1).

Although it is still early, five potentially successful IMS roles are emerging.[1] The first is that of an *IMS company*. IMS companies will serve as the single, integrated focal point for bringing IMS to the consumer. These companies will be national in scope with local subsidiaries or franchises in each of the communities they serve. They will provide the consumer and industrial marketing required on the local and national levels. In many cases, they will generate local content and pursue local advertising through subsidiary affiliations with many locally powerful telephone companies, cable TV operators, newspapers, banks, and broad-

[1] Adapted from concepts first developed by Michael J. McLaughlin in "HIS—Business or Bunk," *Information Industry Insights*, Booz, Allen & Hamilton Inc., issue 8, pp. 3–8.

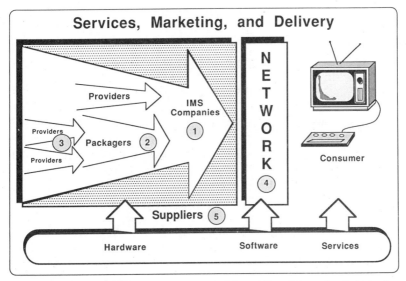

Figure 8.1. Evolving IMS structure. SOURCE: *Adapted from* Information Industry Insights, *Booz, Allen & Hamilton Inc., Issue 7, p. 7.*

casters. Many will also operate software publishing operations, using their electronic delivery and consumer franchise. IMS companies will encourage all information, transaction, and entertainment companies to use their network regardless of their owners' core businesses.

Several major joint ventures have been formed to date that appear to be presecuting the "IMS company" role. They include such powerful and diverse combines as IBM/CBS/Sears, Time Inc./AT&T/Bank of America/ Chemical Bank, and GE/Citicorp/NYNEX. The roster from which other ventures may be formed includes such as yet "uncommitteds" as Chase Manhattan, Dun & Bradstreet, American Express, AMR, North American Philips, and Comp-U-Card.

A second major role will be that of the *service packager*. Service packagers will provide the technology and marketing required to bring such services as banking and shopping to the market. Integrating services across companies is an extraordinarily difficult task. They will provide small- and medium-sized businesses with the expertise and scale required to compete. For example, a financial services packager will help the smaller banks and independent insurance agents to offer services to local communities. Chemical Bank, Bank of America, and Chase are just three financial service firms already offering such packages. Companies that are service packagers in one geographic area may be the IMS companies in other areas. Eventually both information service and entertainment service packagers will merge as the infotainment theme prevails.

The *information or transaction provider* will be the third major role. Information providers will participate in IMS for both defensive and offensive reasons. Over time they will find the shared economies of an IMS systems far more attractive than trying to operate their own networks. Providers will literally range from cottage businesses (for example, a specialized newsletter) to billion dollar companies such as Dow Jones and ADP.

A fourth major role is that of the *telecommunications network operator*. The principal contenders are the cable operators and data-telephone network companies. We believe the network facilities and IMS companies have strong, complementary interests. Cable and telephone operators are looking for the profitable growth associated with IMS content. Yet, such capabilities require expensive upgrades to existing systems. And the skills and resources required to be successful in the facilities and content businesses are dramatically different. For these and other reasons (e.g., regulatory restrictions), we do not believe that any network companies (even telco-cable combines) will be successful in offering IMS services unilaterally. Rather, we expect IMS companies to work closely with local cable or telephone companies.

Electronic suppliers will play the fifth IMS role. Some will sell mainframes, network equipment, development systems, and software to the other players as systems components. Others will attempt to supply electronics, supplies, and services directly to consumers.

This latter group will face a pivotal distribution issue as IMS matures. Will the IMS companies leverage their scale and standard interests to become the prime distribution channel or will conventional retail and mass merchandising channels prevail?

Until many consumers can be attracted to the new media, businesses will not justify the funding and other support necessary. At the same time, a robust IMS service, even on a limited geographic scale, will involve cumulative investments not fully recoverable from consumers. Therefore, the successful IMS company will have to—in some way—catalyze early mass-market acceptance of high-tech IMS, triggering a critical reaction cycle. If initial consumer demand can be stimulated, content providers and advertisers will broaden the range of available programming and subsidize consumer subscription fees. These actions, in turn, will further swell consumer demand, attracting still more business support.

We strongly believe that several vehicles are already securely established that will provide the necessary stimulation to both consumers and business services. All of these new vehicles will drive off the mounting popularity of direct-marketing channels. Over the past 5 to 10 years, direct-mail letter solicitations, specialty catalogs, telemarketing, and the distribution of coupons have all mushroomed as marketing techniques. Indeed, these and other related direct-marketing mechanisms now account for some $200 billion worth of goods and services. Of this, some 12 to 15 percent, about $25 billion, represents the value added or the take of the firms providing marketing services. Marketing is the center role of the three roles depicted in the IMS model (see Figure 4.2).

Fueling these marketing firms are "pure" information providers—providers of lists, directories, behavior data, credit-standing—accounting for roughly another $20 billion annually. And finally, a long roster of banks and other entities play a key fulfillment role and in the process garner many billions of additional revenue dollars.

Nearly all these existing services are relatively low-tech, although the growing use of sophisticated IT in manipulating buyer databases and operating telemarketing centers is greatly boosting productivity. Building on the success of these low-tech channels are several early high-tech vehicles which are bridges to the ultimate in-home videotex system.

One bridge, briefly mentioned in Chapter 2, involved locating stand-alone or communicating devices in public places (i.e., electronic kiosks). Using blends of videotex and videodisc technologies, these kiosks can play one, two, or all three IMS roles. Some only dispense tourist and other "directory" *information*. Others issue coupons, travelers checks, and event tickets (i.e., fulfillment). And yet others play the marketing role by displaying catalog-type merchandise and, in some cases, taking the order.

As "transactions" become the principal focal point of these kiosks, the term "transtations" might be a more appropriate label for these devices. (There is more about transtations in Chapter 10.)

Another new IT means is audiotex. This involves interactive retrieval of information in voice formats using ordinary TouchTone telephones. As such, audiotex can be viewed as a high-tech extension of telemarketing. Early examples include DowPhone and People's Express reservation service.

When combined with spot advertising services, conventional telemarketing and direct mail, new higher-tech "electronic retailing" channels can be developed with little or no marketing risk.

Critical Success Factors

However appealing IMS is as a target opportunity, information service providers need broader success guidelines to deal with the full platter of emerging intrabusiness, business-to-business as well as business-to consumer challenges. Here are those we think will be the most important qualities of winning information services players:

1. *The insight of content companies to anticipate potentially successful new distribution methods.*   Historical examples abound in both information and entertainment service clusters. Surviving newspaper chains and magazine publishers moved successfully into broadcast and cable to complement their print businesses. Conversely, movie studios failed to see the potential of pay cable until HBO and Showtime had built formidable barriers to entry. Also, certain videogame producers did not recognize the rapid migration from dedicated videogame machines to more versatile home computers until it was too late to convert their software. As described earlier, some of the most promising new IT channels are interactive compact discs, audiotex, and videotex.

2. *The ability to leverage the value of previous investments.*   A database or library created for a traditional distribution channel is often reusable through new distribution media. The quintessential examples come from the entertainment service cluster. These are the film libraries owned by the major studios which re-release films on tape and for pay TV at huge profits. Newspapers, magazine, and book publishers have recently come to realize that they have created important databases. Selling databases is like mining an inexhaustable lode. Moreover, as the database grows and deepens, barriers to competitive entry become virtually insurmountable.

Cumulative investment in nurturing *customer bases* may allow "crossselling" of new and different products. McGraw-Hill appears to have seized on this in their late-1984 reorganization from the product to the market dimension. Yet, many other multitype content suppliers allow their divisions to operate independently with little or no marketing synergy. Some have one customer franchise for their broadcasting or cable properties; another for books, newspapers, or software; and yet others for prerecorded audio and video.

3. *The ability to instill and nurture the creative process in large organizations.* No matter how the IT value added *grows*, the content side of information services will continue to be people intensive, and commitment to top talent is a critical success factor. Nurturing a known author or a skilled computer hacker is a skill well practiced by certain publishers and software producers. Yet this practice is often at odds with the sense of self-importance built up as a content business bureaucratizes. Keeping top people from defecting to competitors or going independent is a continuing challenge for managers in the content business.

4. *Tighter control over content development costs.* Content companies will have to find new ways of minimizing failures in the creative process. The stakes at risk—for example, investments of tens of millions of dollars for a new high-tech IMS service—compel greater attention to improving market testing of new information products. The fact that creative people may find such input counterintuitive does not excuse content companies from seeking new methods.

5. *Successful management of the joint venture.* These ventures are established either to round out a new service offering (i.e., the IBM/Sears/CBS Trintex venture) or to better distribute existing products (i.e., the ATT/EDS agreement in the systems integration market). Each partner must be clear on the ground rules of the venture as well as on the possible terms of divorce. Joint ventures should not be looked on as a panacea for every ill. Indeed, they are fundamentally unstable structures—unstable to the extent that initial consensus between partners can quickly diverge or atrophy depending on their own corporate fortunes or misfortunes. Therefore, joint ventures should be used only when diverse skills cannot be developed internally or acquired outright.

Summary

In summary, aggressive information services players should set three goals to ensure a healthy share of the business: *expand* participation in all three content value-added stages—development, synthesis, and distribution (as described in Chapter 2); *defend* current value-added roles and content types against existing or likely competitors; and (3) *enhance* the creative process while exercising fiscal prudence.

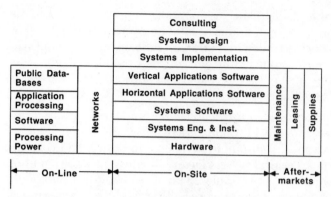

Figure 8.2. A value-added marketplace model for information services.

To enable existing information service firms as well as would-be information services players to analyze and to select the most attractive, desirable, and doable positioning, we have developed a simple marketplace model (see Figure 8-2).

It depicts the interrelationships of the various product-service elements associated with information services. By mapping alternative positionings versus those of established and potential players, information service planners can envision which elements could be primary, which secondary, and which are to be avoided. Together with more rigorous quantitative techniques, information service firms can resolve the most basic strategic issue of "what business am I in?" Similar modes can be readily constructed for other clusters. Indeed, the same model can be applied readily to all but the two consumer-oriented clusters, entertainment services and consumer electronics.

9

Entertainment Services: For the Fun of IT

By comparison with other clusters, the lineup card of major-league players and the bases of competition in entertainment services will be more stable, although individual properties will continue to be traded as draft choices are. Also, joint venturing will expand because of the added skills and resource imperatives of the trend toward infotainment, described in Chapter 2.

The successful entertainment producers and distributors of the 1990s will have brought their costs under tight control. They will have aggressively commercialized participative media such as pay-by-view, telegaming networks, and interactive compact discs. This means substantially boosting technology competency and investments. Often this will have been accomplished through external rather than internal development, especially among content and facilities suppliers and across national boundaries.

Winning content companies will increasingly be sourcing and managing a new breed of creative entertainment software developers, often physically dispersed "on location." These relationships will not be fully internalized but rather involve equity incentives and attractive contingent payouts that share the risks and rewards across otherwise independent large and small players.

Therefore, despite some continuing consolidations among larger players in the traditional cable TV and broadcasting areas, ownership of the entertainment services cluster will have to become even less concentrated than in the past to match the increasingly eclectic demands of a more participative, IT-literate global marketplace.

Entertainment services will generate $100 billion in domestic revenue in 1990. Of this, broadcasting and cable TV will account for 60 percent and prerecorded software on tape and disc media for 22 percent; the balance will be in other distribution channels such as movie theaters.

Segmenting the Market

The entertainment media market can be segmented based upon the flexibility of the entertainment scenario and the consumer's role in interacting with that scenario; that is, to segment between *performance* media and *participative* media.[1] Performance media (radio, records, television, and movies) are passive. Although consumers may be emotionally engaged by such media, they can *do* nothing to influence the inevitable outcome of linearly predetermined scenarios—that is, Rhett is going to leave Scarlett, the Maltese Falcon is going to be a plaster fake, and E.T. will go home no matter how much a viewer wishes otherwise.

In contrast, participative media allows consumers to *influence* the direction of the action and proactively to choose the outcome of a scenario and alternative paths leading to that ending. Thus, participative media are *interactive*. Today such media are limited to selective off-the-air audio and video taping, a scattered handful of optical discs, some computer-driven musical " instruments," and the latest generation of videogames. However, they are growing and will be an important and lucrative force in coming years.

Given the overall importance of the video marketplace and the integral role consumers play in it, the balance of this chapter addresses these principal subsegments of video—performance and participative. From a strategic perspective, video performance media are based on proven and well-matured content. Innovation is focused therefore on distribution techniques. Participative video media is an emerging segment, and therefore the focus is on innovative product development.

Video Performance Media

IT has sparked an explosion in video distribution channels. Up until the early 1970s, only three distribution channels existed for films and two for television. Movies were released sequentially: first to theaters, second to network television, and third to independent television stations. Television series appeared on networks and then, after completing their runs, were syndicated to independent TV. Now, cable, videocassettes, video-

---

[1]This segmentation concept was first advanced by Joseph R. Garber, "Video Entertainment Tonight," *Information Industry Insights*, Booz, Allen & Hamilton Inc., issue 8, pp. 8–17.

discs, subscription television, low-power television, direct broadcast satellite, satellite master antenna TV, multichannel multipoint distribution service, and others have emerged to carry movies, sports, concerts, news, and series to consumers.

These distribution channels have an insatiable appetite for programming, and, consequently, not only consume virtually the entire output of the major film studios but also foster the growth of new producers and impresarios. Additionally, these channels have given new life to older syndicated television series. *The Honeymooners, My Little Margie, The Life of Riley*, and other popular programs from television's "golden age" are seen again on various cable channels. A principal motivation for Ted Turner's acquisition of MGM was to ensure that his Atlanta superstation would be refreshed with new content.

But these new, competing distribution channels have provoked considerable controversy. Heated debate rages over the impact of the new media on traditional broadcasters and the real or perceived economic and technological tradeoffs between cable television and its emerging competitors. Our analysis suggests that broadcasting and cable television are and will remain the dominant video distribution channels. Other media will, at best, serve niche markets.

Traditional Broadcasting

Broadcast network audience shares, however, will continue to slip because of three competing distribution channels. One is *independent television*, a $200-million business in 1970 and a $2-billion-plus business in 1985. While typical VHF station audience shares were stable for 15 years, UHF station viewing mushroomed. UHF shares tripled from under 3 percent in 1970 to nearly 9 percent by the early 1980s. The growth of independents can be attributed to a large after-market in retreading successful networks series. And as this distribution channel attains its own critical mass in audience size, it, too, is now attracting original programming.

Another force is *consumer programmed media*. This includes off-the-air videotaping, videogames, and video camera taping and playback. A study by Stanford University indicates that the participative media already siphon up to a half hour of daily viewing. And a high proportion of U.S. VCR use is traced to time-shifting, otherwise considered as a highly specialized form of consumer participation.

And the third force is *pay television*, already a $3-billion business for such services as HBO and Showtime. Pay television captures 18 percent of viewing in pay cable homes, and broadcast network share in these homes is down close to 50 percent. Pay channels now have over 30 million subscribers, many of these subscribers are spending well over $400 per year for their basic pay cable services. (More on this is in the next section.)

Nevertheless, even under a highly pessimistic scenario, passive network television still will represent the majority prime-time audience share (55 to 60 percent) for national advertisers. And with the raising of the "7-7-7" ownership limits (on TV stations and AM and FM radio stations) in 1984, group broadcasters with a large number of stations inevitably will wield more power over TV syndicators and the TV networks.

Cable TV

In contrast with broadcasting, cable television will grow in size and even more rapidly in profitability. Three factors will continue to fuel its expansion: (1) the completion of major market wiring, (2), a deepening penetration of existing and rebuilt markets, and (3) an expanding portfolio of entertainment and information services.

Cable has clear-cut strategic superiority over its proximate "narrowcast" competitors (Direct Broadcast Satellite and Multichannel Multipoint Distribution System). This holds in most of its major market segments. Cable has enormous economies of scale; it controls 45 million subscribers—20 times or more the share of other news media, excepting videotape. This translates to an overwhelming and growing edge in purchasing films and programming.

Cable offers the best "price-performance ratio" to consumers. On average, consumers pay less than $0.60 per channel per month for cable services versus more than $3.50 per channel for DBS and up to $20-plus for other services. In addition, it is subject to few federal and state regulatory constraints. Yet, it has considerable political muscle and wields it effectively.

And cable is gaining from new technologies. Addressable converters, pay-by-view switchers, stereo hi-fi, and data transmission are being added to backbone cable systems modularly. By the early 1990s, "transputers," a new form of microelectronics, will facilitate a flexible range of switched video services. This will enable consumers to tighten control over the timing and selection of programs. All this greatly expands the range and quality of services and the revenue potential.

Cable's traditional weaknesses have been related to its long construction lead times, its up-front capital intensity, its fragmentation, and its inexperienced and often IT-illiterate management. With over 70 percent of the nation wired and a meaningful block of the balance under construction, the first two of these weaknesses will soon be moot.

Today's fragmentation presents interesting possibilities. Basic economics are pushing for intensified consolidation over the next 5 to 10 years.

The wave of new cable construction crested in 1982 and industrywide cash flows turned positive in 1985. Most operators have begun to generate sizable amounts of cash. The cable operators garnering these rewards have begun to recognize that: (1) minimal opportunities exist for unit growth through "greenfields" construction, (2) upgrade investment opportunities will increasingly relate to technologicial skills and cumulative experience, and (3) the most obvious opportunity for further growth and disposition of cash is to acquire other less effectively managed, IT-illiterate, and hence undervalued cable companies. Aggressive players such as Tele-Communications (TCI) are already heavy acquirers. Moreover, cable companies will be targets of opportunity to some communications services firms as a means of controlling wideband access to the consumer. Given such circumstances, further consolidation seems inevitable.

The scenario raises a strategic issue of considerable importance: What should a cable company do now to position itself as an effective acquiror— or to ensure that, if it elects to be an acquiree, its shareholders receive good value? How can large cable companies effectively use scale, such as clustering contiguous franchises, to optimize the economics of the business? To what extent will utility companies, such as electric and telephone, wield economies of scope to acquire or build cable backbones? Will smaller independent companies be economically disadvantaged and become highly dependent "clients" of larger, strongly integrated enterprises once true scale or scope is achieved?

Participative Video Media

The likes of *Gorf*, *Pac-Man*, and *Zaxxon* generated a $9-billion windfall in profitable home and arcade revenues back in 1982, but they cost Warner, Mattel, Coleco, Texas Instruments, and Bally aggregate losses approaching $1 billion in 1983 and 1984. These are hardly levels of risk for the fainthearted.

Technology improvements and retail price wars have turned low-end home computer and videogame hardware into a commodity business. During one 12-month period from late 1982 to late 1983, average low-end prices plummeted 43 percent. Most games software companies, spawned in the early 1980s, have folded or been acquired.

Looking back, the participative media have rapidly evolved through four generations, all within the past decade. Compact disc products are heralding a fifth generation. The first three generations consisted of increasingly sophisticated versions of action games. The fourth generation melded the videogame and home computers, expanding the range of entertainment to include thought games and interactive music and art.

Now, in the latest round of innovations, animation is becoming more refined, and entertainment will soon involve human actors and more complex plot lines. A few recent optical discs that offer viewers multiple decision points during the action are primitive first steps toward fifth-generation products. One leading-edge example is *Eat or Be Eaten*. Produced by the Firesign Theatre, *Eat or Be Eaten* is an interactive comedy version of an existing game with mixed graphics and audio.

Compact discs will spur development of "edutainment" software—stories and games that teach while they entertain. Telegames—thought and limited action games pitting two (or more) households together—will also emerge during the next 5 to 10 years, as will telegambling—lotteries first, to be followed by horses.

This next-tech generation is a certainty. IT's profit potential is not. Four factors cloud the strategic outlook. One is *behavioral*. Passive performance media are still the path of least resistance for consumers. Conventional wisdom says that "Joe Six-Pack" is perfectly content to exert no more physical effort and thought than needed to turn the TV channel and belch during the commercial break. Participative media offer a choice—a choice between being entertained or entertaining oneself. Early consumer acceptance is strong, but more market research is needed to determine both its staying power and the market's yet untapped potential.

Infrastructure is a second factor. Next-generation participative media require extensive computer and random accesss storage power and display clarity and flexibility well beyond that affordable to the mass market today. The videodisc, based on analog technology, has had the potential to satisfy most of these needs but was totally mispositioned as a passive medium at the starting line by RCA and others. The interactive compact disc, based on digital technology, shows the most promise. Its ability to store vast amounts of data, images, and sound promises to develop hybrid hi-fi, video, and data media, i.e., infotainment. Digital-chip television sets now penetrating the market have the potential to enhance the visual impact of infotainment.

The challenge facing digital-chip and disc suppliers is to enhance the price and/or performance of the hardware and to facilitate the availability of related content. Alternatively, cable or fiber-optic-based full motion video-on-demand, using transputers at the head-end and microchip-driven addressable converters in the home, could become the infrastructure by the late 1990s. Under either scenario, consumers appear to be seeking higher quality sight and sound systems in modular but interoperable media configurations to match individual budgets, self-gratification objectives, and physical environments. These demands might eventually be reinforced as new interactive videophotography applications, such as those being pioneered by Kodak, and digital audio and video systems meld.

Finally there is the question of *software*. It is the ultimate pacesetting factor. More than one promising entertainment technology (e.g., Cinerama and quadrophonic stereo) died an expensive death because of trite or inadequate quantities of software content. The challenge is to marshal sufficient talent to sustain development of "videocomp" software that can be distributed to the home economically.

Segmentation in the Changing Video Marketplace

Until the early 1970s, most TV viewers had four or five viewing options from which to pick; three networks, PBS, and in some markets an independent station or two. Today most cable-connected viewers face up to as many as fifty choices. The shifts in viewer habits can be startling. In one 1985 survey of viewer satisfaction, the three networks placed tenth, eleventh, and thirteenth behind such cable services as Cable News Network, MTV, WTBS, Nickelodeon, and others. Now audience segmentation is a major and perhaps *the* major issue.

Segmentation schemes were traditionally used by advertisers, researchers, and programmers to attack television's massive market. These approaches have the benefit of mirroring advertisers' product segmentation approaches. But they are vulnerable to the implicit assumption that product preferences correlate with viewing preferences—and they yield such canonical wisdom that all beer drinkers watch football and that all football viewers drink beer. As audiences have fragmented into smaller and smaller subsegments, these over simplistic approaches are waning. It now makes more sense to segment on the basis of factors which correspond much more closely to viewing preferences.

One such segmentation scheme[2] classifies each individual into one and only one of fourteen interest segments. This is based on data from a nationally representative survey of 2476 individuals in 1333 TV households. These fourteen segments were redefined only after an exhaustive analysis of consumer patterns of leisure interests and activities and underlying psychological needs. Table 9.1 profiles these fourteen segments along with their sizes and a sampling of the associated demographic descriptors.

Detailed comparisons of the segments' television behavior, as well as their usage of radio, newspapers, magazines, books, and movies reveal clear and coherent patterns of differences. Some were quite surprising. For example, the "mechanics and outdoor life" segment, a group of

[2]Marshall G. Greenberg, Ph.D., "Segmentation in the Changing Video Marketplace," *Information Industry Insights*, Booz, Allen & Hamilton Inc., issue 5, pp. 8–10.

Table 9.1. Overview of Fourteen Interest Segments

	Population (%)	Average age (years)	Females in each segment (%)	Females in total population (%)
Adult male concentration				
Mechanics and outdoor life	8	29	4	1
Money and nature's products	6	53	23	3
Family- and community-centered	6	47	17	2
Adult female concentration				
Elderly concerns	8	61	71	11
Arts and cultural activities	9	44	69	11
Home- and community-centered	8	44	84	12
Family-integrated activities	10	35	87	16
Youth concentration				
Competitive sports and science/engineering	7	22	5	1
Athletic and social activities	4	19	83	7
Indoor games and social activities	4	22	91	7
Mixed				
News and information	5	47	43	4
Detached	9	46	47	8
Cosmopolitan self-enrichment	8	36	59	9
Highly diversified	8	34	51	8
Entire population	100	40	52	100

SOURCE: Marshall G. Greenberg, Ph.D., "Segmentation in the Changing Video Marketplace," *Information Industry Insights*, Booz, Allen & Hamilton Inc., issue 5, p. 9.

young adult males (96 percent males, average age 29) who are primarily in blue-collar occupations, view relatively little sports programming on TV. Despite its somewhat "macho" image, the group watches less professional sports than do most of the segments that contain a majority of women. The explanation is that these young men's interests focus on *noncompetitive* physical activities involving personal accomplishment, thereby belying a stereotype often associated with their demographic characteristics.

Here are a few of the many surprises this survey uncovered:

- Soap operas do surprisingly well in the "news and information" segment.
- The rather elderly, male, and rural population making up the "money and nature's products" segment shows a preference for adventure and documentary programs.
- The "highly diversified" segment, a low-income segment with a large concentration of minorities (33 percent Black), ranks among the highest in viewing public TV.

As audiences become increasingly fragmented in response to the proliferation of choices available, strategies for "narrowcasting" are likely to emerge as the most effective means of identifying and reaching targeted market segments. This phenomenon is not new to mass media. A similar pattern evolved in radio and magazine audiences during the past 3 decades.

This poses some delicate issues for advertisers and programmers. Can new program formats be developed which strongly appeal to multiple segments (since many advertisers need to reach the widest possible market)? Should the networks continue to rely on their "tried and true" traditional sources, or will these sources be unable to respond to the dynamics of a rapidly evolving marketplace?

Or will economics of programming against smaller or less affluent segments be prohibitive (with programming costs growing at a rate far exceeding inflation)? Could the multitude of special-interest channels ultimately eliminate mass-market network and PBS media (much as the special-interest magazines survived the original *Life*, *Look*, and *Saturday Evening Post*)? And how will independent television (which relies on repeat showings of the most popular network shows) survive as consumers are exposed to programming targeted at their special interests?

Summary

Overall, advertisers and marketers will need to grasp how to develop more complex media plans resulting from shrinking sizes of mass audiences. However, proper segmentation of their target markets should lead to greater cost efficiency in reaching and "grabbing" selected audiences with persuasive messages.

As entertainment and information services converge, even more complex segmentation challenges emerge. For example, how should an individual's experience with and/or attitudes toward technology be factored into a segmentation scheme?

10
Consumer Electronics: Home Is Where IT's At

The consumer electronics business is currently out of vogue. Most long-time players have only modest returns to show for their cumulative experiences. Therefore, the relatively low growth rates and profitability of the more traditional product areas will attract few if any major players.

Lacking size, growth, or above-average profits, some long-standing players could deemphasize their role or even defect unless they find ways to boost their profitability.

The vigorous growth of certain "hot" products such as compact discs and home robots will attract some new niche players from other clusters, but they, too, will face the challenge of sustained profitability in a volatile and faddish marketplace.

Indeed, consumer electronics will continue to be the smallest of the IT clusters at $60 billion in 1990. Two-thirds of that will be in audio-video and photographic products, and the balance mostly in information and two-way communications devices.

The successful consumer electronics manufacturer of the early 1990s will leverage rather than be leveraged by its distribution channels. It will have established, through skillful promotions and superior product configuration, a distinctive "pull" branding among consumers rather than relying on the somewhat less discriminating "push" of merchandisers.

Consumer electronics will continue to have been one of the few high-tech fields in which the pioneers win more often than they lose. And pioneering in the later 1980s will consist of introducing innovative modular media centers that we call playstations with audio, video, and information processing components. As the gateways to both entertainment and information services, the most successful products will have enabled consumers to create, manipulate, time-shift, and archive all types of content (see Figure 10.1). The "smart house" is another pioneering notion that will develop slowly until the mid-1990s. A house is smart when it has automated security and temperature and humidity control integrated with infotainment functions.

Scale and scope will prove to have been even more of a critical success factor than in the past. The winners will mass their scale through worldwide distribution and their scope by downsizing and upsizing their most popular components. Broad product lines will increasingly be found not only in living rooms and dens but also in automobiles, bedrooms, kitchens, and hotel rooms. And miniature versions of flat-screen TV-sets, pagers, and telephones will join radio-cassettes and watches in the pockets and pocketbooks and on the wrists of many upscale consumers.

Despite the power plays of world-scale manufacturers, successful retailers will have pushed volume at the mass market. They will have sourced their own product supply from a broadening array of willing low-cost suppliers in developing countries. Much of their merchandise will be plug-compatible component clones of well-known brands. They will have expanded beyond store fronts to absorb and control other channels such as mail order, public transtations, and telemarketing. Increasingly, they will have placed their sales people on incentive compensation schedules.

Infotainment: Is IT There?

Few private sector businesses are as faddish as consumer electronics. Witness the boom-bust cycles of electronic calculators, CB radios, quadraphonic sound, and, more recently, $9.95 telephones.

During the early to mid-1980s, the consumer electronics cluster turned frenzied. Deregulation of telephone sales brought with it a whole new product line to retailers' shelves. The home computer boom—especially for low-end machines—more than compensated for the bust in the video-game console market. And an array of digital audio and video components, especially the VCR, brough new vitality into the previously stagnant TV and hi-fi markets. But the VCR market is rapidly reaching a plateau and the first-generation home computer market turned into a bust. So where is the real action?

We see some new booms emerging, and, despite some early travails, they are likely to sustain their success well into the 1990s. One area of rapid sustainable growth is the automobile. As of the mid-1980s, a typical American-made automobile contained $500 worth of electronics. By the early 1990s this will triple as in-auto screens, navigation aids, and info-tainment systems proliferate. "The whole thrust of marketing autos will be technology,"[1] according to Trevor O. Jones, group vice president at TRW, Inc. N. V. Philips is already demonstrating a CD-ROM based system with synthesized speech that "talks," routing information to the driver. The same unit also can play entertainment discs but will interrupt that program when it has updated information to "tell" the driver.

Looking to the 1990s, three developments are particularly intriguing and are discussed in this chapter. First is the next-generation home computer—and its sustainable "fit" in the home environment. Second is the emergence of all-digital playstations creating integrated audio-video environments within the home. Finally, outside-the-house transaction stations—transtations—offer consumers a low-risk environment in which to experiment with participative media while conducting financial, communication, and entertainment transactions.

Home Computers: Proving IT

Early pundits who relished a $5-billion home computer market by the mid-1980s did not address the classic question: "What business are we in?"

[1]"Next From Detroit: The Computer on Wheels", *Business Week*, February 11, 1985, p. 114.

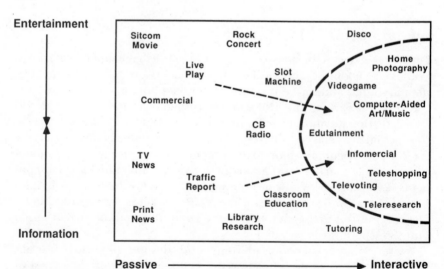

Figure 10.1. The trend is towards interactive infotainment. (SOURCE: *Harvey L. Poppel, "A Special Look at the $130 Billion Electronic Home Market,"* Information Industry Insights, *Booz, Allen & Hamilton Inc., issue 7, p. 2.*)

They perceived the business much like railroad boxcars, i.e., raw facilities, when it is really more akin to freight transportation, i.e., a blend of content and facilities.[2] Today's home computer is viewed substantially as a hardware box. Yet, potentially its real value is that it can serve as a vehicle for transporting useful business services to the consumer.

First-generation home computers, to the extent they were only a box, were a very short-lived phenomenon. They cost too much, did too little, and were not really what most people needed. They were, in fact, very nearly a toy for the upper middle class and the technocrats. And like most toys, many first-generation home computers were closeted after a flurry of play.

Currently, there are two major segments: *mass-market* devices and *high-performance* machines. Mass-market models, known as such only because these units are sold by mass merchandisers, are little more than glorified game machines. Substantially more than half the time spent on these units is used to play videogames. And the term "mass market" is a misnomer. Despite basic unit prices of $100, total consumer expenditures tally to an average of $1000 for a typical configuration—hardly within reach of a large majority of consumers. In fact, until recently, the majority of purchasers have been upscale—white collar workers with an average income of more than $30,000—and eight out of ten have had some work-related experience with computers. High-performance models cost even more. Buyers of these machines spend at least $4000 within the first 2 years of ownership.

Thus, until recently, a "real" home computer mass market had not developed. Rather it had been a high-ended gadgetry niche occupied by "pricey boxcars." To expand this niche into a genuine mass market, considerable improvements in technology, price, and functionality are emerging. First, home computers are becoming more interoperable— giving consumers a window on the world, rather than an electronic closet. With low-cost modems, new responsive local and national packet network services, and easy-to-use communications software, consumers are beginning to discover the wide world of public databases and bulletin boards as well as the ability to stay in touch with other business and personal relations. Second, price performance is rapidly improving. This is making the $1000 to $1500 configuration fully functional for most consumer users. Third, applications software linked to public databases demanded by users is proliferating. And fourth, new low-cost peripherals—most importantly the compact disc and low-cost printers—are extending utility and flexibility as well as moving toward the third generation.

---

[2]These analogies and the segmentation scheme described in the next paragraph were first suggested by Mary E. Kirson, "Market Evolution of the Home Computer", *Information Industry Insights*, Booz Allen & Hamilton Inc., issue 7, pp. 12–14.

Based on high-performance 16/32 bit microprocessors and visually powerful graphics, drivers, and extremely simple but fast communication interfaces, these new third-generation home computers are emerging as the engine for IMS services. IMS companies are likely to package the home computer with their basic services, thus assuming primary responsibility for home computer distribution and standards.

We forecast that 15 million (interoperable) IMS−compatible home computers could be installed by the early 1990s, representing penetration of 15 percent of U.S. households. But, this will only materialize if current and would-be suppliers begin seizing opportunities now, and this requires repositioning products (from boxcars to transportation) and developing new relationships.

Regardless of how quickly hardware sales grow, we estimate that home computer software revenues will overtake hardware by 1991 or 1992.

Playstations: Having Your Cake and Eating IT

Today's proliferation of audio-video devices is giving way to integrated componentry offering high-quality audio and video display and record and playback capabilities from a single unit. The availability of new home information and entertainment services—such as IMS, prerecorded software, and pay-per-view cable TV—will further spur demand for interoperable all-digital playstations. These playstations will be the center of family activity. As Roy Mason, one of the founders of the World Future Society predicts, ". . . the home of the future will become more like the home of the past."[3] He believes that the computer-controlled electronic center of the home will serve as the new "hearth."

Digital-chip receivers, large-screen monitors, and compact discs will be the boom playstation devices of the late 1980s and early 1990s. Digital-chip-driven TV configurations will offer greater picture clarity, multi-program windowing, freeze framing, and zooming among the earlier features. Consumer and content supplier acceptance of compact discs has rekindled home-use optical storage technology following the naive initial mispositioning of home videodisc players. Compact discs already offer unparalleled sound quality. By 1990, we see more new audio programs distributed on compact discs than on audiotape and vinyl records combined. And new uses are emerging as compact disc control units facilitate multimedia interactivity. This includes database and software storage as well as still-frame video.

[3]"Turning to Needs of Homes", *International Herald Tribune*, October 26, 1983.

The duplication and inconvenience of maintaining separate devices—each with its own tuner—is driving toward the integration of all these components into an infotainment center operating through a unified receiver-CPU. Its principal components will be digital-chip TV monitors evolving into larger and flatter screens offering better resolution; remote tuner keyboards allowing data to be retrieved and input; compact discs; newly emerging digital audio tape units and digital VCRs with recording cameras; and an array of plug-compatible peripherals such as floppies, printers, joy-sticks, and speakers. Smaller, less costly, and more compact configurations will be increasingly prevalent in bedrooms, home offices, and cars—especially among the affluent.

Transtations

Shared transaction stations in public places—transtations for short—are hardly new to the U.S. consumer IT market. The earliest transtation (first generation) has been the coin-operated telephone. Many decades ago, it served the same purpose as today's transtations, namely to allow access to an interoperable system, providing consumers with a cheap and non-threatening means of experimenting with a new medium before bringing IT into their homes—learning its value while conducting any of a variety of communications, financial, information, or entertainment transactions. Other more recent second-generation transtations include automatic teller machines (ATMs) and video arcade games.

Although the basic market is not new, what is new is the expanding range of applications for which transtations are being used. Expansion of the ATM market has led to third-generation point-of-sale transtations that vend information or goods directly to consumers. Today's examples include ticketing and travel insurance kiosks in airports and bus and train stations; rental car check-in and check-out terminals; department store or mall kiosks tied into inventory and delivery systems; hotel lobby tourist information and reservation terminals; and credit-card-reading telephones.

On the near horizon are fourth-generation public gaming machines tied into state-controlled gambling networks, public transportation information networks providing best-route and carrier selection schedules, gasoline dispensing pumps activated by the insertion of a credit or debit card, and enhanced public telephones offering linkages to data networks and public databases.

The consumer benefit of transtations is greater convenience in conducting transactions—realized through time savings, more convenient locations, and immediate completion of the transaction (no out-of-stock situations). Businesses, however, stand to gain even more. Transtations are in many instances a lower-cost product or service delivery vehicle than traditional forms. Additionally, transtations can provide revenue that would otherwise not be realized. For instance, a kiosk in a department store can provide a full range of colors and styles of an item, while the physical department can only display a small sample. And this also reduces inventory and carrying space costs as well.

As a result of these benefits, businesses such as banks have successfully subsidized the initial acceptance of transtations. The best example is ATMs. The ultimate gain is measured in bigger marketshares and operating benefits. By 1989, Thomas Rauh, a retailing consultant with Touche Ross & Co., predicts that 50,000 transtations will account for $5 to $10 billion of retail sales annually.[3] This exposure and acceptance is paving the way for direct delivery into the home via high-tech IMS.

Public access is helping to familiarize consumers with high-tech IMS; it demonstrates to business sponsors that they can share the benefits of making information or merchandise available through this channel. Critical success factors include packaging the content and technology for durable and self-teaching public access, deploying in highly trafficked areas, and providing simple pricing and payment schemes. Among the leading transtation providers to date are such otherwise disparate firms as McKesson, R. R. Donnelley, Southern New England Telecommunications, and AT&T.

[4]"Automatic Shopping Is Coming," *The Arizona Republic*, February 4, 1985.

11

Office Equipment: IT's Wonderful, IT's Marvelous, But. . .

The office equipment cluster will continue to be among the most competitive. Existing players, newer entrants from other customers, and start-ups are vying for pieces of a strong growing market but one that is vulnerable to substantial price erosion.

Just as consumer electronics will have become the gateway to infotainment, so will office equipment become the gateway to knowledge work. Successful office equipment suppliers of the early 1990s will have greatly expanded the range and versatility of their systems, using 32-bit and 64-bit processors and 256K and 1 megabyte storage chips. The most important facilitating innovations will have been the incorporation of electronic image handling and the emerging interoperability of local area network configurations with integrated services and digital wide-area networks.

Electronic imaging, in particular, will be facilitated by a proliferation of optical disc workstation peripherals, most notably the interactive compact disc. By the early 1990s, as many as 5 million PCs and other workstations will have a low-cost read-only or write-once optical disc peripheral. The spread of electronic image storage and transmission will continue to fuel the hot market for image printers, most of which use laser technologies. Another image product with market potential is an integrated low-cost facsimile-telephone device which has begun to sell well in Japan.

Also winning suppliers will have brought multifunction, multimedia capabilities within the economic reach of the mass market by incorporating new special function chips into their architecture. These chips will reduce the cost of interactions between terminals and LANs, between microcomputers and high-resolution displays, and between human voice and machine intelligence. Although not universal, most larger systems will be exhibiting some fault tolerance. Like their consumer electronics counterparts, successful world-scale microcomputer manufacturers will have downsized their desktop-based products into compatible traveling models, under $1500, with easy-to-read flat screens. IBM's entry into this field with their PC convertible laptop adds considerable legitimacy to the compact PC market.

But other than strong component-niche players, worldwide success will have proven to have been more a function of superior content than facilities. Winning suppliers will have fostered the integration of their facilities with vertical application software and databases laced with artificial intelligence. During 1985 alone, such office-equipment and CAD suppliers as Alpha Microsystems, Convergent Technologies, Intergraph, Hewlett-Packard, Tektronix, and Wang made content-related acquisitions.

Much of this integration will have been accomplished through external development, at a minimum by encouraging and supporting small entrepreneurial software and database developers and VARs. More aggressive hardware suppliers will have funded these vertical partners with a combination of money, R&D assistance, hardware discounts, and comarketing arrangements.

Growing smartly at 15 percent per year, the domestic office equipment market will surpass $100 billion in 1990. Half of that will come from PCs and other microcomputer and data storage systems. Voice and data communications networking products including PBXs and LANs will account for nearly 15 percent. Paper, blank magnetic media, and other supplies will be slightly over 15 percent, and the remaining 20 percent will consist mainly of copiers, printers, and other data and image input-output equipment.

Many traditional office products and systems are mature and intensely competitive. Telephone systems, copiers, and stand-alone word processors are among the biggest traditional categories. Much of their focus is to support clerical and secretarial workers. The real excitement in office equipment relates to interoperable, multifunctional, and multimedia systems aimed at knowledge workers.

Three professional-functional segments account for over 80 percent of the knowledge-work market—marketing and sales, technical design and analysis, and operations management. Four other segments account for the remaining 20 percent. Each has intrinsically different attributes. They are purchasing, personnel, finance, and legal.

Where should IT suppliers target their efforts? As we previously identified, marketing and sales is particularly attractive. Not only does it account for 27 percent of all U.S. knowledge work but it is the least IT-intensive to date. A mid-1985 survey by Pacific Bell found that of those small businesses planning to purchase computers, 42 percent intended to use them for marketing and sales.[1] Among European CEOs[2] this segment was singled out as a priority for productivity improvement. Moreover, the potential benefits are most leveraged. They go beyond cost savings and enhanced coordination to revenue and marketshare gains as well as enhanced customer satisfaction. Also, marketing and sales remains the wellspring of a content stream critical to the entire enterprise. Performance of almost all other functions in the firm depends on how well marketplace information is captured and leveraged.

Lessons Learned

Success in the knowledge-workers arena will take more than selecting the attractive segments. As with consumers, a principal issue is user acceptance. We disagree with Ulric Weil, formerly Morgan Stanley's computer industry analyst, who just before the 1985 computer slump argued that customers remain willing to buy "pie in the sky" and that gullible users do not seem—or want—to learn. His mistaken conclusion was that they just keep ordering and installing.[3]

What can be done to deepen or expand internal IT acceptance? Part of the answer can be found in the Booz-Allen study described in Chapter 2. The study showed that acceptance of the new technologies varied according to two criteria: participants' familiarity with the application and the potential for reduction of less productive activities. For example, most participants, especially those who did heavy analytical work and created many documents, were enthusiastic about using such well-known aids as electronic information retrieval and text processing. Conversely, less familiar applications, such as videoconferencing and electronic mail, appeared to face greater resistance, One market survey indicates, however, that persons who attend many task-oriented meetings are more receptive to videoconferencing because of the time it will save them.

Only a handful of participants would be likely to resist all applications. Those with more company tenure, less education, and lower-level positions tended to be less receptive. Surprisingly, once separated from tenure, age was only a minor factor.

---

[1]"Small Businesses Surveyed on Computer Technologies," *Mini/Micro-Computer Report*, vol. 9 no. 9, September 1985, pp. 1–3.

[2]Findings from the 1984 survey of European chief executives, "Productivity in the Office," sponsored jointly by Booz, Allen & Hamilton Inc. and *The Wall Street Journal/Europe*.

[3]*Computer Research Note*, Morgan Stanley, February 19, 1985, p. 1.

Such attitudes tell us something. We think that organizations can gain maximum acceptance of office automation among knowledge workers by:

- Using it to reduce less productive time, the greatest source of knowledge-worker dissatisfaction

- Involving users and getting their opinions early when selecting and developing new automated systems

- Making no demands for universal acceptance, avoiding personnel shifts that might appear to reduce support service levels, beginning with easy-to-use applications, and starting with intensive user training

We believe that in as little as 1 to 2 years, interoperable office systems investments can yield an attractive return. On the average, the one-time up-front investment runs $5000 to $10,000 per professional within the first 18 to 24 months. Based on average productivity gains of 15 to 20 percent (established by the Booz-Allen study and subsequently validated in before-after comparisons), the up-front investment can be generating compensation savings or offsets of $7000 to $10,000 annually once users have learned how to use the system to their fullest advantage. On an operating basis using 5-year equipment amortization, the annual *net* operating savings per knowledge worker is an impressive $6000 (see Figure 11.1).

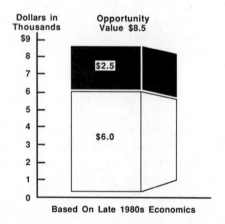

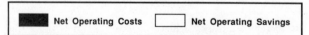

Figure 11.1. The potential net operating savings per knowledge worker is impressive.

But, hard-dollar realization of professional time savings can be elusive. One way an organization can reap tangible benefits from time saved is by reallocating that time toward achieving specific departmental goals based on the firm's overall strategies. "Most companies," notes David Ness of the University of Pennsylvania's Wharton School, "would prefer a 15 percent improvement in managerial effectiveness to a 10 percent cut in clerical overhead."[4]

In field selling, for instance, the time sales professionals can save by simplifying or offloading servicing and administrative tasks and by reducing travel and time spent with low-probability prospects should be reinvested in calling on high-potential accounts. Indeed, simple arithmetic shows that effective prospecting and selling time, which averages about 18 percent across many industries, can be roughly doubled if 15 to 20 percent readily achievable time savings derived from nonprospecting and selling activities is reallocated properly (see Figure 2.3).

The cost-benefit linkage between IT and the performance of knowledge workers, proven in leading-edge installations, is compelling. But how can mainstream offices get IT there?

Roadblocks

Until very recently, products suffered from a combination of interrelated shortcomings. One was *insufficient functionality*. This applies in particular to the "heavy-use," vertical-application needs of some professions, such as physicians, or of functionalized departments, such as marketing and sales. Also, most IT-systems have been *too expensive in relation to the perceived benefits*, especially those benefits associated with the casual or sporadic usage patterns of most knowledge workers.

Unifunctional products, such as stand-alone microsystems, have, in comparison, appeared "cheap," and therefore have proliferated. But their potential is limited. They often *lack interoperability* both among applications on the same system and with traditional systems such as reprographics, telephone, and transaction processors. At the same time, most "integrated" office systems have not related to conventional non-automated practices (such as meetings) and paper resources (file, mail, etc.) that will continue to support most knowledge-work activities for the balance of this century. But nearly all office-equipment suppliers recognize this roadblock, and by the early 1990s we forecast that at least 3 to 4 million local area network server units will be installed to facilitate office-equipment interoperability.

---

[4]Parker Hodges, "Fear of Automation," *Output*, August 1980, p. 38.

Furthermore, the marketing of integrated office systems has tended to *intimidate* the IT illiterate. This is quite visible in the required operational training, the complexity of training documentation and procedures, and the behavioral changes needed to gain the full benefits. The new systems are perceived as *threatening* to customer EDP/MIS and telecommunications managers relative to their perceived influence over system development, operations, and end-users in general, or as *wasteful* in the selling time and pilot-project effort spent on "office automation" managers. Yet, these often self-anointed zealots rarely have corporatewide decision making power and are personally unable to persuade end-user executives (other than in their own systems and administration areas) to install extensive configurations. Moreover, they tend to be more concerned with technical issues (such as transmission protocols) than with the quality of database availability, applications support, and tangible end-user benefits.

The bottom line is that only a small minority of business customers have placed large orders for integrated office systems.

What Can Users Do about IT?

To tap the potential advantages offered by office automation technologies, users can consider five lessons learned from successful experiences in leading-edge firms. For this purpose we will use examples that are drawn primarily from the marketing-sales field but are relevant to nearly all professional segments.
They are:

1. *The aim of all applications is to maximize effective knowledge work.* Within IBM for example, marketing reps in the North-Central Marketing Division have a wealth of on-line tools available to shorten or improve marketing preparation. Using a program called LEASCALC, reps can rapidly analyze all available lease terms and options. Or, at the touch of a key, reps can peruse detailed lists of support personnel, education offerings, applications descriptions, calendars of events, and bibliographies of materials for any of sixteen industry groups. Time saved in seeking information, calculating, printing, and verification has been in excess of 50 to 1.

While applications like these are almost universally appealing, many firms have been stymied in justifying new systems by a lack of hard sales-rep time-profile data for their business case. Appropriate time and behavior studies are required. For some 15 years, IBM had surveyed the time profiles of its marketing reps as well as its systems engineers.

2. *The benefits of IT-assisted knowledge work grow exponentially with the scope of functions supported.* In IBM's NCMD, the marketing rep is

only one of five players on the field selling team. Others who directly interface with the customer are the systems engineer and the administrator; all three "up-front" players are supported by the manager and the secretary.

Shared systems and information flows enable each player to feed and support others in the workstream. For example, a systems engineer can transfer a computer-assisted configuration design electronically to an order entry system. Here, the administrative team member picks up accurate order-ready data, saving considerable time and avoiding costly errors. A secretary charged with scheduling a six-person meeting can electronically match the calendars of every participant and leave explanatory messages as well. Just this one relatively simple task would normally take some twenty telephone calls.

Pepperidge Farms and Citicorp, among others, have invested in decision-support systems for their marketing and sales managers. Chrysler's district sales managers now carry portable terminals to plan and track activities while on the road. Uniroyal's chemical division reports a boost in sales rep productivity by providing direct order entry for its customers and automated support for its customer service reps. Wrangler is yet another showcase for successful field sales-rep systems. Other firms, such as PPG, Frito-Lay, and TRW's Optical Electronics Divisions, are now using voice mail systems to ease internal selling-related communications. At AT&T Information Systems, North American Philips, and Avon, more effective and less costly sales-rep and/or sales engineer development is the objective of interactive videodisc-based training systems.

3. *Computerized knowledge work is a five-staged process in which each stage builds and expands upon previous successes (see Figure 11.2).* Each

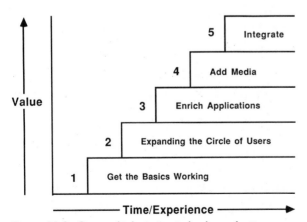

Figure 11.2. Stages of information technology adoption.
(SOURCE: *Booz, Allen & Hamilton Inc., 1983.*)

stage is a synergistic collection of modest yet powerful applications. For the present, no single application can, by itself, achieve a majority of the objectives.

a. *Stage 1.* Get the basics working: Install a pilot or prototype system with limited scale and scope and make sure it is working properly before heightening exposure.

b. *Stage 2.* Expand the circle of users: Most generic applications have been aimed at a single player. This cannot work to the company's full benefit. At IBM's marketing divisions, a 1960s administrative system was focused initially on assisting administrative personnel. But later on, marketing reps and managers were given in-branch access to the system. Then IBM installed terminals at larger customer sites to extend access by IBM sales reps, systems engineers, and customer engineers visiting or located at these sites. More recently, customers have piloted limited direct access as well. In fact, many other firms including McKesson, American Hospital Supply, Cameron & Barney, and RKO Networks are now allowing their customers to enter electronic orders directly to their computers.

c. *Stage 3.* Enrich the content: When executed properly, stages 2 and 3 are virtually indistinguishable. Once stimulated by their exposure, new users want new uses. And new applications attract new users. NCMD's in-branch information center applications have also burgeoned. The information center enables all the NCMD players to develop their own applications, data files, and job-related support services. Managers now use these systems for such diverse purposes as preparing forecasts, tracking the pivotal expense-revenue ratio, planning account coverage, mass mailing, and salary and personnel administration.

d. *Stage 4.* Add media: Data as a medium is the focus of only 5 to 10 percent of sales rep time. New uses of other media—voice, video, electronic image, and sensor—can exert even more productivity leverage as we noted in Chapter 2. Many other companies have also introduced new media systems for marketing purposes. Both Procter & Gamble and Johnson & Johnson have used videoconferencing successfully for advertising and public relations purposes. J. C. Penney uses teleconferencing to help its buyers meet changing customer needs.

e. *Stage 5.* Integrate: The most important dimension is interoperability, enabling linkages of information flows among systems. IBM's Corporate Common Data Network enables team players with proper security codes to "pass through" local systems and reach processors (or other individuals) throughout the network. A less glamorous but necessary dimension of integration is the technical rationalization and updating of disparate architectures.

4. *The success of each system is a direct function of commitment, initially by innovative zealots followed by a "guts guy" willing to be an early adopter.*   Ultimately, it is the user group that owns and further enhances the system. Therefore, the quest for technical purity and elegance takes a back seat to getting the system, even prototypically, into the user's hands. Behind all this, however, must be the firm commitment of senior management.

5. *The pursuit of performance gains is a never ending process.*   Once the user chooses to "be driven" by the new technologies, the process of introducing IT and improving IT's reach and efficiency is both never ending and all encompassing. No member of the workgroup can be left out.

IT's Urgent

Despite compelling economic arguments, only a few businesses are likely to hurdle all the obstacles described in the previous sections and achieve larger-scale interdepartmental multiapplications installations until the early 1990s.

Nevertheless, by starting serious planning and pilot programming now, organizations can benefit early and lay the groundwork for long-term payoffs. Conversely, a laissez faire approach is likely to result in a flood of localized, ad hoc, and uninteroperable systems.

What Can IT Suppliers Do?

Clearly suppliers need to overhaul their product development and marketing efforts if they are to remove the blocking factors cited earlier and help spur their customers to follow the program outlined above. And there are some specific product, marketing, and sales imperatives.

One product development imperative is in the area of electronic information storage and retrieval systems. In the future, these systems should readily accommodate speech messages and annotations and voluminous noninternally generated paper-based documents, as well as conventional databases. To mitigate the cost per professional, initial access to these systems could be sharable at the departmental or cluster-group level. Some specific features required include:

- Simplified artificial-intelligence-based indexing schemes and ease of media conversion between speech, paper, and electronic storage
- Compatibility with conventional database management systems (such as ADR's Datacom DB or Cullinet's IDMS) and display software (such as spreadsheet and graphics packages)
- Images and speech retrievable at both professional and secretarial workstation levels and transmittable to other colocated and remote departments

Also of critical importance is a need for better interoperability between systems and technologies:

- Dyadic and other fully compatible small cluster configurations of professional, secretarial, and clerical workstations
- Concurrent use of full voice, speech message, and workstation image and data functions
- Laptop (and home) workstations that are fully compatible downsized versions of desktops
- The ability to transfer information or processing to and from conventional host-based internal and external data processing services in applications-compatible formats (e.g., IBM's LU6.2)
- Common desktop and portable terminal access to department-level shared resources such as a medium- to high-speed image printer, a large-capacity magnetic and optical disk storage, and a medium-speed paper-image and photograph reader (i.e., digitizer) with simplified indexing and entry

The second set of supplier imperatives has to do with *marketing and sales.*

- Clearer presentations to the decision maker on "how it all fits" in terms of coexistence with current IT environments, e.g., PBX-key systems, conventional transaction processing applications, word processing, microfilm, stand-alone personal computers, reprographics, and external database access terminals
- Migration path(s) to eventual full interoperability
- Critical mass considerations and interdepartmental and multilocation connectivity

Indeed those suppliers willing to nurse this customer through the early stages of development will reap the much larger follow-on sales. But even then most customers are likely to use multiple suppliers to some extent.

Far more selling efforts must be directed toward end-user decision makers. Whether to a neophyte user or a leading-edge one, the key selling justification should be based on cost justification to new users and value added to experienced ones. Customer sales and support emphasis should include computer and office systems literacy courses; emphasis on heavy-use vertical applications rather than calendars, keyboard messaging, and other user-perceived "bells and whistles"; assurance of low-risk, modular growth, completely off-the-shelf solutions (or assuming the systems integration turnkey responsibility); and full training support. Education for EDP/MIS practitioners concerning user value added (what we call the "value curve") should include documented model cost-benefit cases and feasibility studies, showcase before and after installations, fuller perception and appreciation of the needs and paranoias of the IT illiterate, and shift of emphasis from technical distractions to vertical application benefits.

12

Business Operations Equipment: Embedding IT

With a few notable exceptions, the success of larger firms will have become less a factor of their technology leadership and more a factor of their market leadership. To achieve critical market mass, some hardware firms will merge with others. The Burroughs-Sperry merger is one example. It and others to come will succeed only if the combined market position is sufficient to sustain an integrated research and product development program.

Most mainstream technology leadership will have derived more from modular architectures that bridge interoperably across component generations. Few larger business customers will be making outright massive replacements of their operations equipment, opting instead to replace or upgrade specific components frequently. Manufacturers ignoring modularity and interoperability will not make IT for long. In the early 1980s, Sord, a previously successful Japanese computer manufacturer, failed in the small business market in part because of lack of interoperability with IBM software.

Consequently, the business operations equipment cluster will see fewer broadly based new entrants from other clusters, but the high growth rate should attract a plethora of industry-specific niche players.

As in the past, new smaller firms will have surfaced suddenly with a "better box." Among the latest better boxes are reduced instruction set computers (RISC), parallel processors with associative memories, low-cost fault-tolerant configurations, database processing machines, and all sizes of optical storage. Just emerging in the early 1990s from the development stage will be optical processors and switches.

The world-scale leaders of the 1990s will be measured principally on the basis of their marketshare of specific industry segments rather than grosser or coarser measures. Other than participating indirectly through their OEM business, even the largest players will opt to have invested their specialized software or hardware in only a limited number of verticals. Even here, much of the product and market development will be externalized as with office equipment suppliers. But in contrast with office equipment, many of these strategic alliances will have been struck with leading-edge customers, eager to control the disintermediation of their industries. Two notable examples will have been communications equipment manufacturers with larger carriers and financial industries' IT suppliers with leading money-center banks.

Getting to the Heart of IT

Despite the computer slump of the mid-1980s, business operations equipment remains the largest and fastest growing (16 percent compounded annual growth rate) of the clusters. It may not be the most glamorous, but by 1990, this cluster will account for over 30 percent of domestic IT revenue.

Normal business operations in any corporation can be viewed as a series of value-added stages from development through distribution. It is these stages that are being revolutionized. Embedded IT is altering both the marketing and physical distribution stages of business operations. Other systems are affecting the development and production stages as well. Just a few of the production examples are shown in the following table:

Industry	Embedded IT system
Manufacturing	Computer-aided design and manufacturing
Banking	Automated teller machines and smart cards
Health care	Computer-assisted diagnoses
Brokerage	Automated trades
Education	Computer-based training
Retailing	Electronic point-of-sale systems
Publishing	Computer-assisted makeup and imaging
Lodging	Electronic inn management
Transportation	Automated guidance systems
Utilities	Energy management control systems
State government	Lottery systems

Most are already widespread. The others loom on the horizon. All of the examples above represent one of two fundamental types of business equipment, that which is industry-specific, what IT suppliers typically call "vertical" and that which is generic, or "horizontal." Most general-purpose computer configurations and systems software used to process business transactions are generic, at least until users add applications software to tailor the computer power to their specific needs. Some of the exciting developments in the generic segment will be the introduction of larger and more powerful mainframe configurations surpassing 200 MIPS (millions of instructions per second) of processing power and trillions of bytes of optical storage by 1990, as well as scientific computers whose power is measured in multibillions of floating point instructions per second (gigaflops). Overall, the market for such supercomputers will be growing at over 40 percent annually through the early 1990s.

But while both industry-specific and generic IT can wind up serving user needs, sharp strategic differences mark the two segments. Industry-specific products and services provide more added content value to customers. Because they have already been tailored to the idiosyncracies of end-user segments, they are more apt to be of immediate utility, i.e., require less customer effort, time, and risk to implement. Indeed some industry-specific products such as automated teller machine and certain industry-specific services such as credit databases go far beyond any single customer's ability to develop them. Industry-specific systems are also typcially more efficient since they do not bear the overhead associated with generic devices and software.

Despite the greater value to customers, the industry expertise needed to accomplish this is often difficult and expensive for IT suppliers to amass. To be successful, such systems must be developed by firms concomitantly expert in both IT and in the streets and subways of a vertical application and its customers. Hence, industry-specific segments not only yield a premium from value-conscious customers but also are more competitively sheltered. Therefore, providers of generic IT facilities such as general purpose computers and telecommunications networks increasingly are trying to acquire or collaborate with industry specialists. And as Ed Diamond, a telecommunications consultant with the Eastern Management Group says, "Hardware isn't the name of the game, software is the name of the game."[1] (Successful information service veterans have guarded this insight as a trade secret until it recently became obvious to most hardware players.) One rapidly growing type of specialist is the independent value-added reseller who typically procures generic hardware and adds industry-specific application software, databases, and/or peripherals and terminals before selling the configuration to eager customers.

As a result, the industry-specific segments of the business operations equipment cluster are the fastest growing. By 1990, they will reach close to $165 billion, more than generic business equipment ($135 billion) and almost as much as consumer electronics and office equipment combined.

[1]*The Report on AT&T*, January 28, 1985, p. 9.

One big industry-specific type of equipment worth about $40 billion annually will be sold within the IT industry. This is communications networking equipment sold to the communications cluster. Given the trials and tribulations of telecommunications carriers, communications equipment suppliers face especially formidable challenges which we describe below. The other largest vertical market is the discrete manufacturing segment. And here, as in most other smaller segments, incisive market planning is a prerequisite to success. Therefore, we follow our discussion of communications equipment with a further illustration taken from the IT-integrated factory market.

Network Telecommunications Suppliers: Getting IT Out There[2]

For network equipment suppliers, the first test is how well they understand in what ways their carrier customers will be responding to their challenges (as described in Chapter 7), i.e., "Do we grasp the strategic environment of our customers, and how can we use this major strategic upheaval to build our relationships, add values, and shape decisions, such as network strategy, critical to suppliers?" Once armed with that strategic insight, they then face their own set of five challenges (see Figure 12.1).

Network equipment suppliers must consider whether a competitive advantage can be gained in new market segments. This first challenge means knowing why new market opportunities have opened up. Is it carrier imperatives for new services, competitive actions, or capital efficiency? Is it new technologies, architectures, and standards or shifts in operating practices? Might it be a result of removing trade restrictions or just different buying perspectives? Is it simply demand fluctuations? Are these new opportunities an outcome of competitive skills in differentiating products, economies of scale or scope, or from vertical integration efficiencies?

A second challenge for equipment suppliers lies in determining which traditional products are more or less vulnerable to new entrants. Weaknesses and strengths might be attributed to an ISDN systems approach subsuming existing niche markets or to technical obsolescence. "It is clear now that the objective of telephone companies in the U.S. and Postal Telephone and Telegraph (PTT) authorities in Europe is the implemen-

[2]Adapted from Robert J. Cymbala, Steven P. Nowick, and Harvey L. Poppel, "The Trials and Tribulations of the Telecommunications Industry," *Information Industry Insights*, Booz, Allen & Hamilton Inc., issue 8, pp. 9–10.

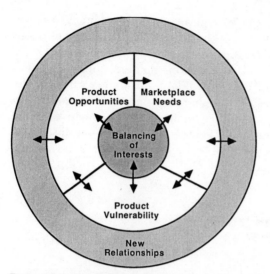

Figure 12.1. Network equipment suppliers face five interrelated sets of strategic challenges. (SOURCE: *Adapted
from "The Trials and Tribulations of the Telecommunications Industry,"* Information Industry Insights, *Booz, Allen
& Hamilton Inc., issue 8, pp. 9–10.*)

tation of an integrated services digital network (ISDN)," Marc De Villepin, assistant vice president of France Telecom, Inc., asserted in early
1985. He predicted "by 1995, 95 percent of France will be covered by an
ISDN. Three million ISDN lines at 144 kilobits per second will be installed. (That would roughly equate to a staggering capacity of 2×10^{17}
bits per year)."[3]

Powerful joint ventures, shifting buyer loyalties, or distribution channel discontinuities might also be the cause of shifting entry barriers.

Third is a realignment of relations with carriers. We see many causes
for realignment: shorter lead times, more competitive initial procurements and replenishment, more volatile demand forecasts, joint funding
of R&D, more technical sales and service support requirements, stream-
lined materials management and physical distribution, and revamped
procurement procedures. All of these imply changes in management style
and procedures.

A fourth challenge is in developing an internal picture of the evolving
view of end uses instead of relying on carriers' procurement forecasts.

---

[3]Marc De Villepin, "Europe Focuses on Public ISND, Extending Satellite Nets," *ComputerWorld Special Report*, February 25, 1985, p. SR/10.

This is particularly so given that carriers are still maturing their own planning and forecasting processes and that intense local carrier bypass and interexchange carrier price competition could lead to unforeseen booms or busts. In addition, reliance on purchased off-the-shelf market studies often means too optimistic, extrapolative, and global forecasts. And although end users are a generally good source for near-term demand analyses, more sophisticated end-use forecasting techniques are also needed for longer-range planning input.

And fifth, product-market and manufacturing strategies for end users and carriers and for customer-premise equipment and networks must be balanced and rationalized. This means leveraging R&D and manufacturing investments across multiple product-market segments or developing modular, customer-premise equipment-network synergistic products. And efforts should be made to mitigate business cycles' effects on capacity, cash flow, and earnings. But network suppliers who also manufacture customer-premise equipment will need to balance certain unilateral marketplace thrusts with the maintenance of friendly distribution partners to reach other segments.

All of these five challenges will induce a substantial consolidation among both network and customer-premise equipment manufacturers. Recent deals between GTE and Siemens and between ITT and CGE are a direct outgrowth of facing up to these new challenges. Nevertheless, suppliers seeking strategic partners should heed the conclusion of L. F. Rothchild's Karen Mulvaney, "Most joint ventures are a disaster. I can't think of one in the communications field that has ever worked."[4]

Industry-Specific Market Segmentation: Taking IT Apart[5]

All the fanfare that has surrounded GM's new Saturn car is but the tip of an immense iceberg. This project represents a radical shift by U.S. companies into full-fledged automated manufacturing. The IT-integrated factory is one of the largest and most dramatic industry-specific sectors of the business operations equipment cluster. Therefore, we will use it to illustrate how a vertical market can be segmented. In this case, two dimensions of the market establish the segmentation framework:

[4]*Electronic Business*, March 1, 1985, p. 599.

[5]Derived from concepts first advanced by Robert J. Mayer, "Segmenting the Factor of the Future", *Information Industry Insights*, Booz, Allen & Hamilton Inc., issue 6, pp. 3–5.

1. *Manufacturing characteristics.* They are used to spotlight attractive categories of manufacturers. Two factors are most relevant (see Figure 12.2). One is the *process type* which is divided into batch, high volume, and mass production. The other is the *product-process innovation rate* or stage of maturity. Is it fluid, transitory, or specific?

When mapped against one another, these two factors reveal eight categories of the $1 trillion "discrete parts" manufacturing shipment volume. The best choice for broad IT manufacturing products and services include oil field equipment, machine tools, and electronic office equipment (2); internal combustion engines (3); construction and farm equipment (5); and photographic equipment (7). These comprise a substantial portion of manufacturing sector value. Industries within them are sufficiently established to be predictable, yet they are dynamic enough to generate market opportunities.

The fluid state companies (1, 4) represent only 1 percent of the value of U.S. shipments in discrete products and are too dynamic (e.g., genetic engineering and microprocessor development) to provide a reliable market. Companies in the remaining categories (6 and 8) have facilities and products unlikely to change substantially over the next 15 years—for example, wood furniture, foundries, and textile products.

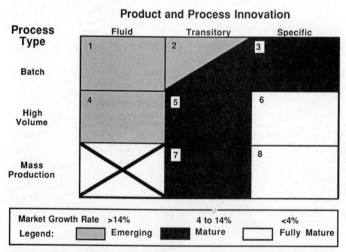

Figure 12.2. Successful penetration of the IT-integrated factory market requires a careful segmentation of the manufacturing marketplace. (SOURCE: *Robert J. Mayer, "Segmenting the Factory of the Future,"* Information Industry Insights, *Booz, Allen & Hamilton Inc., issue 6, p. 4.*)

2. *Product-market characteristics.* They fall into three common segments. We can call these strategic operations units in that each has similar traits and critical success factors that are closely linked to product and market strategy.

The first type of strategic operations unit in the manufacturing vertical is composed of standard products with a relatively stable design. These products have a constant marketplace demand, and they require a fast response time on orders. Price is the key critical success factor, and this type of business would benefit from IT products and services that help integrate production lines.

The second category of strategic operations unit relates to manufactured products that are less standardized, have more variable features, and are produced in moderate to low volumes. Because the marketplace demand for these products is highly variable, they are not volume produced nor carried in heavy inventory. Flexibility is the critical success factor; therefore, flexible process technologies and manufacturing information systems are pivotal.

Engineered customized products are a third type of strategic operations unit. Like the second category, these products experience highly variable marketplace demands. In this category, product innovation is the critical success factor, and computer-aided engineering systems are important.

Manufacturing is not necessarily limited to three strategic operations units, but virtually any discrete-parts manufacturing industry can be decomposed into a short list of such units. For example, the motors industry, part of manufacturing segment 5, has all three, with motors ranging from high-volume standardized models to custom-engineered special orders. Others, like textile products in 8, would fall primarily in the second unit category—moderate volume and somewhat variable products.

Indeed the strategic operations unit segmentation method can be applied to other industries. For example, banking branch offices can be segmented into those that serve the mass market and are hence efficiency driven and those that serve the higher net worth customer and are service quality driven.

Essentially, this segmentation concept enables IT customers to plan their future manufacturing facilities on a unit-by-unit basis by identifying investments required to achieve competitive success. By analyzing scale and logistics economies, each strategic unit can be translated into specific factory configurations, each having automation requirements tailored to its volume, customization, and production requirements.

Accordingly, an IT supplier can derive the percent of the industry asset base in each strategic operations unit. Supplier product investment can then be estimated as a percent of each unit's asset base. Thus, this concept enables each IT supplier to configure and target its products and services to meet specific customer needs and to size the market potential.

This segmentation method is also useful for sizing industry-specific markets for functional hardware, such as controllers, at the physical operations level. Conversely, we can forecast the market for most software technology and interoperability products on a macro or top-down basis rather than bottom-up because these products are generic.

Summary

In this and the previous five chapters of Part 2, we have forecast the principal product and market dynamics that will separate the IT winners from the losers. But we really have not explained what we mean by winning.

How do we know when a company is successful? What are the principal ways of judging an IT-supplier's performance?

One way is the proven ability to generate *shareholder* rewards. As we will describe in Part 3, this is a fully quantifiable, highly analytic measure. A second, more qualitative and subjective measure is the perception of its major *stakeholders*—customers, suppliers, investors, employees, and collaborators. The next chapter deals with each of these two measures at some length.

PART 3
Succeeding at IT

13
Measuring IT

Many different categories of stakeholders are vitally concerned with measuring the performance of IT suppliers. Senior managers are typically compensated and advanced based on performance measures. And many customers and suppliers are increasingly wary of doing business with poor-performing companies. But ultimately the most important performance watchers are the public and private shareholders, who establish the relative value of companies based on proven and anticipated performance.

Shareholder Rewards[1]

For-profit corporations exist mainly to generate returns to stockholders. Ultimately, these returns may be in the form of cash dividends. Realistically, however, appreciation in the stock price provides much of the potential motivation for today's IT stockholders. This is particularly the case for the high-growth IT companies. Where strong growth potential exists, current cash is better used to fund profitable new investments than to pay dividends. Indeed, the stock market should reward this emphasis on investment growth for companies which have superior investment opportunities.

But does it really work that way? And, if so, is there a quantitative relationship which can be measured, or better yet, anticipated? We are now convinced that the answer to both questions is a definite "yes!"

Market to Book: The ROE Factor

For many years, the relative value of publicly held corporations was expressed in terms of current market price versus annualized earnings,

---

[1]Adapted from concepts first advanced by Paul A. Branstad, "Is Market/Book Ratio the Ultimate Measure of I^2 Corporate Performance?," *Information Industry Insights*, Booz, Allen & Hamilton Inc., issue 4, pp. 1–3.

the P/E ratio. But P/E ratios are intrinsically volatile. The underlying growth in earnings per share on which they are presumed to be based is volatile and subject to currency fluctuations, tax strategies, and special adjustments. Moreover, attempts to manage consistent earnings growth through creative accounting practices are eventually discounted by the market, thus perpetuating instability.

A more meaningful comparative measure has gained currency among sophisticated investors—the ratio between a company's stock market value and its book value (market to book or MB). The MB ratio is a measure of the markup or markdown of book value. The up or down direction and magnitude are a reflection of the corporation's underlying profitability, assuming that book value accurately reflects shareholder interest in the accumulation of net assets. In contrast to earnings and earnings growth, book value and book value growth are inherently more stable, especially once a company survives its start-up and early capitalization period.

MB ratios which exceed 1 to 1 reflect investor confidence that future returns on equity will exceed required levels. Conversely, MB ratios less than 1 to 1 imply that shareholders expect future returns from the company's investment base to be below required levels.

Empirical Results

Empirical analysis of the IT industry in general and of the information services cluster specifically does indeed support the thesis that the MB ratio does reflect the specific performance criteria of growth and return on equity.

Historical financial performance can explain almost 90 percent of the observed variation in MB ratios among larger IT suppliers. This finding holds true for MB ratios ranging from slightly below 1 to 1 to nearly 7 to 1. We have found, however, that superior performance must be sustained for a long period if the market is to regard it as a legitimate basis for future performance. In this context, short-term manipulation of earnings or public relations are transparent.

Growth in the shareholders' investment base and return on equity (ROE) are the performance measures which best explain MB ratios. Higher ROEs consistently yield higher MBs. But the market may reward or penalize strong growth performance depending on the level of ROE. Companies whose return on equity exceeds minimum shareholder requirements typically receive an MB ratio greater than 1 to 1. This premium tends to expand with higher rates of asset growth. Similarly, companies whose past performance augers that their investments will earn less than the minimum required return are actively penalized by the market for pursuing additional growth.

ROE has more leverage than growth on stock market performance.
Figure 13.1 plots lines of constant MB ratio for a combination of office
and business equipment companies as a function of growth and ROE.
Each of the hardware companies is plotted based on a weighted average of
its ROE and growth performance during a sample period (1981). To
illustrate the primacy of ROE, Data General, a company with an average
MB ratio at that point, could have expected that a 5 point gain in ROE
(line E) would boost the MB ratio from 1.5 to nearly 2.0. The potential
from a 5-point gain in growth (line G) was clearly lower. True, exceptional
asset growth rates, above 35 percent, can yield high MBs even with only
slightly above average ROEs, provided that the market expects ROE to be
maintained.

Therefore, the lines of constant MB ratio plotted at specific points in
time can provide a frame of reference for evaluating the degree to which a
company's performance was explained well and also the degree to which
that ratio was the result of superior ROE, superior growth, or both.

This approach can also be used to understand whether the stock market anticipates future performance which is different from past per-

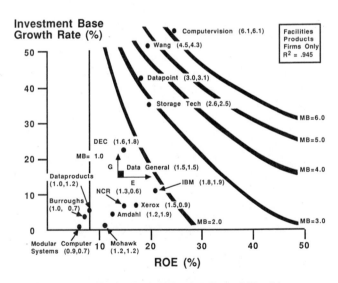

Legend: (a,b)* = (predicted MB [as plotted], actual MB ratio)
*rounded to the nearest tenth

Figure 13.1. Of the two performance measures, ROE has a stronger
influence on the M/B ratio. (SOURCE: *Paul A. Bransad, "Is Market/Book
Ratio the Ultimate Measure of I^2 Corporate Performance?,"* Information
Industry Insights, *Booz, Allen & Hamilton Inc., issue 4, p. 2.*)

formance. For example, Figure 13.1 shows that the actual 1981 MB ratio for Xerox was lower than predicted. This suggests that the 1981 stock market was anticipating some future deterioration in Xerox's ROE and/or asset growth rate—which did occur in 1982 through 1984. Revenue, as opposed to asset, growth is not a reliable measure of successful performance. For example, a spot analysis of some 1984 and 1985 results points up intriguing dichotomies between revenue growth and ROE. Of the nineteen fastest growing IT firms over $160 million in 1984, only five materially surpassed the overall industry ROE average. In 1985, thirteen of these firms reported at least one losing quarter.

On an unweighted average basis, companies operating principally within the three product clusters—consumer electronics, office equipment, and business operations equipment—grow at a 14 to 15 percent rate while entertainment, information, and communications service firms average only 10 to 11 percent. Yet, in 1985 for domestic companies over $100 million, "pure" service firms clearly outgunned pure product suppliers on ROE—16 percent versus 11 percent.

But, some growth is healthy. Few firms we have studied with shrinking revenues manage to eke out even a minimal 10 percent ROE. For facilities-based firms, especially those lacking the natural advantages ascribed earlier to many content-based companies, growth may be vital to ROE success.

A 10-year long analysis of primarily facilities-based, high-growth IT niche firms shows that ROE deteriorates as growth slows (see Figure 13.2). Our diagnoses of companies experiencing this slowdown find that management overconfidence is the disease. As Stephan McClellan warns in his book, "The bigger their egos, the harder they fall. Beware of smugness or cockiness in management. Lack of humility is dangerous. Those who have overly high opinions of themselves usually have other blind spots as well."[2]

This type of overconfidence spreads during the early entrepreneurial stages of robust growth and leads to ill-conceived attempts to sustain very high growth rates. Symptoms include naivete about new businesses, insular attitudes toward shifts in core business competitive dynamics, and, most frequently, glaring inabilities to migrate business and organizational strategy. The results are indiscriminate diversifications, competitor inroads into core businesses, and, inevitably, a plummeting ROE. Examples of the most recent niche players, previously exalted by the business media, that have been "niched" themselves include Cullinet, Televideo, Tandon, Daisy Systems, DSC, Apollo, and TIE. Some come back. But the list of near or total fatalities lengthens daily.

[2]Stephan T. McClellan, *The Coming Computer Industry Shakeout: Winners, Losers & Survivors*, John Wiley & Sons, New York, NY, 1984, p. 324.

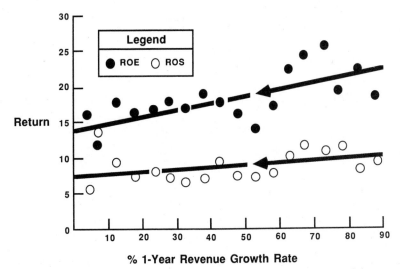

Figure 13.2. Today's niche players face the challenge of eroding margins and slower growth which historically have beset those niche players attempting to diversify. (SOURCE: *Based on Booz-Allen analysis of 1972–1981 published data for thirty-seven rapidly growing IT niche players.*)

Strategic Differences

The most important conclusion derived from our quantitative research is that the relationship between ROE and MB is governed principally by product-market factors.

As it turns out, the IT industry as a whole has sustained a higher ROE and hence a greater MB than the average of other industries (see Figure 13.3). This, despite some cyclical slumps such as that of 1985. This is because of the relatively high (12 percent) secular growth rate sustained by the industry's marketplace and the continuing opportunities for above-average profits triggered by new technological developments.

But the real product-market distinctions do not clearly show until we examine the ROE-MB correlation for each of the six IT clusters. Although the linear correlations for each are quite strong, each has its own intercept and slope (see Figure 13.4).

Information service firms enjoy the strongest premium of market over book, while communications service firms show, on average, almost no premium. Valuation premiums derive more from intrinsic product or market factors than from financial factors.

Communications services receive a low premium because of regulatory-capped pricing, very high fixed (and indeed often inflexible) asset in-

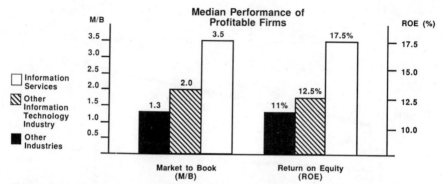

Figure 13.3. Despite its growing pains and challenges, the information service sector rewards its shareholders handsomely. (SOURCE: *Broadview Associates.*)

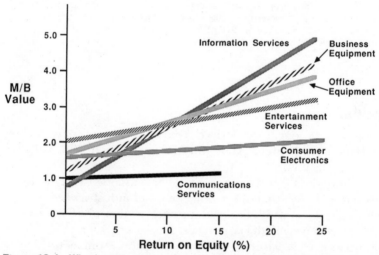

Figure 13.4. What business you are in has a dramatic effect on shareholder value. (SOURCE: *Broadview Associates, based on data available April 1986.*)

tensity, regulatory uncertainties, and as yet unproven abilities to move ROE up beyond 16 to 17 percent. In contrast, we attribute the strong premiums of information services to:

- The inherently more stable subscriber revenue stream (the volatile software package segment is an emerging exception to this).

- The value-based pricing that most information service firms enjoy based on the heavy content (versus facilities) mix of their services.

- Relative insulation from technologically induced short product life cycles (also a function of rich content versus facilities' value added).

- Limited, if any, competition in the sourcing and synthesis of their content and, in some cases, virtually insurmountable entry barriers.

- Little or no foreign competition.

- The strong potential in most information services segments to earn very high ROEs (even if a given firm at a specific point in time is not). This high ROE potential exists without leveraging debt-equity ratios as much as it does in all the other five clusters.

Indeed, 1986 data show that a hefty 25 percent of all publicly held information service firms were earning over 20 percent ROE, a level rarely achieved by companies in other segments of the IT industry, much less in other industries (see Figure 13.5). Among publicly held hardware product firms only 7 percent were earning superior ROEs over 20 percent. Nearly half showed anemic returns of less than 5 percent (see Figure 13.6).

Product-market distinctions even lead to some modest valuation differences among some of the principal segments within information services (see Figure 13.7). The integrated market services segment has the highest premium. It is generally the most rapidly growing and the most content-intensive, and it includes many highly valued emerging IMS players such as Safecard and Information Resources, Inc.

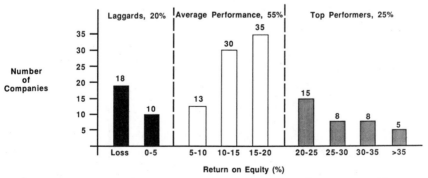

Figure 13.5. One out of every four publicly held information service firms earns over 20 percent return on equity. (SOURCE: *Broadview Associates, based on latest 12-month results of 142 "pure" I.S. firms as of January 1, 1986.*)

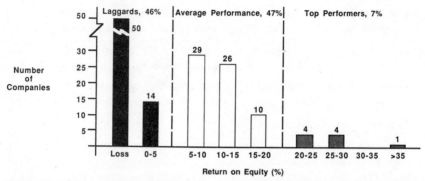

Figure 13.6. Relatively few publicly held hardware product firms earn a superior return on equity. (SOURCE: *Broadview Associates, based on latest 12-month results of 138 "pure" IT hardware firms as of April 4, 1986.*)

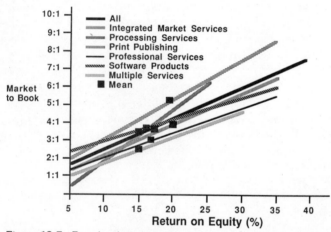

Figure 13.7. Even for above-average performers, what business you are in can account for big differences in market value. (SOURCE: *Broadview Associates, based on January 1, 1986, market values for 111 profitable companies, latest 12-month ROE, and most recent quarter book value.*)

Professional services firms, which lack pricing leverage and whose growth is tempered by human resource development considerations, have a lower, albeit still considerable, premium. Firms with mixed identities also fall nearer the bottom, just as less-focused firms, especially conglomerates, do in other industries. Investors like to be clear about what they are buying into.

Some Final Observations

Bigger, then, does not mean better. ROE—not revenue growth—is the principal driver of shareholder value, as measured by the MB ratio.

But, placed in proper perspective, targeted growth is important to most companies. If targeted at relevant markets, growth can translate to marketshare gains and economies of scope. If targeted at cumulative production volume, growth is the means to achieve experience-curve cost reductions. If targeted at organizational development, growth can stimulate cultural and human resource evolution. The key is that when growth is targeted on higher-return products, markets or value-added segments, it can drive corporate ROE upward.

All performance factors taken together still need to be seasoned with qualitative outlooks and a keen sense of the idiosyncracies of a particular company within a particular IT cluster (see Figure 13-8).

Stakeholder Perceptions

However revealing ROE, MB, and growth measures may be, they do not always jibe with stakeholder perception. That is one of the principal findings of a 1984 Booz-Allen study[3] of stakeholder perceptions. Some 200 senior executives were surveyed about those IT firms most familiar to

---

[3]Harvey L. Poppel, "Successful Companies and Contributing Attributes," *Information Industry Insights*, Booz, Allen & Hamilton Inc., issue 10, pp. 1–3.

	Performance	Outlook
Strategic drivers	Proven value ■ ROE ■ Asset growth ■ Marketshare	Potential value ■ Technology change ■ Marketplace change ■ Management change
Economic forces	Relative Values ■ Stock market cycle ■ Cost of money	Potential relative values ■ Customers' economic cycle ■ Suppliers' economic cycle

Figure 13.8. The timing and thrust of shareholder investment is a function of numerous performance indicators. (SOURCE: *Derived from technology investment matrix, Morgan Stanley.*)

them. Executives rated up to ten such firms on a 1 to 10 scale by two measures: customer satisfaction and shareholder satisfaction. From their responses, findings were compiled on the fifty companies which were most often cited and from these a top-ten selection was made:

The Top Ten

Customer satisfaction rank	Shareholder satisfaction rank
1. IBM	1. Microsoft
2. Matsushita	2. IBM
3. Apollo	3. Dun & Bradstreet
4. Hewlett-Packard	4. Dow Jones
5. Sony	5. ADP
6. The New York Times	6. Matsushita
7. Eastman Kodak	7. 3M
8. Tandem	8. Hewlett-Packard
9. Dow Jones	9. Intel
10. Apple	10. Wang

Getting to be one of the top ten is tough enough. Staying there is even tougher. Only 1 year later, the earnings of six of the top ten in shareholder satisfaction were flat to nonexistent. This is especially so in an industry full of surprises—well-known stories of companies seemingly taking off, like Osborne Computer, but which plummet with equal haste and declare bankruptcy. Or there is EDS seemingly headed in one direction but then unexpectedly acquired by GM. (An event not painful to EDS' shareholders.) Some high flyers of yesteryear fell flat on their faces with aborted efforts such as Xerox with XDS. And there is little doubt that severe market quakes will continue to shock the microcomputer and telecommunications equipment sectors.

In fact, there is so much volatility that a prediction of individual company futures is hazardous. It is no accident that *Institutional Investor* regularly changes its selection of the best computer industry analyst. That is why it is one thing to describe the more predictable trillion dollar gross opportunity, as we have done in Parts 1 and 2. And it is quite another to forecast who will cash in on those opportunities.

Nonetheless, to update as well as complement the survey's top ten, we fearlessly nominate another ten publicly held firms, representative of a much longer list of well-managed firms of which we are aware, whose shareholders should be highly "satisfied" and who have promising outlooks, as of this writing:

BDM International	Dynatech
Comp-U-Card	General Motors Class "E"
Computer Associates	Information Resources, Inc.
Cox Enterprises	Metromail
Cray Research	Telex

Even the companies presently or previously cited as most successful have, or have had, problems. Their corporate leaders and managers cannot rest for a moment on the laurels of past achievements. We will pinpoint the major management issues they will have to master in order to be on the 1990s top-ten list. Here are some glimpses and doubts about the top ten in 1984.

Dow Jones was high on the 1984 top-ten list, but does it have the technology muscle to migrate successfully into electronic information services alone? At present, the company is much smaller in overall size and shallower in management depth than Dun & Bradstreet and McGraw-Hill. Much like The New York Times, another top-ten player, its cash flow and profits depend largely on one service, in this case *The Wall Street Journal*, whose revenue and profits have come under some pressures of late. Complicating its future is that the firm does not have the lock on electronic distribution that they have on certain print distribution. Their recent investment into Telerate helps give the firm expanded presence. But as only a partial owner, Dow Jones may not be able to leverage the opportunity fully. Despite these issues, we believe that Dow Jones would still be an attractive acquisition for certain larger IT firms, were Dow Jones willing.

Even at *Dun & Bradstreet*, with size and good management depth, there are uncertainties. The firm must achieve potential synergies at a time when both the traditional Dun & Bradstreet and newer Nielsen organizations are trying to leverage IT in traditional businesses or face being disintermediated. For example, A. C. Nielsen's current methods of collecting its syndicated TV and other market information will give way to new on-line information gathering systems whether they lead the way or not. Similarly, such successful Dun & Bradstreet businesses as telephone directory sales, credit databases, coupon distribution and clearing, and the airline guide face new competitive challenges.

Hewlett-Packard faces choices between sustained success based on marketing generic electronic components, micros, and minis to mass markets versus focusing more narrowly on a series of industry-specific niches, such as factory automation, in which they have built experience, a market franchise, and can leverage their strong instrumentation position. Moreover, they have placed many of their "chips" on a new RISC-based computer series with unproven long-term market acceptance.

Wang is attempting to balance its resources between slugging it out with IBM in generic office equipment and building a very sizable information service position.

Wunderkinds like *Microsoft* face the classic "passages" challenge of migrating from a single product, privately held, entrepreneurially run firm to something else capable of breaking well above the $100MM to $200MM range that seems to mire most formerly high-flying IT firms. Does anyone remember what became of Visicorp? (We do. It is gone.)

Among the "rising suns," companies such as *Matsushita* and *Sony* could be making a big mistake in emphasizing the business arenas for most of their future growth (as they have publicly stated) rather than investing more to gain marketshare in the home arena, in which they are strongest and know best how to compete on a worldwide basis.

Can *3M* and *Kodak* successfully outpunch the Japanese on blank media products, such as videotapes, floppies, and optical discs, in which the Japanese excel? The size, growth, and intense price competition of these markets and the lack of either an overwhelming customer franchise, as Kodak has in film, or a defensible niche position (as 3M has in many other of its markets) cast doubts on their success. Both firms have spotty track records of previous IT diversifications. 3M clearly failed to make a mark in word processing and certain copier products. And Kodak has had well-publicized problems with its Atex (computer-aided publishing) acquisition and in ceding emerging markets such as instant photography to Polaroid and 35-mm cameras to the Japanese.

ADP stands out with its unbroken 25+-year record of growing profitability in the face of fundamental restructuring of the computer service business. But as the value of telecommunications and other high technology in computer services grows, ADP may find itself on less familiar ground that may require more internal development initiatives and risk taking. Or one might consider *Tandem's* future. Can it maintain market leadership in fault-tolerant transaction systems as IBM rallies behind Stratus, the number 2 firm, or as other powerful computer companies such as AT&T and DEC start offering similar capabilities? Can fallen superstars like *Apollo* reestablish their growth curve if their market niches just are not big enough to satisfy them and all the other aggressive players? Should *Intel* stabilize the impact of the feast-famine cycle in electronic components through diversification even though they already have divested at least one earlier diversification effort (in the database management software area)?

And can *Apple* maintain its "Avis-like" number 2 PC position into a generation beyond MacIntosh without a major collaborating partner or two? To date, it has not been notably successful in penetrating either the Fortune 500 or most non-North American markets. What happens if IBM one-ups the Mac?

Many analysts and consultants consider IBM the best-managed company in the U.S. And after performing listlessly during the latter 1970s, it has roared back during the early 1980s. But for all the success it has amassed, the past has not been faultless. Their diversification track record is far from exemplary. During the 1970s, IBM's penetration of the copier market was shallow and attempts to become a leader in the PBX market stalled in its European roll-out stage. Their videodisc-production venture with MCA is bygone, abandoned after a few years. Their early- to mid-1970s push into private sector custom design and programming (for profit and growth) slackened until very recently. They threw hundreds of millions of dollars into SBS without any returns to date. More recently, IBM's PC_{jr} failed to penetrate the consumer arena successfully. The giant's entry into computer services (Information Network) is not yet notably successful. And internationally, Big Blue has run into big problems with the Bundespost, the British government, and other European governments on specific products and standards issues.

Most recently, IBM failed to forecast the computer and PBX equipment slump of the mid-1980s, thereby raising skepticism about its avowed intention to achieve $100 billion by 1990. That means growing faster than the IT industry as a whole, i.e., gaining share. And there is the catch-22 of another potential round of antitrust actions, beyond the Reagan era, especially if large numbers of IBM competitors continue to withdraw from direct competition (e.g., CDC) or go Chapter eleven (e.g., Storage Technology).

So, in the face of all these uncertainties what is it that we can learn about success from the top ten?

Perceptions versus Performance

Despite its fallabilities, IBM has posted an enviable record of high (over 20 percent) returns on equity while sustaining an unsurpassed image for quality. So they and the other highly regarded IT firms must be doing something right. Yet on balance, financial performance records hardly justified their high position. For example, of the ten IT leaders in return on equity at the time of the Booz-Allen study, eight do not appear among the survey's top ten. Indeed, only IBM and Dow Jones were able to match financial achievements with perception. And if one takes another financial performance measure, namely market to book, IBM drops off the list and only Dow Jones remains. Only for those companies with superior sustained earnings over longer periods of time do shareholder rankings and actual performance data match up well.

For some companies, the correlation between customer satisfaction and shareholder satisfaction is also weak. Among those listed above in the customer top ten, several including The New York Times, Sony, and Eastman Kodak had weak shareholder ratings. And among the balance of the fifty most often cited, several others including Mitel, L. M. Ericsson, and Tandy also show almost no link between customer and shareholder satisfaction.

Bigness is also no a priori indicator of making the top ten. Although IBM is certainly big and makes nearly every top-ten list, six of the top-ranked companies were under $1.5 billion in sales. Apollo, The New York Times, Tandem, Microsoft, ADP, and Dow Jones all ranked below the 100 largest IT companies, yet they were among the perceived most successful. If neither narrowly defined shareholder performance data nor sheer size in the marketplace contribute measurably to customer and shareholder perceptions of satisfaction, what general conditions or characteristics do?

Success Attributes

Five special qualities, or success attributes,[4] do appear to drive customer and shareholder rankings. One success attribute, *people-culture*, outweighs the others as the most important determinant of success. Following it in descending order of correlation strength are product quality, senior management competence, corporate strategic vision, and marketing-sales capabilities (Table 13.1).

Two other attributes used in the Booz-Allen survey emerged as important but less vital determinants in establishing customer and shareholder rankings. One was *financial strength* which is understandably correlated with shareholder rank but not with customer rank. The other, strong *customer franchise* ratings, tended to characterize only the top-ten customer-ranked or shareholder-ranked companies, while both strong and weak customer franchise ratings were sprinkled among the other forty most-cited firms.

Four other attributes did not contribute materially to overall customer and shareholder rankings—and in some cases detracted from them. *Product innovativeness* is often stressed by public relations people as a successful attribute. Yet only Apollo and Tandem, among the top-ten customer-ranked firms, were also among the ten ranked as most innova-

---

[4]"Critical Success Attributes," *Information Industry Insights*, Booz, Allen & Hamilton Inc., issue 10, pp. 3–4.

tive. Many firms with strong innovation ratings placed low on the overall customer and shareholder lists. Indeed, this was one of the very few categories in which IBM failed to rank among the leaders.

Many of the laggards in *R&D-technology* ratings ranked above average in the overall customer and shareholder categories; in fact, none of the information service firms, except Microsoft, ranked above thirty-fourth in R&D-technology. Communications service firms ranked relatively high in *physical distribution*, yet the cluster finished last in overall customer and shareholder rankings (cluster rankings are interpreted in the next chapter).

And as far as being *least-cost producers*, consumer electronic firms, on average, had the most favorable image in this category but still fared poorly in overall shareholder ranking. In many other ways, the ratings given this attribute did not seem to fit other perceptions. In general, respondents did not think of IT companies as least-cost producers. Far more rated that as a weakness than they did any other attribute. This may be a result, however, of their reacting to the prices they were charged, because respondents lacked adequate knowledge of the cost structure behind these prices.

We find no other common threads. No single quantitative or other immediately discernible characteristic, such as size, business mix, geographic base, maturity, or market to book, that accounts for the high ratings of the ten firms.

Table 13.1. Attributes and Successful IT Performance

Success attributes	Limited correlation	Little or no correlation
People-culture	Financial strength	Product innovation
Product quality	Customer franchise	R&D-technology
Senior management competence		Least cost
Corporate strategic vision		Physical distribution
Marketing-sales capabilities		

14
Doing IT Right: The Strategic Management Challenge

Future success or failure, whether in the top ten or contenders for the top spots, means but one thing: strategic management, which translates into being in the right businesses in the right ways. In the last chapter, we identified what we called the five principal success attributes. Two of these, strategic vision and senior management competence, are intertwined with the issue of strategic management. Strategic vision is the soul of senior management competence. But vision is not enough; superior managers knowingly take risks and marshall resources to fulfill their vision. That is strategic management.

Managing IT

A 1982 Booz-Allen survey[1] of more than 200 senior IT executives helps us to interpret the strategic management challenges. With strategic management at the core, that survey pinpointed three other management processes as also vital both currently and in the future: (1) people-culture management, (2) market management, and (3) technology management. Three other management processes—productivity, financial, and regulatory—trailed far behind in future mentions. Not that these are not important, but in the dynamic IT industry, they are secondary.

---

[1] "I^2 Critical Success Factors: An Analysis of a Booz-Allen Survey," *Information Industry Insights*, Booz, Allen & Hamilton Inc., issue 3, pp. 1–4.

The flywheel issue is how to be in the right businesses in the right ways. That is what strategic management is all about. Strategic management is the basis for the other three vital processes (see Figure 14.1). It is what integrates, unifies, and energizes all the others.

Strategy is of course important to all companies, regardless of industry. But it is of particular importance to IT suppliers because the tempo of change is so rapid, the number of possibilities for new directions is so vast, and the net in-flow of capital redeployed from smokestack and energy industries is so huge. The less stable and deterministic an industry is, the more players in that industry need strategic management to outflank less competent firms who do not see what lies ahead. And the IT industry is one of the least deterministic and most unstable. According to Stephan McClellan, "Companies that stand pat, go broke. Any company that is not constantly changing and adjusting to this rapidly changing industry is on a fast track to obsolescence. Don't believe the axiom: 'If it isn't broke, don't fix it.' "[2] We agree.

The survey[3] tells us something more. For one, the relative importance of management processes is "a-changin'." As executives compared future

[2]Stephan T. McClellan, *The Coming Computer Industry Shakeout: Winners, Losers, & Survivors,* John Wiley & Sons, New York, NY, p. 325.

[3]"I[2] Critical Success Factors.

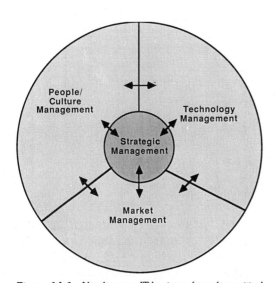

Figure 14.1. Nearly every IT business faces four critical interrelated sets of issues.

importance to past importance, strategic management was more than twice as often cited the most vital overall area of concern. Human resource management designations also more than doubled. And clearly this relates to why people-culture is at the top of the critical success attributes list. The market management process held its ground in relative importance while technology management lost just over half of its most critical mentions.

Within each vital area, survey respondents also highlighted specific critical success factors. The importance of these factors and improvement needs tended to differ by company size, geographic base, and the management role of the respondent. In general, larger companies seemed more concerned with success factors addressing new product and market opportunities, i.e., new product development and segment selection. Understandably, they also placed more importance on organization and general and administrative productivity than did smaller companies that typically have less management processes and less overhead. In addition, capital investment and R&D funding levels were rated more important by larger companies that typically plan these expenditures more rigorously.

In contrast, the entrepreneurial nature of smaller companies influences their far more frequent selection of senior executive compensation and selection, stock and bond market valuation, and acquisition and merger as critical success factors. Also, many of these smaller companies are younger than their larger counterparts. This earlier stage of maturity doubtless contributes to placing greater importance on achieving vertical integration. In addition, they were more concerned with critical success factors relating to gaining near-term marketshare such as enhancing existing products, funding marketing and sales, and attracting and retaining good marketing and sales people.

The responses received from European and Japanese executives differed dramatically from those of U.S. companies. The European responses, mainly from France and the United Kingdom, showed far less concern about planning processes did than either U.S. or Japanese responses. Conversely, European executives place more importance on exogenous factors. Government policies and regulations, lobbying, and financial and economic forecasting were more frequently cited by the Europeans.

Although not as concerned as the Europeans, the Japanese valued government policies and regulations more highly than did U.S. respondents. The Japanese also cited capital investment and R&D success factors more frequently than either European or U.S. executives. Conversely, their greater dependence on noncaptive distribution systems outside Japan lead them to deem internal marketing and sales people and productivity as considerably less important than either of the other two geographic groups did.

CEOs and COOs saw things a bit differently from other executives who responded. They were less concerned—and probably feel more confident—about their ability to deal with the integration of planning efforts and organization issues. CEOs and COOs did, however, have five identifiable hot buttons—attraction and retention of good technical people and of good marketing and sales people, the development of proprietary technology, demand forecasting, and financial control over operations.

No notable differences in priorities of concerns existed among IT executives based on their cluster. But there should have been. Other research gives dramatically different marks to the six clusters in terms of their strategic management performance.

Different Views of IT

In Chapter 13, we showed that ROE and shareholder performance differed markedly among the six clusters. How well are these differences perceived by IT executives and what do they suggest about the critical success factors for each cluster?

To get the answer to this, we turn again to the results of Booz-Allen's 1984 successful company survey,[4] introduced in Chapter 13.

Overall, sharp differences existed among respondent perceptions of IT firms when analyzed by their principal cluster (see Figure 14.2). This is

[4]Harvey L. Poppel, "Successful Companies and Contributing Attributes," *Information Industry Insights*, Booz, Allen & Hamilton Inc., issue 10, pp. 1–3.

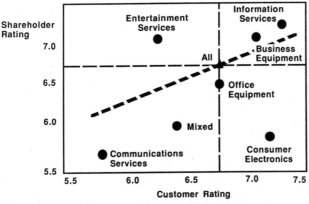

Figure 14.2. Information service firms had the highest customer and shareholder ratings; telecommunications service providers, the lowest. (SOURCE: *Booz, Allen & Hamilton Inc., 1984.*)

so even though the top-ten firms listed earlier cut across nearly all the clusters. Indeed, outstanding firms could transcend the limitations or negatives of the business clusters they had chosen to pursue. Nevertheless, positives or negatives intrinsic to certain clusters do clearly influence average or below-average perfoimers within those clusters.

In fact, the two clusters most highly regarded by our respondents—information services and business operations equipment—also received the largest MB premiums while the communications service cluster came out at the bottom of the pack both in the survey and in MB performance.

Most Admired

Information service firms were the most admired. They received the highest customer and shareholder ratings. Nevertheless, they ranked below business equipment suppliers in respondent perceptions of three of the five successful attributes, namely product quality, senior management, and strategic vision. And, only one information service firm, EDS—still independent when the survey was taken—made the top ten in a fourth success attribute—people-culture. It appears, therefore, that the top customer and shareholder rank of information service firms derives from a combination of outstanding ROE performance and from the one remaining critical success attribute—marketing-sales.

Business operations equipment firms, led by the strong images of IBM and Hewlett-Packard, ranked either first or second in nearly all categories. The one exception was shareholder satisfaction in which they trailed both information and entertainment service firms. And this is understandable, given the substantially lower average ROE (about 12 percent in 1983–1984) earned by this product cluster in comparison with those two service clusters.

Indeed, the top nine domestic computer manufacturers, excluding IBM and Hewlett-Packard, only showed a 9 percent pretax return on assets from 1980 to 1985 according to Wertheim & Company, Inc. This is a full percentage point under the Standard & Poor's 400 Stock Index.

The Middle of the Pack

Office equipment suppliers ranked nearly even with business operations equipment suppliers in people-culture and had a better image for product quality and strategic vision. But they fell down markedly on marketing-sales and their senior management received below average grades.

We suspect that both of these low rankings were related and that they stemmed from a widespread perception that the identities and hence marketshares of office equipment suppliers were being subsumed by at least two trends. Business and telecommunication suppliers, such as Hewlett-Packard, AT&T, and Digital Equipment, are increasingly encroaching the turf of traditional office equipment suppliers as processing, transport, and storage element values associated with integrated office systems rise. Meanwhile, Japanese companies have been gaining share of the more mature, low-end office markets such as copiers and typewriters.

Consumer electronics suppliers and *entertainment service companies* also received checkered ratings. Both of these consumer-oriented clusters got high marks for marketing-sales, especially in comparison to the other clusters which market more to business. This reinforces our perception that the state of the art in consumer marketing is generally more advanced than in industrial marketing.

But beyond consumer marketing-sales, ratings for these two clusters contrasted sharply. This, despite the obvious connections between such entertainment services as prerecorded music and television and the electronic devices through which these services are accessed.

Consumer electronics firms received moderately higher customer satisfaction rankings, probably because they have had to perform for customers consistently well to have survived in what has been a world-scale thin-margin, mass-market business.

In comparison, nearly all producers and distributors of entertainment content both score hits and make errors, leaving their customer with mixed impressions. This kind of up and down performance probably contributes to the very low ratings entertainment firms got in people-culture, senior management, and strategic vision.

Consumer electronics firms did much better in the people-culture category, probably because of their consistency over time. Yet, they were poorly regarded in terms of shareholder satisfaction, senior management, and strategic vision. These perceptions were undoubtedly fed by their sustained record of lower-than-average ROEs.

In contrast, entertainment service firms scored with investors. Their shareholder rankings were only slightly lower than the leading cluster, information services. And, indeed, the average ROE of this cluster is only 1 to 2 percentage points behind information service. But individual company financial performance tends to be highly volatile. Clearly, then, one critical success factor in entertainment companies is the ability to stretch hits into home runs while quickly erasing errors.

And Those with Nowhere to Go But . . . ?

Companies with *mixed identities*, spanning more than one cluster or with primary interests outside the IT industry, also fared poorly. Apparently, the fuzziness surrounding their identity contributed to their dead-last showing in both senior management and strategic vision. It suggested, too, that diversifications into unrelated businesses can be quite risky but even when successful, can leave shareholders confused and underwhelmed.

In nearly all of the ratings categories, *communication services* finished last among the clusters. In addition, six of the bottom-ten companies in shareholder rank had substantial stakes in telecommunications services or equipment or both. (Note that this roster of poorly regarded firms did not include any of the regional Bell holding companies. The survey was taken too soon after divestiture for respondents to rate them in comparison to other firms or to each other.) Senior management and strategic vision were the only two of the five principal contributing attributes in which communication service firms did somewhat better, albeit still below average. These ratings do suggest some confidence in the ability of top communication executives to boost performance, especially as the aftershocks of divestiture subside.

Summary

Recapping the survey results, no cluster was perceived as flawless. Each one clearly faces the challenge of improving its people-culture, product, or market performance. The balance of this book will describe lessons to be learned in these three vital management areas that contribute to sustained strategic success.

15
Humanizing IT: The People-Culture Challenge

By definition, people-culture values permeate the entire fabric of a business entity·—embracing all of its human resources and the structure that knits them together. For many IT businesses, the entrepreneurial and often charismatic style of their first-generation leaders establishes these values, and many IT firms are young enough to have retained them. Most more mature IT businesses also attempt to challenge both senior executives and employees at all levels to sustain and enhance performance.

How effective are these challenges and the motivational techniques that accompany them? In this chapter, we will address this question from two vantage points. First we will examine the linkage between IT executive compensation programs and corporate values. And then we will assess how well IT firms are implanting and retaining important cultural values at all levels in their enterprises.

On Top of IT

The infotrends are testing the skills and motivations of many IT executives. IT is no longer business as usual. Indeed, this raises the question of what inspires managers to take new risks. Clearly, it seems, such risk taking should ultimately satisfy the shareholders, but studies[1] of executive compensation practices among IT companies highlight major discon-

---

[1]Derived from concepts initially advanced by Steven J. Heyer, "Is Your Compensation Program Rewarding Executives for the Wrong Performance?", *Information Industry Insights*, Booz, Allen & Hamilton Inc., issue 5, pp. 1–3.

nects between the shareholder value creation process and executive reward generation. Moreover, by precluding these disconnects, financial and stock market performance is enhanced. We conclude that most IT suppliers can strengthen corporate performance through a refocused, strategically driven executive compensation program.

The corporation's ultimate mission is to expand shareholder wealth—through dividends and common stock appreciation. Therefore, the goal of top corporate executives, elected by a board of directors representing the shareholders, should be to develop and implement strategies that create shareholder value. Common stock appreciation, expressed in terms of market-to-book ratios, was the thrust of Chapter 13, which linked it to the return-on-equity measure of performance. This relationship provides a critical context for thinking about basic management processes.

Executive compensation is one management process whose impact on the market valuation process has been long underutilized by IT companies. Executive compensation programs are pivotal to the success of the value creation process in two ways. First, these programs induce strategic management—supporting strategic and operating actions which create and sustain shareholder value. Second, such programs, when properly designed, pay either directly or indirectly for the value created.

Perhaps most importantly, a suitably focused executive compensation program can actuate executives to deal with the tough management challenges facing most IT companies at both the corporate and business unit levels.

Setting corporate direction involves difficult portfolio and asset management decisions. Compensation programs should reward each corporate-level executive in a manner consistent with that executive's role in the value creation process. That role is to make a subset of the strategic and operating decisions that determine the business's *real* bottom line—ROE, asset growth, and ultimately, stock value. The best programs tailor the mix and priority placed on each of these measures to the business's overall positioning objectives, competitive marketplace, and economics. Furthermore, when the performance measures are cast in comparative terms, the target-setting process becomes more dynamic, market sensitive, and reflective of "true" performance.

At the business unit level, key decisions typically relate to products, markets, and productivity—the strategic and operating factors that produce competitive advantage and, thus, support corporate performance and shareholder value creation. However, business unit executives can only partially influence market valuation. Therefore, business-unit compensation programs are most effective when they are "unbundled" from overall corporate plans and based upon the strategic ingredients specific to that unit and controllable by unit management.

Ultimately, executive compensation programs harmonized at both the corporate and business unit level can enhance the business by putting teeth into setting priorities, communicating new directions, changing or retaining values and cultures, and generating appropriate and "defensible" rewards.

Disappointingly, most IT firms do not utilize long-term incentives as the valuable management tool they could be:

- The majority of all performance plans are driven by dysfunctional earnings-per-share targets, either exclusively or in combination with other measures. Earnings are inflation, and currency-rate sensitivity may not reflect the true cost of generating earnings and are therefore illusory in many ways. Earnings per share does not drive market-to-book ratios in IT companies. Most importantly, earnings measures may provide incentives for management to make decisions not in the best long-term interest of the enterprise.

- However, most IT companies appropriately do use some form of stock appreciation-based plan for corporate-level executives (e.g., incentive stock options, stock appreciation rights, or phantom stock). Executive gains with these plans are tied directly to shareholder value creation. Moreover, many of these companies utilize longer-term performance-based plans—providing companies with the opportunity to reward management for actions which indirectly generate stockholder returns, e.g., return on net assets, asset growth, or other success factors at the business level.

- Nevertheless, very few companies use ROE or asset growth directly as the primary measure for funding or awarding longer-term incentives to corporate managers and few have developed individualized unbundled programs at the business-unit level.

- Furthermore, only a small percentage of the IT companies with performance plans use return measures as a primary funding factor.

A strong empirical relationship appears to exist between strategically appropriate compensation plans and strong financial and market results. Within the three product clusters, for example, companies relying solely on option plans or option plans in conjunction with return-based incentive plans markedly outperform other companies within their peer group.

Companies with option plans and those with return-based performance plans (some in conjunction with options) tend to have ROEs well above average. In contrast, companies with other, less shareholder-oriented long-term plans average below ROE norms. Similarly, option-only and option and return-based companies grow their assets faster on average than peer companies. Most importantly, companies with option and return-based plans experience faster growth in total market values than companies with other incentive plans.

Compensation program design cannot single-handedly explain performance. However, we do believe that thoughtful compensation programs are conducive to the successful implementation of well-articulated corporate and business unit strategies. As a result, the "right" performance measures are essential to sound strategic implementation. These measures are: shareholder value and relative, or real ROE (ROE adjusted for a company's cost of equity), growth at the corporate level, and business unit targets tied to business economics and each unit's portfolio role.

Once the CEO and board have determined what has to be done to strenghten their businesses and create shareholder value, the reward system should be tailored to provide the support and motivation to do it. Creating value for shareholders may not be as difficult a task in the coming years as creating a culture and environment focused on value creation. And that leads us to consider the rest of the employee roster.

What Is in IT for the Rest of Them?

"Assembling and nurturing people with talent and skills is the prerequisite to growth for any business and the most challenging task facing any management,"[2] according to Donald N. Frey, Chairman of Bell & Howell Co. Progressive IT firms, successful at strategic market and technology management, are tuning in to strategic human resource management.

A 1984 Booz-Allen study[3] of office and business equipment firms showed that a few leading firms are developing programs to implant and foster valuable cultural attributes. The same study identified four such attributes.

A set of *well-understood values*, consistent across all organizational units and levels, was the most common cultural characteristic shared by the better performing firms. Hewlett-Packard's statements of corporate philosophy range from "management by walking around" to "everyone is treated with dignity." These statements are widely distributed and continually reinforced to ensure universal understanding. Another highly successful firm placed customer service as the top priority. Employees from

[2]Donald N. Frey in a speech to American Society for Training & Development, "Developing Corporate-Classrooms," Dallas, Texas, May 23, 1984.

[3]Reported by Julie M. Wulf, "Improving Human Resource Performance," *Information Industry Insights*, Booz, Allen & Hamilton Inc., issue 10, pp. 1, 9–11.

the executive suites to the mailroom and from manufacturing plants to retail outlets know to "drop what they are doing to serve a customer." This is difficult given the growth and change characteristics of many IT suppliers. As Bill McGowan of MCI put it: "We must hire 40 percent of our new openings from outside the company. At every level. This is a new business. We can't worship the old one."[4] Automatic Data Processing succeeds by maintaining an entrepreneurial environment even after passing the $1 billion mark in size.

But turnover is not the only culprit. Some surveyed firms failed to reach their full potential, in part to inconsistent interpretation of mission and approach among different levels and units. Fuzzy communications of missions and guiding principles usually resulted from the absence of a clear, common purpose, rather than from outright confusion.

A second success attribute is the emphasis placed on *strong people-management skills*. Managerial skills (such as staff development and equitable treatment) and leadership ability (such as directly motivating staff) are both critical to upwardly mobile managers. Career progression aborts if flawed people-management skills are discovered. Within successful IT companies, a manager's worst offense, outside of a breach of ethics, is mismanaging subordinates.

Third is a *healthy attitude toward risk*. Leading IT firms encourage and support risk taking when decisions are based on sound logic and thorough analyses. These firms sponsor strong upside recognition, yet do not severely penalize mistakes. The "you bet your job" approach rarely yields innovative ideas. "Correct" decisions are greeted with considerable fanfare (such as promotions, monetary rewards, employee-of-month awards); mistakes resulting from sound decision-making processes are seen as learning experiences and rarely lead to demotions or terminations. This approach yields an effective blend of entrepreneurial risk taking for the firm and downside protection for the individual. It also contributes to a "lifetime career" concept instead of short-term commitments.

Overriding reliance on teamwork is the fourth common success attribute. Employees who feel they have contributed to the firm's prosperity exhibit great pride. The competitive spirit energized by "us versus them" comparisons surfaces when they discuss rival firms. Also, employees display a refreshing sincerity when they talk about teamwork. In contrast, employees of firms without this sense of camaraderie generally display a "me-first" rather than "us-first" attitude. Mark Shepard, Jr., former CEO of Texas Instruments, claims, "TI's company-wide People Effectiveness

---

[4]Bob Stoffels, "Telecommunications Leader of the Year," *Telephone Engineering & Management*, December 15, 1984, p. 66.

Program is based on involving TIers to the greatest extent possible in the planning and controlling, and not just the doing, of their work. This is backed up by recognition, training and periodic attitude surveys."[5]

Hewlett-Packard's project team system was one example that surfaced during the study of the teamwork ethos. Individuals worked together on a daily basis to create new products. Hewlett-Packard employees valued the project team's common purpose and still recognized the company as the true team; in one instance, a project team decided to disband temporarily so that resources could be redirected to a higher priority.

Also, teamwork reduces overhead. As Jack MacAllister, CEO of U S West puts it so well, "What we don't need are checkers checking checkers who check checkers. What we do need are the skills, ideas, and knowledge of *all* employees—an atmosphere in which everyone contributes, in which new ideas can flourish and levels don't get in the way of human interaction."[6]

Planting the Seeds for Success

No doubt, this set of cultural success attributes is a valuable tool. More important, however, is understanding how high-performance companies lay the groundwork to grow and nurture these attributes. A four-pronged approach of training programs, appraisal processes, communications channels, and compensation practices seems to work best.

Leading IT firms offer *multifaceted training programs* to develop technical, marketing, and managerial skills. Training is especially important given the rapid pace of technological and market obsolesence in the IT industry. In addition to developing skills, top management uses classroom setups to transmit corporate philosophy and values. Attentive participants are indoctrinated with company beliefs, mottos, and slogans. For example, a customer service firm emphasizes and repeats its customer credo through introductory handbooks and training program content for both entry and senior management levels. In addition, training program leaders cite anecdotes that describe top executives who individually call or write letters in response to customer requests. One highly successful firm uses all of these techniques to ingrain their statements of corporate philosophy. Less successful firms lack this coordinated effort and consequently send out mixed signals.

---

[5]Mark Shepard in a speech to Harvard University, "The U.S. Corporation within the Competitive Environment," Cambridge, Massachusetts, April 25, 1980.

[6]Jack MacAllister in a speech to Options Club annual dinner, "Wide Open Spaces—Wide Open Opportunities," Seattle, WA, May 17, 1983.

A second step is a *proactive appraisal process*. High performing companies focus employees on key success factors through dynamic, supportive, and interactive appraisal techniques. Leading IT firms place importance on people management by specifying the ability to manage people as a key performance measure. These "qualitative goals" (staff development, employee motivation, etc.) are explicit measurements of each manager's performance. In those firms in which customer service is the number 1 objective, account representative performance is based upon quality of service. 3M's long-standing emphasis on innovation is reinforced by how they focus and evaluate their managers and engineers on the basis of successful new product innovations.

In these environments, appraisal processes are an integral part of operations rather than a bureaucratic ritual enforced by corporate personnel. The design and completion of appraisals are typically the responsibility of line management. For example, 3M allows operating units to tailor the appraisal format to best fit their needs. It may be a structured management-by-objectives format with explicit comments on each objective, or it may be a comprehensive discussion covering categories of performance. Leading firms also use supportive, rather than punitive, appraisal techniques which highlight employees strengths and include constructive professional criticism and suggestions for development areas instead of ruthless personal assaults.

Third, IT high performers *encourage open two-way communication*. While most communication is channeled through a well-structured system, opportunity for informal communication is ample. Formal mechanisms, such as newsletters, bulletins, monthly magazines, and regular meetings, transfer the bulk of information. Employees are generally well aware of important events and change in focus. Encouragement of informal communication creates an open and honest environment in which employees feel they can discuss concerns or make suggestions. One such technique is a deliberately designed, open-office environment that promotes an unrestricted workplace and helps to keep the work force well informed. Another is the weekly Friday afternoon beer party which encourages informal communication in a social meeting. Leading IT firms listen to their employees—"why hire them if you don't listen?"

By comparison, less successful firms usually are cautious about sharing information. Their secretive, "behind closed doors" manner creates suspicion among employees. For example, one firm not only monitors information flowing from rank to file, but it also is secretive in the information it sends upstream. The company's suggestion box is carefully gleaned of controversial or "problem" suggestions.

The fourth part of the plan involves *team-oriented compensation prac-*

tices. Rather than providing exorbitant pay packages to attract top talent, many leading IT firms offer compensation plans that are less leveraged than one might expect. Employees' sense of pride and identification with the company philosophy seem to offset some of the need for highly leveraged pay.

To reinforce teamwork, better-performing companies offer broad equity programs, granting stock options to relatively low levels within the organization. Leading firms balance this corporate-based reward by recognizing individual contributions through special awards. Individual accomplishments such as cost-saving measures and suggestions for improvements frequently merit cash bonuses, employee-of-the-month awards, and stock grants.

In keeping with a risk-oriented, yet safe, career-employment environment, leading IT firms typically pay above-average salaries. Higher salaries combined with moderate incentives neutralize individual competition in a team-oriented workplace and provide a safety net. This downside protection helps to support risk taking.

By comparison, less successful firms must offer even more lucrative pay packages to attract top talent. Highly leveraged cash incentives encourage individual competition rather than corporate identification and a team philosophy.

Strong Human Resource Management

Successful IT firms exhibit common traits and use similar techniques to build and reinforce them. However, a strong human resource function is the fundamental cultural attribute which drives it all.

Leading firms do not strengthen the human resource function by building an extensive staff. Instead, they commit to *human resource management.* Believing that "people are our most valuable asset," they accomplish this by positioning the task of managing people equally with other work demands.

Frequently, the more successful firms further integrate human resource management into business operations through the selection of top human resource executives who have extensive line experience and a solid understanding of the business. Customarily, senior management spends some time directing the human resource function, which reinforces the function's importance.

In the midst of the dynamic, quick decision-making and highly competitive IT environment, a host of companies consistently outperform their peers. Although no substitute for quality products and sound strategies, effective human resource management is proving to be critically important.

A strong, cohesive culture, with consistent, communicated, and well-understood values, results in performers who are better equipped to anticipate and capitalize on the ever-changing marketplace.

But good people and nurturing cultures are not enough to assure success. IT firms must also have quality products. This is growing more difficult as information technologies lead to shorter product life cycles. The next chapter deals with the relationships between technological innovation and successful products.

16

What IT's All About: The Product Quality and Technology Challenge

Wanting IT

Mark Shepard, Jr., the former chief executive officer of Texas Instruments, does not hedge in stating his conviction about the importance of technology's role in long-term success: "Technology is the lifeblood of competitive leadership, and successful companies guard it jealously."[1] The implication is clear: The winners in technology investment will win big, and the unwary and the cautious will lose.

Technology investments take two forms: internal and external. Most IT firms, if they are objective, continually choose whether to bet on leveraging their own cumulative internal R&D experiences or to gain access to technologies through acquisition or codevelopment programs. Later on in the chapter we will suggest a program whereby such choices can be managed. But first, we will put the vital importance of technology management into perspective.

The attitudes of Fortune-1000 executives underscores this importance; particularly revealing are responses[2] from "electronics" executives, the survey segment closest to IT.

---

[1]"Technology Strategy: Two Pivotal Issues," *Information Industry Insights*, Booz, Allen & Hamilton Inc., issue 2, p. 5.

[2]Based on a survey conducted by Booz, Allen & Hamilton Inc., in 1981 and reported by John W. Allen and Andrew Messina, "Technology's Role in the Planning Process—An Awareness of Current Perception," *Information Industry Insights*, Booz, Allen & Hamilton Inc., issue 2, pp. 3–5. Survey respondents included some 800 chief operating officers, R&D directors, and planning officers representing seven manufacturing sectors, including electronics.

184

1. *Changing technology followed by capital costs and government regulations and policies were the three exogenous factors electronic executives believed would affect their businesses most deeply.* They identified five specific technologies, led by "microelectronics," as having the potential for making the greatest impact. Not far behind were software engineering, advanced computer capabilities, telecommunications, and CAD/CAM (in that order). IT market planners should note that advanced computer capabilities, microelectronics, and CAD/CAM were also strongly cited by nonelectronics sector (i.e., potential user) respondents.

2. *Electronics sector respondents were far more concerned than those in other sectors about the impact of foreign competition on their future business outlook, with 87 percent specifically vexed by the Japanese and 75 percent by the West Germans.* Domestic electronics executives believed they enjoy distinct competitive advantages around the world because of superior technological know-how. However, they also perceived competitive disadvantages due to government and industry priorities, policies, and subsidies as well as labor costs and productivity. Nevertheless, while 60 percent considered their processes for monitoring technology threats and opportunities in the United States "extremely effective" or "very effective," less than 20 percent were as confident about their ability to monitor technology abroad; moreover, these percentages dropped to 42 percent (United States) and 7 percent (abroad) when respondents were asked how effective their companies were in making more proactive use of their technology scanning—i.e., "long-range technology impact forecasts" rather than simply "monitoring."

This tendency of the industry to view the world only from an inward-out perspective was evident in another way—more than 50 percent claimed they gave "extensive consideration" to *internal* technologies in assessing cost and quality improvements to existing products and in developing new products while less than 15 percent give "extensive consideration" to available *outside* technologies.

3. *A "short-term profit orientation" was considered the strongest barrier to integrating technology into corporate strategic planning.* Two of the five approaches most cited for enhancing technology's business contribution—greater top management commitment to long-term results and higher R&D funding levels—relate directly to surmounting this barrier. Although marketing and sales was perceived as the function most important to the overall performance of electronics companies, new product development, R&D, and manufacturing and engineering were considered to be the most underfunded functions.

4. *Several management process approaches were among the five most important factors in enhancing technology's contribution to the overall performance of the company.* These included improving long-range tech-

nology planning and more integration of technology in both strategic planning and decision making. To underscore the need for other process improvements, only 36 percent of the respondents believed that their technology commercialization process was "extremely effective" or "very effective."

5. *Focusing directly on the technology management process, electronics executives placed different weights on those factors vital to long- versus short-term planning.* New product development, the availability of qualified technical personnel, product performance, and expected technology change were rated most important for the long-term planning process (in that order). But product performance moved up to first place in importance for short-term planning followed by U.S. competitive position, the availability of qualified technical personel, and manufacturing economics.

Overall, the survey results and the authors' personal experiences strongly suggest that many companies should adjust their technology management practices. They need to place greater emphasis on the importance of technology to long-range corporate success, identify the specific means of integrating technology in the planning process, and develop a sound analytical approach to carrying out technology planning. Also, technology management can satisfy what might appear to be conflicting objectives as Dean O. Morton, chief operating officer of Hewlett-Packard, says, " . . .high quality and low costs are *not* mutually exclusive goals. In fact, the lesson we needed to learn was that the best way to reduce costs is to improve quality—*if* you go about it in a systematic way."[2]

Innovating IT

We endorse a seven-step program[3] to strengthen the technology management process and raise the probability of internal development successes:

1. *Develop a new products strategy.* The most successful companies develop a well-defined strategy for each new product they need. That strategy may be an external, market-driven one or it may be designed to exploit a firm's internal strengths. In those cases in which internal

---

[2]Dean O. Morton in a speech to the Montgomery Dorsey Symposium, "Searching for Excellence the HP Way," July 14, 1984.

[3]Adapted from concepts first advanced by William P. Sommers, "Improving Corporate Performance Through Better Innovation Management," *Information Industry Insights*, Booz, Allen & Hamilton Inc., issue 3, pp. 4–6.

strengths are lacking, the strategy leads to acquisitions or codevelopment efforts.

These strategies tend to have the highest batting average:

a. Exploit technology in a new way.

b. Maintain product innovation position.

c. Defend marketshare.

In contrast, strategies to preempt competition, gain a foothold in a future market, or leverage an existing distribution position are more risky and less likely to lead to successful products. Also, the relationship of a new product development effort to existing products—those offered by the company and/or by competitors—appears to influence success.

2. *Analyze market potential at the outset.* Giving greater attention to the initial steps of the innovation process can materially improve the payback on R&D and new product investments. More attention to up-front product strategies, greater investment in market research to determine customer needs, and more probing analysis of the profit potential of a new product can boost the return on innovation investments. William Newport, executive vice president /technical management, of Bell Atlantic describes the rationale for some aspects of digital technology, " . . .deployed to meet customer requirements. Our guidelines for that deployment will be, first, major customer opportunities, and second, the largest cost reduction potential."[4] Another value of market analysis is to determine when market windows, however attractive, may be closing before new products can be commercialized. This, in turn, can spark external product acquisitions that match rather than lag the marketplace opportunities.

3. *Establish a formal evaluation process.* The most successful product innovation firms typically document explicit prescreening criteria for determining which products are to be commercialized and which set aside. In this way, they can review decisions underlying new product programs periodically (even after commercialization) and verify or modify key assumptions and calculations as new information becomes available. Tradeoffs between continuing internal programs and acquiring products externally can then be made on a more rational ongoing basis.

4. *Involve top management in the new product development process.* The intellectual leadership of top management is vital. Not only does this tend to inspire product developers, but the greater scope and depth of top management experience often can help developers avoid technology successes that turn out to be market failures. Too much top management involvement is rarely a major obstacle.

---

[4]William Newport in a speech for a Booz, Allen & Hamilton Inc. conference. "Telecommunication Network Trends," July 25, 1984.

5. *Commit and focus adequate financial resources.* No firm can expect to catch or even equal the market leader's position by investing fewer resources than that leader in R&D or in the external acquisition of new products. But it may be necessary, for instance, to reallocate R&D investments in a firm's mature business to developing areas of greater opportunity. Often this is politically unpopular because a firm's power is often centered in its large and naturally profitable mature businesses. Paying "premiums" for proven products through acquisitions may be much less expensive than cumulative R&D over several years, especially given that only one out of a dozen or more internally developed new product ideas achieves commercial success.

6. *Sustain commitment to innovation.* Most new product developments experience a steep experience curve. This means that the firms that are active in new product development are likely to require less investment per new product, all other factors being equal. In fact, the firms that have created more new products in the past 5 years are twice as likely to be more successful in the next 5 years as those that have engaged in little recent new product innovation. This same relationship holds true for product acquisitions. Firms that routinely acquire new products externally have a much higher success ratio than neophytic acquirers.

7. *Match organization structure and rewards system to the results demanded.* The organization structure needed for success in growth markets is almost always different from that required for success in mature ones. Moreover, managing acquired products together with their original marketers and developers is dramatically different from managing home-grown products.

The process of new product internal development and innovation cuts across departments and, as a result, may require new forms of compensation and incentives based on the entire new product team's performance. This ties back to the conclusions in our earlier chapter on people-culture management.

Therefore, management must be prepared to make use of ad hoc organizations to achieve new product goals. This is because a mounting number of IT firms are finding that new product hyperactivity is putting stress on their internal technology development process—especially with respect to organization structure, management systems, resource management, and culture. Moreover, stresses are being magnified by the growing tendency toward technology "trading" through such vehicles as technology purchases, licences, joint ventures, and second source agreements, as well as the mounting usage of both university and industrial research laboratories.

Summary

In conclusion, successful technology management and the resulting high quality of products depends on meeting six imperatives.

- The product should fit market needs during (not before or after) its life cycle.
- The product should be technologically superior or deliver content in a superior way.
- Top management should provide intellectual leadership and display sustained commitment.
- Both internal and external development vehicles should continually be considered objectively.
- Products should match the internal strengths of the organization, either "original" or acquired.
- Product quality should be a high priority not only of the development program but throughout the life cycle. According to Charles Brown, former chairman of AT&T, "As long as we keep service high on our list of priorities in the competitive environment, move quickly, and continue to emphasize precision and excellence in our work, then I don't have to worry about our people's success."[5]

We do not want to dispute Mr. Brown, but even the highest quality IT firms have at least one more ingredient if they are successful and that is an effective market management process.

---

[5]Charles L. Brown in a speech to The Economic Club of Detroit, "The Challenge to America," October 15, 1984.

17
Working IT In: The Marketing and Sales Challenge

Successful technology and management processes are interwoven. As an information technology evolves, so do the products and services that flow from it. As these products and services develop, so do the markets they address and the nature and productivity of marketing and sales vehicles needed to penetrate these markets.

We begin this chapter by introducing a new technique for analyzing life-cycle changes, and we then follow by explaining how successful IT firms optimize their marketing and sales productivity throughout the life cycle.

Analyzing IT[1]

Conventional product life-cycle analysis is shopworn and overused. Existing techniques—typically depicted as simple time versus volume "S-curves"—are of limited value because they dwell on technology maturity rather than market dynamics. Hence, they tend to be inward rather than outward focused.

Although this inward focus may be acceptable in some stable, mature markets, it is inappropriate to IT firms. Most IT segments can be described as "technologically inspired and market driven." Therefore, we have developed a life-cycle technique that recognizes the interaction between product and market dynamics.

[1]Based on work initially published by Harvey L. Poppel, "Market-Product Life Cycles—A New Strategic Analysis Tool," *Information Industry Insights*, Booz, Allen & Hamilton Inc., issue 6, pp. 11–12.

We depict life cycles as U-shaped curves plotted on market versus product axis. As shown in Figure 17.1, the market axis is the measure of customer sophistication while the product axis describes supplier experience. Every product or service passes through four distinct market-product stages, each with its own critical success factors, although time frames vary markedly.

This life-cycle concept forces strategic analysts to interrelate market and product dynamics and distill critical success factors from these interrelationships. From a product perspective, it enables them to array the complete product-service portfolio including related peripherals and software. From a market perspective, it facilitates behavioral and interest group segmentation, as well as competitive portfolio analyses. The balance of this chapter amplifies the underlying rationale.

Stage 1: Emergence

The earliest buyers tend to be leading-edge pioneers and hobbyists, i.e., "technologically sophisticated," even though they have no specific exposure to the new product or service. Suppliers' cumulative market and production experience is nil, although pioneering suppliers may have built up considerable prerollout technology experience.

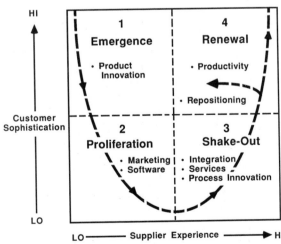

Figure 17.1. (SOURCE: Based on work initially published by Harvey L. Poppel, "Market-Product Lifecycles—A New Strategic Analysis Tool," Information Industry Insights, Booz, Allen & Hamilton Inc., issue 6, pp. 11–12.)

As a result of the technology focus of both early buyers and suppliers, the most critical success factor in stage 1 typically is product engineering innovation. Current examples of stage 1 products include RISC computers and high-tech integrated market services (IMS).

Stage 2: Proliferation

As buying momentum shifts away from early adapters to the mainstream "masses," average user sophistication drops sharply. The average experience and exposure level with the specific product or service is minimal. Suppliers' cumulative experience, however, has risen especially with respect to user needs, benefits, and resulting applications. New entrants multiply, some as spin-offs of initial providers, carrying their exposure with them.

Product enhancement and marketing emerge as the more critical success factors. In contrast with stage 1, product development imperatives are more often related to content than facilities. Marketing savvy is pivotal in alerting and convincing first-time buyers of the favorable cost-benefits ratio. CD-ROMs, integrated voice-data terminals, and relational database management systems are three current examples.

Stage 3: Shakeout

As second-generation versions come on the market, buyers' sophistication rises through first-generation use or media exposure. Suppliers' experience begins to concentrate as strong and marginal players affiliate and weaker players fold. Regulatory and/or standards bodies often influence suppliers' actions during this stage.

New critical success factors emerge. *Integrating* the product with other existing and/or new products is vital as buyers become concerned about interoperability. *Service* acquires added importance as buyers learn that marketing claims do not translate automatically into product and maintenance reliability. *Process innovation* is needed to reduce product-service costs and improve delivery schedules as buyers increasingly discriminate among competitors on the basis of price and responsiveness.

Examples of stage 3 include personal computers, most applications software packages, and cable television.

Stage 4: Renewal

After buyers have experienced several generations of a given product or service, even "trailing-edge" users grow IT literate and price becomes the primary purchasing criterion. The experience of surviving suppliers goes through its third or fourth wave. Relative competitive economics and market positions become apparent to all players.

Depending on the circumstances, two sets of critical success factors become dominant, namely *productivity*, i.e., being the least-cost producer, or *repositioning*. "Dead-end" market-product segments display the commodity characteristics of the classical maturity stage often described in literature. Consequently, productivity becomes the driving success factor. But few IT market-product segments display such dead-end characteristics because IT is dynamic. Moreover, numerous cross-substitution possibilities emerge constantly. Therefore, the most critical success factor is repositioning. This is done either by infusing new product technologies (e.g., component high-definition digital television) or by introducing an existing product or service into a new market segment (e.g., introducing paging services to consumers or telephone service to automobile users).

Experience with this new analytical technique reveals keener insights and more astute strategic market management actions than traditional, less incisive methods. More mileage can be gained by more sensitively managing existing product positions in current markets or repositioning into new market segments. Hard-won market positions can be exploited better by the timely enhancement or replacement of product lines.

Getting More out of IT

No IT firm would dispute that marketing and sales is a critical success attribute. But despite the importance, the associated costs are growing faster than the industry's revenues. Many IT suppliers who sell directly to businesses through their own salesforces spend over 25 percent of each revenue dollar on marketing. This is definitely an urgent problem. In maturing product lines, such as copiers, the ponderous embedded costs of the multi-intermediary channel structure often outweighs the shrinking values these intermediaries add. In high-growth electronic products, such as low-end business computers, eroding unit prices are forcing suppliers to seek lower unit-cost and less traditional distribution channels.

As a result, top management interest in improving marketing productivity is mounting rapidly. However, translating the quest for marketing productivity into results can be difficult. To many IT marketing executives, improving productivity means nothing more than cutting costs per unit, e.g., salesforce cuts, branch closings, salary freezes, and product line rationalizations. All too often, this myopic interpretation enervates the enterprise's fundamental strategic underpinnings.

Instead, here are the six most relevant strategic questions an executive should ask:[2]

1. Is market positioning strategically sound, aligned with customer needs, and economically defensible?

2. Should the pricing strategy be revamped to achieve improved contribution and/or higher marketshare?

3. Should there be a switch to a more specialized or to a more consolidated salesforce or possibly to less expensive distribution channels?

4. Should service to smaller accounts be sustained and if so, how?

5. Can branch sales and service network costs be reduced especially in terms of the best mix of direct sales and support personnel?

6. How can productivity of the individual field sales personnel be raised?

Our recent IT client experience shows that an expanded multilevel view of marketing productivity best answers these questions. It allows the executive to attack the full range of available marketing leverage points sequentially (see Figure 17.2). Within most market arenas, variations in the value added differentiate competitive positioning.

Although desirable, across-the-board and across-the-life-cycle positioning advantages are usually too costly. The winning market positions achieve demonstrable and sustainable competitive advantage along such selected critical value-added dimensions as marketing scale, superior territorial coverage, lowest delivered service costs, or the tailoring of delivered value to priority customer segments. Often, the selection is based on the stage of market-product life cycle.

The Japanese takeover of the small copier market at its proliferation stage illustrates the leverage inherent in strategic market positioning. It also spotlights the vulnerabilities which develop when a value-added structure shifts away from marketing-oriented functions.

Structural Market Relationships

Fundamental underlying relationships govern buyer and seller competitive dynamics. Careful analysis, based on some straightforward modeling, can uncover these dynamics including price-volume elasticities, product substitution rates, and competitive share shifts versus relative price. These marketplace relationships can then be overlayed with the better-known in-

---

[2]Adapted from concepts advanced by James A. Wolf, "New Concepts in Improving Marketing Productivity," *Information Industry Insights*, Booz, Allen & Hamilton Inc., issue 5, pp. 3–6.

ternal economic relationships—e.g., production scale, experience curves, product mix profitability, and field sales and service economics—to gauge competitive profitability.

By framing the marketplace relationships as continual, structural relationships are recognized and the most effective leverage points identified; sales and share objectives become realistic; and pricing becomes a managed initiative within an overall strategic context.

Resource Deployment

The third tier of marketing productivity is the tight matching of distribution economics against the available contribution potential by business segment. Advantage is more often achieved from a clean-slate evaluation than simply downsizing existing activities.

Selling costs can vary markedly by market segment. Direct sales coverage of small accounts has become particularly expensive. Thus, in many IT product segments, product characteristics and the sales support economics dictate a realignment of channel support. Multiple channels often

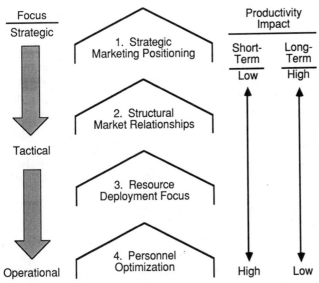

Figure 17.2. Coordinated approach to marketing productivity. (SOURCE: *James A. Wolf, "New Concepts in Improving Marketing Productivity,"* Information Industry Insights, *Booz, Allen & Hamilton Inc.,* issue 5, p. 4.)

can be more productive than putting a broad line through a single channel.

In contrast, larger accounts often get extra, expensive concessions in both price and field service—frequently they are too much. Direct account coverage can be made more effective by building strategic rationale into the individual account coverage guidelines.

Selling costs also go up with the number of selling organizations and down with higher account density. However, in maturing businesses, the diminished need for specialized sales management unleashes overhead consolidation opportunities—provided the supporting systems and incentive programs are strengthened appropriately.

On balance, well-managed, selective, and coherent specialization can frequently generate substantial improvements in both marketshare and net contribution. The optimal resource deployment for a specific company will depend also on such matters as:

- Placement of the defensive perimeters
- Meeting minimum volume requirements
- Willingness to forego areas where not competitive
- Protection and management of different marketing cultures.

Personnel Optimization

Contrary to the widespread emphasis on headcount and expense control, the most critical leverage point in salesforce productivity is uncompromising management of personnel quality and skill mix. As mobility slows at all levels, many companies are prone to institutionalize the noticeable variations in talent within their organizations. This typically accelerates the attrition of exceptional performers and saps the organization of its forward momentum.

In combination, more careful hiring and forced attrition can boost field productivity by as much as 30 percent. Today's hiring practices frequently do not recognize shifting product mixes or channel emphasis. A tough 3-month and 6-month forced attrition program can materially heighten overall salesforce productivity.

Focusing on individual salespeople and their activities can also raise productivity. Sales management routinely overestimates the time spent face to face with customers and prospects and underestimates the time the force spends on administration and planning. More critical performance elements are not highlighted. And the opportunities to off-load work either to more effective specialists or lower-priced marketing support groups are missed.

Implications

This multitier approach to marketing productivity goes well beyond the cost-cutting measures more typically pursued. A systematic, comprehensive marketing productivity program should:

1. Develop a coherent set of prioritized, narrowly focused marketing missions.
2. Ration the delivered customer value to carefully selected price-benefit points.
3. Determine economically based distribution channel alternatives and the tailored cultures and incentives required for their support.
4. Monitor and manage the related economics and day-to-day efforts on a pragmatic, disaggregated basis.
5. Institute aggressive programs to squeeze out the areas of subpar performance with individual personnel or customers.
6. Overlay a more flexible set of management resources and time sensitive decision-making processes.
7. Practice what the IT industry preaches to customers and use IT to boost its own marketing and sales productivity.

Beyond these specifics, planners should periodically confirm the targeted market positioning as strategically sustainable and affordable against the anticipated technological and marketplace developments.

Index

ABC, Inc., 10
Acquisitions, 85, 87, 91–95, 132
Advance Publications, 11
Advanced Datum, 88
Advertising, 28, 30–31, 50–52, 106
Agridata Resources, Inc., 87
Alpha Microsystems, 132
Amdahl Communications Systems, 88, 155
American Airlines, 88
American Can Company, 8
American Electronics Association, 66, 67
American Express, 95, 110
American Hospital Supply, 48, 138
American Microsystems, 75
Ameritech, 9, 88
Anaconda-Ericsson, Inc., 93
Analytical time, 21
Andersen, Arthur, 88
Anixter Brothers, 48
Apollo Computer, Inc., 40, 42, 156, 162, 164, 166
Apple Computer, Inc., 12, 86, 162, 164–165
Applications management, 104
Applications software, 73
Applied Data Research (ADR), 105, 140
Artificial Intelligence (AI), 73
AT&T Company, 9, 33, 75, 80, 85–87, 99, 110, 113, 130, 164, 173
AT&T Information Systems, 137
AT&T Technologies, 88
Atari-Tel, 67
Audiotex, 112
Australian firms, 65
Automated factories, 35–39, 147–150
Automated replenishment, 50
Automatic Data Processing (ADP), 77, 92, 162, 164, 166, 179

Automatic teller machines (ATMs), 129, 130
Automobile, electronics for, 125–126
Avon Products, Inc., 137

Bacon, Francis, 81
Baker, James A., 36
Bally, 119
Bank of America, 87, 110
Baron Data, 87
Bayer (Agfa-Gevaert), 11
BDM International, 163
Bell & Howell Company, 8
Bell Atlantic, 9
Bell Canada, 10
BellSouth, 9
Bergen Brunswig Corporation, 48–49
Bertelsmann, 11
Block, H&R, 108
Boeing, 8, 42
Booz, Allen & Hamilton Inc., 16–23, 41–42, 52–54, 56, 71, 72, 74, 78, 89, 133, 166, 168, 178
Brazil, 69
British firms, 73
British Telecom International, 7, 9
Britton Lee, 67
Broadcast television, 28–31, 33
  independent, 117, 123
  network, 33, 115, 117
Buckley, Robert J., 50
Bull, 12, 73–75, 88, 93
Burlington Industries' Denim Division, 49
Burroughs Corporation, 10, 93, 155
Business operations arena, 81, 84
Business operations equipment, 142–150
  defined, 83

Business operations equipment (*Cont.*):
  generic, 143–144
  industry-specific, 143–145
  IT-integrated factory, 35–39, 147–150
  performance measurement of, 158, 171, 172
  size and growth of, 83–85, 142–144
  telecommunications network suppliers, 145–147
Business-to-business direct links, 48–49
Business-to-consumer direct links, 50–56

Cable News Network, 7
Cable television, 29, 31, 47, 52, 102, 115–119, 121
CAD/CAM technologies, 40–42, 72, 185
Cameron & Barney, 138
Canadian Development Corporation, 69
Canadian firms, 65, 69–70
Canon, 10, 67
CBS, Inc., 10, 31, 80, 110, 113
Centel, 13
CGE, 10, 73, 74, 147
Chase Manhattan Bank, 110
Chemical Bank, 87, 110
Chrysler Corporation, 137
CIGNA, 87
CIT-Alcatel, 73, 87, 89
Citicorp, 8, 49, 110, 137
Coca-Cola Company, 88
Coleco, 119
Columbia Pictures, 31
Commodore International, 12
Communication, informal, 181
Communications services, 99–104
  defined, 82
  differentiation of, 99–100
  performance measurement of, 158, 171, 172, 174
  size and growth of, 83–85, 100
  strategic challenges facing, 101–104
Compact disc players, 52, 70
Compact discs, 119–120, 128
Comparably Efficient Interconnection (CEI), 103
Compensation practices, 175–178, 181–182
Comp-U-Card, 50–51, 95, 159, 163
Comp-U-Serve, 95, 108
Computation theory, 73

Computer Associates, 163
Computer Sciences Corporation, 69, 79
Computer service and software firms, 91–95, 99, 106–107
Computerland, 12
Computers:
  business (*see* Business operations equipment; Office equipment)
  home, 32, 119, 126–128
Computervision, 40, 62, 155
Comsat, 7
Connecticut Mutual, 27
Consortium, 67
Consumer arena, 81, 84
Consumer computing devices, 73
Consumer electronics, 107–108, 124–130
  defined, 82–83
  home computers, 32, 119, 126–128
  infotainment trend in, 125–126
  performance measurement of, 158, 171, 173
  playstations, 128–129
  size and growth of, 83–85, 124
  transtations, 129–130
Consumer programmed media, 117
Content, 3–5, 15–33
  defined, 3
  entertainment, 15, 28–33, 79, 81, 84
  information (*see* Information content)
  interrelation with other infotrends, 4, 5
  (*See also* Convergence)
Continental Telecom, 11
Control Data Corporation (CDC), 10, 14, 40, 87, 165
Convergence, 8–14, 77–95
  defined, 8
  external development and, 85–95
  internal development and, 85–86
  interrelation with other infotrends, 4, 8
  IT Grid and, 78–82, 84–85
  mergers and acquisitions and, 85, 87, 91–95
  service and product clusters and, 82–85
Convergent Technologies, 87, 132
Corona Data Systems, 67
Corvus, 88
CoVidea, 87
Cox Enterprises, 12, 31, 163
Cray Research, 163
Cross-substitution, product-service, 77, 79–80

Cullinet, 140, 156
Cultural success factors, 178–183
Customer bases, 112–113
Customer franchise ratings, 166

Dai Nippon Printing, 12
Daisy Systems, 156
Daiwa Bank, 27
Data General Corporation, 13, 155
Datapoint Corporation, 155
Dataproducts, 155
Dataspeed, 86
Dawoo International Corporation, 67
Dealertalk, 87
Defense, Department of, 41, 43
Demand for IT, 68–71
DeMuth, Laurence, Jr., 69
Development:
    of content, 29–30, 32–33
    (*See also* Research and development)
De Villepin, Marc, 146
Dial-A-Date, 32
Diamond, Ed, 144
Digital Audio Disk Corporation, 87
Digital Equipment Corporation (DEC), 9,
    50, 67, 72, 75, 155, 164, 173
Digital Switch, 93
Dionne, Joseph, 85
Direct Broadcast Satellite, 32, 117, 118
Disintermediation, 6–7, 46–63
    benefits of, 47–48
    business-to-business transactions and,
        48–49
    business-to-consumer transactions and,
        50–56
    within businesses, 49–50
    defined, 6
    external development and, 87–88
    interrelation and other infotrends, 4, 7
    reasons for, 47, 48
    strategies dealing with, 56–62
    (*See also* Convergence)
Distributed systems, 73
Document preparation time, 21
Docutel, 76
Donnelley, R. R., Corporation, 130
Dow Jones, 162, 163, 165, 166
DowPhone, 32, 112
DSC, 156

Dun & Bradstreet, Inc., 11, 27, 86, 88, 92,
    93, 110, 162, 163
Dunsnet, 86
Dynatech, 163

Earnings per share, 154, 177
Eastman Kodak Company, 9, 67, 99, 120,
    162, 164, 166
EDI-Net, 87
EDS, 93, 105, 113
"Edutainment" software, 120
Electronic Business, 35
Electronic Data Interexchange networks,
    43
Electronic imaging, 131
Electronic suppliers, 110–111
Emerson, Ralph Waldo, 15
Emhart Corporation, 17
Entertainment content, 15, 28–33, 79, 81,
    84
Entertainment services, 115–123
    defined, 82
    market segmentation, 116, 121–123
    performance vs. participative video me-
        dia, 116–121
    performance measurement of, 158, 171,
        173
    size and growth of, 83–85, 115–116
Envoy Systems, 27
EPIC, 79
Ergonomics, 72–73
Ericsson, L. M., 10, 75–76, 89, 93, 166
European firms, 64–70, 88–89, 170
European Strategic Program for Research
    in Information Technology
    (ESPRIT), 75, 88
Executive compensation practices, 175–
    178
External development, 85–95, 100
Exxon Corporation, 8

Factories, IT-integrated, 35–39, 147–150
Fayard, Christian, 76
Federal Communications Commission
    (FCC), 69, 103
Financial strength, 166
First Data Resources, 8, 95
Foreign Investment Review Act, 69
Franchise territories, 31

Frazee, Rowland C., 57
French firms, 68, 73, 74, 146
Frey, Donald N., 178
Frito-Lay, Inc., 137
Fuji Photo Film, 10
Fuji Xerox, 13, 88
Fujitsu Micro Electronics, Inc., 10, 67, 88, 93

Gallium Arsenide technology, 73
Gannett Newspapers, 11, 31
GEC, 12
Geller, Larry, 100–101
GEMCo, 49
General Electric Company, 11, 40, 67, 87, 88, 94
General Electric Information Systems Company, 69, 86, 87
General Motors Corporation, 8, 40, 41, 49, 62, 87, 88, 93
  Buick Motor Division, 79
  Class "E," 163
Globalization, 7–8, 64–76
  European market share, 71–76
  external development and, 88–89
  interrelation with other infotrends, 4, 7
  North American vs. Japanese market share, 64–70
  (See also Convergence)
Goldstar, 65
Government support, 68–69, 73–76
Granger, 93
Greenberg, Marshall G., 122
Grierson, Donald K., 36
GTE, 9, 76, 88, 147
GTE Sylvania, 27
Gulf + Western Industries, 12, 88

Hachette, 13
Harris Corporation, 11
Hearst Corporation, 12
Hewlett-Packard, 10, 27, 132, 162–164, 172, 173, 178–180
HICOM, 72
Hitachi, 9
Home Box Office (HBO), 33, 79, 117
Home computers, 32, 119, 126–128
Home Information Systems (HIS), 52–54
Home Shopping Club, 50–51

Honeywell, Inc., 11, 67, 76, 88
Honeywell Bull, 88, 93
Howard, James J., 56
Human resource management, 182–183

IBM Corporation, 9, 18, 40, 43, 49, 67, 75, 77, 80, 85–87, 93, 99, 103, 110, 113, 132, 138, 140, 155, 162, 164–166, 172
  Canada, 17
  Corporate Common Data Network, 138–139
  North-Central Marketing Division (NCMD), 26–27, 136–137
ICL, 75
Independent television, 117, 123
Informatics, 105
Information content, 79, 81, 84
  (See also Knowledge-worker productivity)
Information providers, 110
Information Resource Management, 59–60
Information Resources, Inc., 159, 163
Information services, 105–114
  critical success factors for, 112–113
  defined, 82
  Integrated Market Services (IMS), 105, 108–112
  performance measurement of, 157–160, 171, 172
  size and growth of, 83–85, 106–108
Infotainment, 31–32, 125–126, 129
Infotrends (see Content; Convergence; Disintermediation; Globalization; Interoperability)
Initial Graphics Exchange Specification (IGES), 41–42
Input, Inc., 5
Institutional Investor, 162
InteCom, 87
Integrated Market Services (IMS), 8, 50–56, 95, 102, 105, 108–112, 128, 130
Integrated Services Digital Network (ISDN), 43, 45, 69, 72, 145–146
Intel, 162, 164
Interarena, 82, 84
Intergraph, 132
Intermediaries, minimization of (see Disintermediation)

Internal development, 85, 184, 186–189
International Data Corporation, 35
Interoperability, 5–6, 34–45
  of business operations equipment, 142,
    147–150
  complexity of, 34–35
  defined, 5
  external development and, 86–87
  interrelation with other infotrends, 4, 6
  IT-integrated factory, 35–39, 147–150
  of office equipment, 135, 138–140
  requirements for, 35–39
  standard-setting process for, 40–44
  (See also Convergence)
IT cost-benefit relationship, 68
IT Grid, 78–82, 84–85
IT industry, 8–14
  top 100 firms, 9–13, 64–65
IT-integrated factory, 35–39, 147–150
IT-literacy levels, 68
IT-supplier performance measurement,
    153–167
  shareholder rewards, 153–161, 165–
    167, 171–174
  stakeholder perceptions, 161–167, 171–
    174
Italtel, 87
ITT, 9, 14, 86, 147

Japanese firms, 64–70, 88, 131, 170, 173,
    185
Johnson & Johnson, 138
Joint ventures, 67, 86–88, 93–94, 110,
    113, 146, 147
Jones, Trevor O., 126

Kappel, Larry, 100
Knight-Ridder Newspapers, 12
Knowledge work, 81
Knowledge-work market, 84, 132–133
Knowledge-worker productivity, 15–27
  benefits of increased IT use and, 22–27,
    134–139
  inadequate IT and, 16–17
  time-use studies and, 19–22
  (See also Office equipment)
KnowledgeSet Corporation, 87
Konishiroku Photo, 12, 67
Korean firms, 65

LEASCALC, 136
Least-cost production, 57, 167
LEXIS, 107
Life-cycle analysis, 190–193
Lotus, 86
Low Power Television, 32

MacAllister, Jack, 180
McClellan, Stephan, 156, 169
McCormick & Dodge, 92
McDonnell Douglas Automation Compa-
    ny, 87
McDonnell Douglas Corporation, 40, 77,
    93, 99
McGowan, Bill, 7, 61, 179
McGraw-Hill Book Company, 12, 49,
    112–113
McKesson, 8, 48–49, 88, 130, 138
McKinsey & Company, 94
Macmillan, 31
Management Information Systems (MIS),
    59, 60
Manufacturing, automated, 35–39, 147–
    150
Manufacturing applications protocol
    (MAP), 40, 42, 62, 87
Market management, 168, 169
Market potential analysis, 187
Market-product life-cycle analysis, 190–
    193
Market segmentation:
  in business operations equipment, 147–
    150
  in entertainment services, 116, 121–123
Market to book (MB) ratio, 154–158, 176,
    177
Marketing productivity, 193–197
Marketing professionals (see Sales profes-
    sionals)
Marketplace arenas, 78–82, 84
Marknet, 86
Martin, James, 5–6
Mason, Roy, 128
Matsushita Electric, 9, 162, 164
Mattel, 119
MCA, 13
MCI Telecommunications Corporation,
    11, 69, 87, 88, 93
Media conversion, 78, 81, 84
Meetings, 21

Mentor Graphics, 40
Mergers, 85, 91
Merrill Lynch Pierce Fenner & Smith, Inc., 87
Metromail, 163
Micom, 87
Microelectronics, 73, 185
Microsoft, 67, 162, 164, 166, 167
Mintzberg, Henry, 19
Mitel, 166
MITI, 67, 80
Mitsubishi Electric, 12, 67
Moore Corporation, Ltd., 11
Morton, Dean O., 186
Motorola, 10
Multichannel Multipoint Distribution System, 32, 117, 118
Mulvaney, Karen, 147
Murdoch, Rupert, 65

NAPLPS, 43
National Bureau of Standards, 41
National infrastructure, 74
National Mass Retailing Institute, 48
NCR Corporation, 10, 155
NEC, 10, 66, 67, 88
Ness, David, 135
Network architecture standard, 40
Network development, 102–103
Network equipment suppliers, 145–147
Network television, 33, 115, 117
Networking, 34, 35
New products strategy, 186–189
New York Times, The, 13, 31, 162, 163, 166
Newport, William, 187
News Corporation, Ltd., 13, 65
Nichols, John, 37
Nielsen, A. C., Inc., 93, 105, 163
Nippon Telephone & Telegraph, 9
Nixdorf Computer, 13, 89
Nokia, 89
Norfolk Southern Railway, 88
North American vs. Japanese market share, 64–70
North American Philips, 110, 137
Northern Telecom, Inc., 10, 86
Norwegian firms, 68
NYNEX, 9, 110

Office equipment, 131–141
  blocking factors and, 135–136

Office equipment (Cont.):
  defined, 83
  knowledge-worker productivity and (see Knowledge-worker productivity)
  marketing and sales imperatives, 140–141
  performance measurement of, 158, 171–173
  product development imperatives, 139–140
  size and growth of, 83–85, 132
  success factors in IT application to, 136–139
  user acceptance of IT and, 133–135
Office imaging products, 70
Oki, 66
Olivetti, 11, 75, 76, 89
Omnicard, 80
Open Systems Interconnection (OSI), 40, 43
Option plans, 177–178

Pacific Bell, 133
Pacific Telesis Group, 9, 103
Parsons, Gregory, 47
Participative video media, 116, 117, 119–121
Pay television, 117–118
PBX, 72
Penney, J.C., Company, Inc., 88, 138
Penzias, Arno, 6
People-culture attribute, 166
People-culture management, 168–170, 175–183
  cultural success attributes, 178–183
  executive compensation plans, 175–178
People Express Airlines, 112
Pepperidge Farms, 137
Perfect exchange of content, 5
Performance measurement (see IT-supplier performance measurement)
Performance video media, 116–119
  (See also Television)
Personal computers (see Computers)
Personnel optimization, 195, 196
Philips, 9, 71, 75
Physical distribution of content, 28–30, 32–33
Pioneer Electronics, 12
Pitney Bowes, 11
Planning Research Corporation, 79
Playstations, 128–129

Plessey, 12, 87, 89
Polaroid Corporation, 12
PPG, 137
Prentice-Hall, Inc., 105
Prestel, 69
Price/earnings (P/E) ratio, 153–154
Pricing strategies, 57
Printing, 106
Proactive appraisal process, 181
Process type, 148
Processing, 79, 81, 84
Processor architectures, 73
Procter & Gamble, 138
Product businesses:
  cross-substitution with service busi-
    nesses, 77, 79–80
  marketplace arenas related to elements
    of, 78–82, 84
  (*See also* Business operations equipment;
    Consumer electronics; Office equip-
    ment)
Product differentiation, 38–39, 57–58
Product evaluation process, 187
Product innovation, 166, 184–189, 191
Product life-cycle analysis, 190–193
Product-process innovation, 148
Product quality, 184–189
Productivity:
  disintermediation and, 57–58
  of knowledge workers (*see* Knowledge-
    worker productivity)
  marketing, 193–197
Profit orientation, short-term, 185
Publishing, 106

Quality, product, 184–189
QUBE, 53

RAC, 110
Racal Electronics, 89
RACE (Research and Development in Eu-
  rope), 75
Radio, 28, 30, 31
Rank Xerox, 11, 88
Rauh, Thomas, 130
Raytheon, 94
RCA Corporation, 9, 67, 88
Reach, disintermediation and, 47
Reader's Digest, 12
Redinet, 87

Reduced instruction set computers
  (RISC), 142
Reed International, 13
Repositioning in marketing, 193
Research and development (R&D), 74–75,
  85–95, 100, 167, 184–189
Resource deployment, 195–196
Return-based performance plans, 177–178
Return on equity (ROE), 85, 105, 154–
  161, 172, 173, 176–178
Reuters, 89
Rich, Inc., 89
Ricoh, 11, 66, 67
Risk, attitude toward, 179
RKO Networks, 138
Robotics, 70, 72, 74
Rolm, 93

Safecard, 51
Sales professionals:
  displacement of, 46, 49
  IT applied to activities of, 23–27, 136–
    137
  time-use studies of, 19–20
Sales Technologies, 27
Samsung, 65
Sanyo Electric, 10, 67
Satellite Business Systems, Inc., 27, 93, 99
Satellite Master Antenna Television, 32
Schwab, Charles, & Company, Inc., 47
Sears, Roebuck and Company, 8, 80, 88,
  95, 110, 113
Senior management competence, 167, 168
Service businesses, 6
  cross-substitution with product busi-
    nesses, 77, 79–80
  marketplace arenas related to elements
    of, 78–82, 84
  (*See also* Communications services; En-
    tertainment services; Information
    services)
Service packagers, 110
Shareholder rewards, 153–161, 165–167,
  171
Sharp, 11, 88
Shepard, Mark, Jr., 179–180, 184
Siemens, 10, 72, 75, 76, 87–89, 147
Singapore, 65
Software and computers service firms, 91–
  95, 99, 106–107
Software AG, 73
Software engineering, 185

Sony Corporation, 10, 67, 94, 162, 164, 166
Sord, 142
Southern New England Telecommunications, 12, 130
Southwestern Bell, 9
Sperry Corporation, 10, 93
Stakeholder perceptions, 161–167, 171–174
Standard-setting process, 40–44
Standardization, 69
Stanford University, 117
STC, 11
Sterling Software, 49
Storage, 79, 81, 84
Storage Research, 65
Storage Technology, 155, 165
Strategic management, 168–174
Strategic marketing positioning, 194, 195
Strategic operations units, 149–150
Strategic vision, 167, 168
Stratus, 164
Structural market relationships, 194, 195
Success attributes, 166–167
Supply of IT, 64–67
Swiss firms, 68
Synthesis of content, 29–30, 32–33
Systems integration, 43–44, 79, 80
Systems solution, 79

Taiwanese firms, 65, 70
Tandem, 86, 162, 164, 166
Tandon, 156
Tandy, 11, 166
Teamwork, reliance on, 179–180
Technology availability, 70
Technology cross-substitution, 70
Technology management, 168, 169, 184–189
Tektronix Corporation, 94, 132
Tele-Communications (TCI), 119
Telecommunications, 72, 185
Telecommunications carriers, 101–104
(*See also* Communications services)
Telecommunications network operators, 110
Telecommunications network suppliers, 145–147
Teledelivery, 29
Telefonica, 11
Telegames, 120
Televideo, 156

Television:
broadcast (*see* Broadcast television)
cable, 29, 31, 47, 52, 102, 115–119, 121
pay, 117–118
viewing preference segmentation, 121–122
Telex, 163
Texas Instruments, 17, 119, 179–180
Texas Peripherals, 93
Thomson Group, 11
Thomson-CSF Group, 73, 74
Thorn EMI, 11
3M Corporation, 10, 88, 162, 164, 181
TIE, 156
Time, Inc., 10, 31, 80, 87, 110
Time-use studies, 19–22
Times Mirror, 11, 31
Toppan Printing, 12
Toshiba, 10, 67, 88
Toto, 46
Toyota Corporation, 88
Training programs, 180
Transac, 74
Transaction providers, 110
Transport, 78, 81, 84
Transtations, 112, 129–130
Tribune Company, 12
TRW, 11, 88, 93, 137
Twentieth Century-Fox Film Corporation, 31
Tymnet, 103
Tymshare, 93, 105

UAL, Inc., 110
Uniroyal, 137
United Kingdom, 69, 74
United States market share, 65, 69–70
United Telecommunications, 10
UNIX, 43, 87, 107
U S West, 9

Value-added resellers, 107
Venture capital, 90–91, 94
VHS, 43
Video media:
participative vs. performance, 116–121
(*See also* Television)
Videocassette recorders (VCRs), 52, 70, 125, 129
Videodiscs, 116–117, 119–120
Videogames, 117, 119–120

Videophotography, interactive, 120
Videotex, 31, 32, 72, 111, 112
Volkswagen, 8

Wall Street Journal, 56, 71, 163
Wall Street Journal/Europe, 74
Wang Laboratories, 11, 77, 86, 87, 132, 155, 162, 164
Warner Brothers, 31
Warner Communications, 11, 119
Weil, Ulric, 133
Weiler, Robert K., 92

Wertheim & Company, Inc., 172
Wescar, 27
West German firms, 72–75, 185
Western Union, 13
Westinghouse Electric Corporation, 67
Wrangler, 137

Xerox Corporation, 9, 14, 88, 94, 155, 156

Zenith Electronics, 11

About the Authors:

HARVEY L. POPPEL has been widely recognized as a pioneer in the information technology industry for nearly 30 years. Currently a partner with Broadview Associates—a leading IT mergers, acquisitions, and venture capital firm—he was formerly with the international management and technology consulting firm of Booz, Allen & Hamilton Inc. Mr. Poppel holds B.S. and M.S. degrees from Rensselaer Polytechnic Institute.

BERNARD GOLDSTEIN was chairman of the board of National CSS, Inc.—an international information services company now owned by Dun & Bradstreet, Inc.—before assuming his present duties as a partner at Broadview Associates. Mr. Goldstein has spent his entire professional life in the information services segment of the IT industry in a variety of roles, including founder of such firms as Computech, Inc., and United Data Centers. He holds an undergraduate degree from the University of Pennsylvania Wharton School of Finance and Business, as well as a graduate degree from the Columbia University Graduate School of Business.